DATA COMMUNICATIONS
AND
INTEROPERABILITY

DATA COMMUNICATIONS
AND
INTEROPERABILITY

Richard W. Markley

Azusa Pacific University
Azusa, California

Prentice Hall, *Englewood Cliffs, New Jersey 07632*

Library of Congress Cataloging-in-Publication Data

Markley, Richard W.,
    Data communications and interoperability / Richard W. Markley.
      p.   cm.
    Bibliography: p.
    Includes index.
    ISBN 0-13-199340-2
    1. Computer networks.   I. Title.
  TK5105.5.M359 1990
    004.6--dc20   89-34747
                                                      CIP

Credits: Permission to use portions of the EIA-232-D Standard, "Interface Between Data Terminal Equipment and Data Circuit-Terminating Equipment Employing Serial Binary Data Interchange" has been granted by the Electronic Industries Association, 2001 Eye Street, N.W., Washington, D.C. 20006. Permission has been given to use material from Digital Equipment Corporation's Digital Network Architecture (DNA), DDCMP protocol, DEC net routing layer protocol. DNA is a trademark of Digital Equipment Corporation. Permission has been given to discuss Recommendations X.21 and X.25 and adapt in part or whole, selected definitions from International Telegraph and Telephone Consulative Committee, ITU/CCITT, Place des Nations, 1211 Geneva 20, Switzerland. Portions of this text have been reprinted from ANSI/IEEE Std 802.2-1985, ANSI/IEEE Std 802.3-1985, ANSI/IEEE Std 802.4-1985, and ANSI/IEEE Std 802.5-1985, copyright ©1985 by the Institute of Electrical and Electronics Engineers, Inc., by permission of the IEEE Standards Department. For information on purchasing these documents, call 800/678-IEEE.

Cover design: Diane Saxe
Cover art provided by permission of Racal-Milgo, designer and supplier of Integrated Communications Systems and Services.
Manufacturing buyer: Bob Anderson

©1990 by Prentice-Hall, Inc.
A Division of Simon & Schuster
Englewood Cliffs, New Jersey 07632

Printed in the United States of America

10 9 8 7 6 5 4 3 2 1

ISBN 0-13-199340-2

Prentice-Hall International (UK) Limited, London
Prentice-Hall of Australia Pty. Limited, Sydney
Prentice-Hall Canada Inc., Toronto
Prentice-Hall Hispanoamericana, S.A., Mexico
Prentice-Hall of India Private Limited, New Delhi
Prentice-Hall of Japan, Inc., Tokyo
Simon & Schuster Asia Pte. Ltd., Singapore
Editora Prentice-Hall do Brasil, Ltda., Rio de Janeiro

This book is dedicated to my loving wife, Betty

CONTENTS

PREFACE

The purpose of this book is to present undergraduate engineering and computer science majors with an introduction to computer-to-computer data communications. Because the book is self-contained, it can be used for self study. Also, it should be useful to professionals who need to become familiar with this rapidly growing field.

The book is organized to cover five general areas: (1) a short introduction to networking applications (Chap. 1); (2) fundamentals of digital communications (Chaps. 2–3); (3) protocol layering concepts (Chap. 4); (4) physical, link, and network protocols (Chaps. 5–8); and (5) host-to-host protocols (Chaps. 9–11). Useful guidelines for system planning are included in an appendix, and a lengthy list of references is provided for students who are interested in further study.

In Chaps. 5–11, the emphasis is on international protocol standards based on the Open Systems Interconnection (OSI) concept. Each layer of the OSI reference model is addressed, and the latest OSI standard protocols are explained. Also analyzed are Department of Defense (D-D) standards and a few of the widely-used proprietary protocols. Local area networks are covered in Chap. 8.

Performance trade-offs for protocols in several layers of the OSI model are explored using the "transfer rate of information bits" (TRIB) concept. This easy-to-understand concept provides a useful tool for a quantitative comparison of protocols. For example, TRIB is used to evaluate differences in link protocols, point out trade-offs between various LAN protocols, and determine the throughput impact of the Data Encryption Standard (DES) in data link encryption.

Each chapter supplies an ample number of problems, with answers to odd-numbered problems included at the end of the book. An instructor's solution manual is available that contains solutions to all the problems. I have found it useful to assign to students a semester project based on guidelines in the appendix.

I wish to thank Prentice Hall and their reviewing staff for many helpful suggestions. To Dr. Jack Holmes, George Wells, Marvin Miller, Mel Roberts, and Mike Spitz, I want to express my appreciation for their pertinent comments and for the time they gave to the perusal of this work. I am especially indebted, also, to Joan Perry for her effective and painstaking editing.

I also thank Wendel Scarborough at Azusa Pacific University for his initial encouragement, and my parents, Bill and Thelma Markley, for their continued support.

Heartfelt thanks go to my wife, Betty, and my children, Steve and Susan, for their patient forbearance and encouragement during the long days in which I was dedicated to the preparation of the manuscript.

Richard W. Markley

DATA COMMUNICATIONS
AND
INTEROPERABILITY

1

INTRODUCTION

The capability for two or more computers, from the same or different manufacturers, to transmit data and to carry out processes as expected by the users is called **interoperability**.

To achieve interoperability, it is important that a receiver consistently understands the information that a sender transmits. Interoperability requires mutual agreement between the sender and receiver to use certain types of signals, data formats, and procedures. The formal set of rules governing formatting and relative timing of the information exchange is called a **protocol**. In this text, after first introducing the basics of digital communication, we will cover protocol requirements to achieve interoperability.

Every human and automated information exchange has a sender, receiver, and communication system (Fig. 1.1). Each of these components may introduce errors into the information exchange. In common voice conversations, people are the senders and receivers, and they usually rapidly adjust to accommodate problems in the communication system and minor misunderstandings between themselves (in other words, *errors*). In computer-to-computer communication, the senders and receivers are annoyingly inflexible; hence the designers of the system must establish well-defined protocols that can recover from errors.

Automated communication components may be rather complex. The sender or receiver may be a keyboard terminal, sensor, microcomputer, minicomputer, or mainframe computer. The communication system may be a dedicated link digital or an old telephone system that was originally designed to only carry voice conversations. The system may be a national data network with links over optic fibers or satellite links, a local network with company-owned and company-maintained communication links, or a combination of several systems.

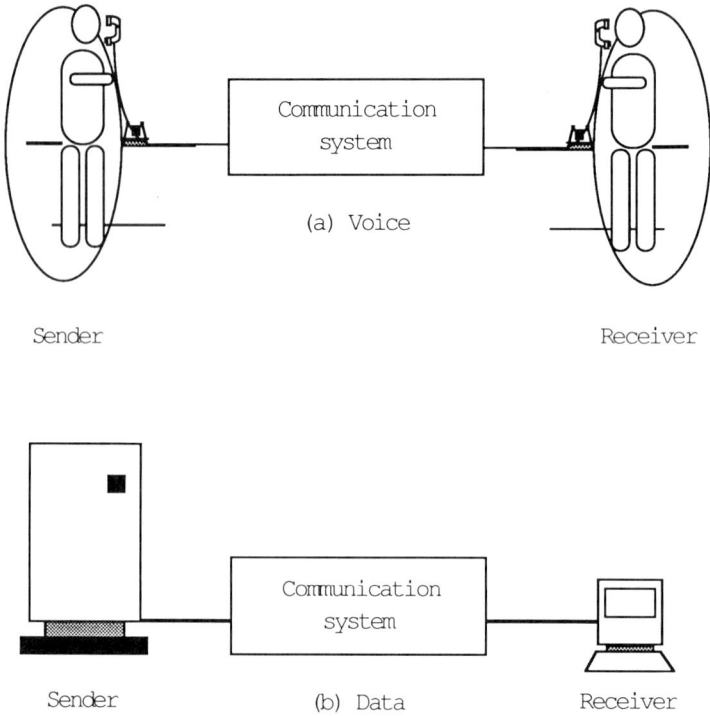

Figure 1.1 Components of information exchange

On individual links between computers, voltages and signaling rates must match. The data format must also be carefully designed.

If the data must be routed over intervening computers, the rules for routing must be defined. The users may expect other services from the network that range from checks for integrity to encryption of sensitive data. The software that provides these services must also have consistent output formats and user procedures.

The obvious solution to achieve interoperability among computers is for each system in the network to implement identical protocols. However, over the years, computer manufacturers have developed proprietary protocols that permit their own systems to interoperate, but exclude interoperability with computers from other vendors. There have been many efforts to overcome this problem. One of the most significant and far-reaching is a worldwide effort under the auspices of the International Organization for Standardization (ISO) to design standard international communication protocols that can be implemented on computers from any manufacturer. The result of this effort is the focus of most of this book.

What impact does the selection of a protocol have on network performance? We will discuss performance as we discuss interoperability because there are often trade-offs between the speed of information transfer and services that a protocol provides. For example, some networks are designed to enable users to query a remote database and receive a rapid response, but heavy protocol overhead can seriously delay the responses, often at the worst possible time. In another example, errors introduced by noise in the communication system have a more profound impact on a financial network engaged in electronic funds transfer than, perhaps, electronic mail. The overhead of additional error detection for financial networks is more important than speed of data transfer.

1.1 NETWORKING APPLICATIONS

Depending on the need for timeliness of the information exchange, networks can be classified into two types:

1. A *real-time* application, i.e., where a fast response from the remote computer is needed before further progress can be made in a process or interaction between people
2. A *non-real-time* application, i.e., where data is transferred from one system to another with less demand on timeliness

The real-time application that involves people, such as bank tellers or airline reservation agents, usually requires responses in a few seconds or less. This puts demands on both the communication system and the computers to meet the timeliness requirements.

Other real-time applications may involve the automation of equipment. Custom software for communication and end-system processing is often designed for minimum protocol overhead. Applications range from automobile engine control to spacecraft guidance and control.

The non-real-time application may not require a fast response, but it still requires accuracy and reliability. Electronic mail and office automation are examples of non-real-time applications. When computers are networked in some offices so that the users can share a printer or file server, the equipment receiving the information may be relatively slow, so the speed of transmission is not critical.

1.2 NETWORK CONNECTIVITY

Network **topology** is a description of a computer network showing specific relations of component parts in regard to interconnection, functionality, and geographic position. A topology is usually the result of much design and evaluation.

In the following section, we describe five common topologies. Each computer that participates in passing data across the network is called a network **node**. The node may be a standalone computer (or a board within a computer) dedicated to moving data through the network. The **node** may also communicate to a larger local computer, a **host**, that supports user functions by storing or processing user data. In some applications, there may be network functions that are accomplished on the node and others in the host. For example, the node may route the data across the network, but the host may ensure that the total volume of data that the sender transmitted has arrived intact with no errors, or may provide recovery procedures if the node's network circuits are temporarily disconnected.

Specific topologies depend somewhat on the geographical scope of the network. Networks limited to a company's or university's local facilities are called **local area networks (LANs)**. They have *horizontal topologies* and interconnect computers that are *peers* with similar capabilities. They are introduced in this chapter and discussed in more detail in Chap. 8. Networks that cover long distances are called **wide area networks (WANs)**, and they often have *vertical topologies* because certain hosts may have greater data-processing capabilities, and less capable hosts funnel data to them for processing. In practice, a particular application may be one pure topology or a mix of several topologies.

There are three common horizontal topologies that are often used in LANs that are described next.

1.2.1 Horizontal topologies

1.2.1.1 Star topology. A **star** is the simplest topology and describes a network with nodes that are linked to a central switching node (Fig. 1.2a). All traffic in the network must travel through the central node. The central node is acting primarily as a communications controller, facilitating communication among the nodes on the outside of the star. Getting data between end nodes requires that it pass through a central node. An advantage is its structural simplicity; it is easy to add or remove nodes by simply upgrading the central node. A major disadvantage is that it is vulnerable to failure because the central node represents a single point of failure; the central node is often backed up to improve reliability of the network. The central node of a star network is also a potential performance bottleneck.

1.2.1.2 Bus topology. In a **bus** topology all network nodes communicate through a common transmission medium (Fig. 1.2b), and the data and control signals are simultaneously signaled, or *broadcasted*, to all the nodes. Each node has a unique address. Although each node senses every message on the bus, it only transfers data to its associated host when the message is addressed to itself. There are a variety of ways for the nodes to gain access to the medium for transmitting their messages. The computers may contend, take a turn when given permission by another computer on the network (*token-passing*), or, given a turn by a master node (*polling*).

Some advantages to the bus topology are: (1) the simplicity of adding and removing users and (2) the high data transfer rates because there is no need to route data through intervening nodes.

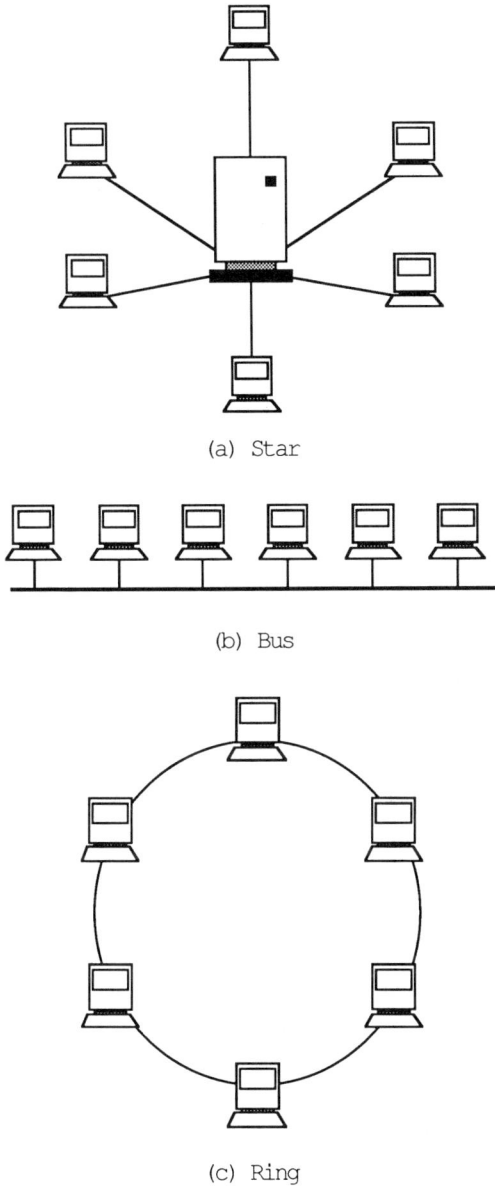

(a) Star

(b) Bus

(c) Ring

Figure 1.2   Horizontal topologies

1.2.1.3 Ring topology.   A **ring** topology (Fig. 1.2c) is characterized by a path between network nodes that forms a complete circle, with each node connected to two adjacent neighbor nodes. The data flow may be unidirectional or bidirectional. Two methods of sharing the ring are

1. Letting each potential sender contend for use of the medium
2. Taking turns through the use of a token

Token-passing is the most popular ring topology method in the United States. Token-passing causes a delay as each node checks to see if the incoming data is a token or some other type of message. An advantage of token-passing rings is that their performance is relatively stable, even under high loads. (This will be demonstrated in Chap. 8.) Thus, performance can be predicted with some accuracy. Disadvantages include a potentially long delay between a need to access the medium and receipt of the token, and, if the token is lost, a time delay until recovery.

1.2.2 Vertical Topologies

1.2.2.1 Hierarchical topology.   A **hierarchical** topology (Fig. 1.3a) describes networks that interconnect hosts that have increasing data management responsibilities. Such a network is not characterized by how it controls access to a medium but, instead, how it supports the users. A key characteristic is that the data-processing capability of the host computers increases at each level. For example, a business transaction taking place at the lowest level, perhaps at the point of sale, may be performed on a microcomputer system, but the transaction is not complete until general-purpose systems higher in the hierarchy update their inventory databases.

1.2.2.2 Mesh topology.   Many WANs have a **mesh** topology (Fig. 1.3b), where there appears to be no recognizable organization or geometric pattern to the network. The nodes are not all peers; in fact, they may range from personal to mainframe computers. The geographic distribution of computers may have developed historically. An example of this type of network is the Department of Defense (DoD) Internet (often called the ARPANET, its original name when it was used for networking research). In the Internet a number of users with different size hosts from different manufacturers exchange data with each other.

1.3 EXAMPLES OF NETWORKS

In the following section are three hypothetical computer network application examples to demonstrate connectivities and topologies.

1.3.1 Small Business

A small business with modest manufacturing facilities may apply computers to assist in the following applications:

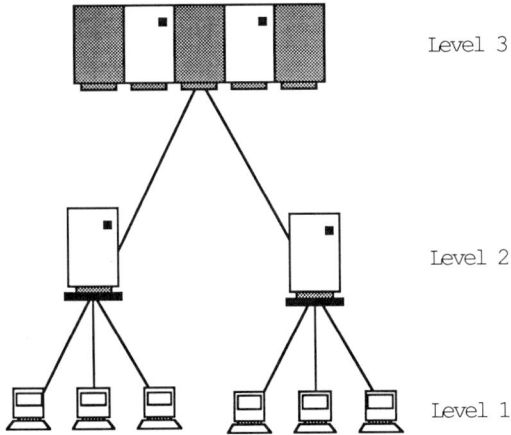

(a) Hierarchical

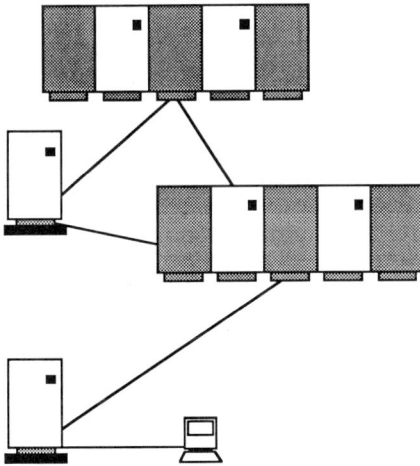

(b) Mesh

Figure 1.3   Vertical networks

1. Accounting (i.e., payroll, billing, tax information, cost forecasts, and order summaries)
2. Manufacturing (i.e., inventory information and manufacturing schedules)
3. Purchasing (i.e., parts inventory, supplier information, and pricing information)
4. Engineering (i.e., technical data, design information, computer-aided design (CAD), and problem solving)

5. Marketing (i.e., schedules, availability, product costs, customer database, and proposal preparation)

6. Personnel (i.e., personnel records, basic payroll information, and access to a travel service)

Each office has its own personal computers, minicomputers, and workstations to meet its own basic responsibilities, with word-processing and database capabilities. The accounting, purchasing, and marketing offices may have spreadsheet software. The engineering office may have a certain degree of computer-aided design capability and FORTRAN software. The personnel office may have on-line access to a travel service.

Within given offices, the computers may stand alone. A more effective business operation is possible by networking the computers together (Fig. 1.4). A

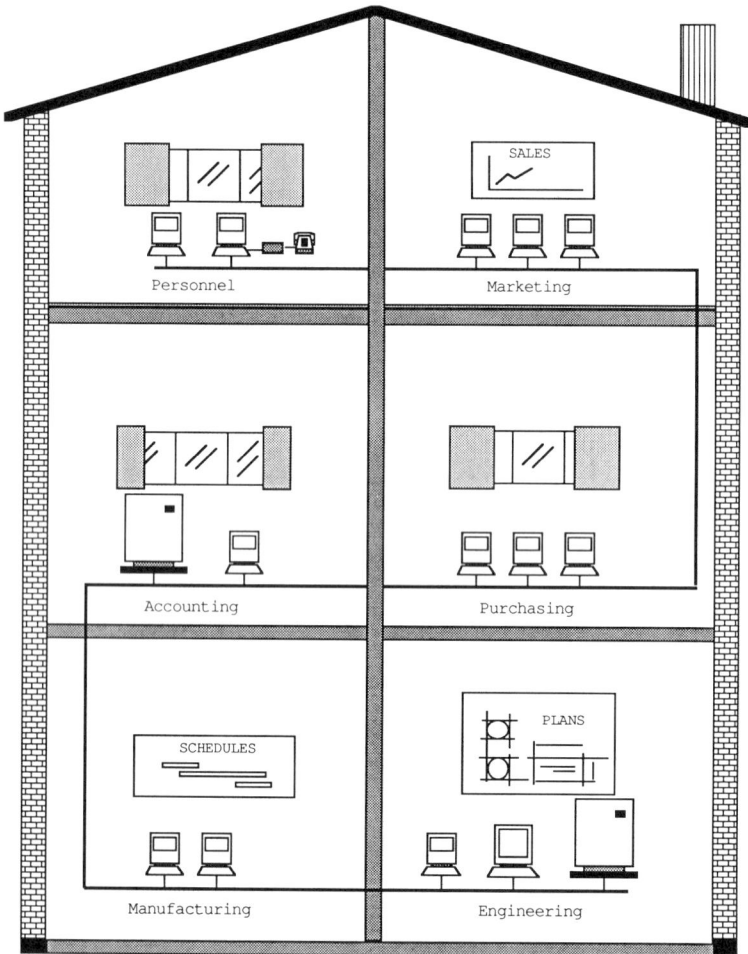

Figure 1.4 Small-business application

companywide network permits the individual offices to meet their basic responsibilities but share data and other resources when necessary. Memo distribution is simplified by providing each computer with electronic mail software. Proposal preparation in the marketing office is simplified by transferring cost and schedule data from accounting and manufacturing, and graphics data from engineering. Certain resources, such as a high-quality laser printer and a scanner, may be shared among offices.

Some business data are sensitive, such as data in personnel files and cost information. For this reason, security measures must be implemented before all the files are accessible from other computers on the network.

1.3.2 Scientific Research

A typical scientific environment may require the following capabilities:

1. Real-time data acquisition
2. Data reduction and presentation
3. Laboratory data comparison with model predictions
4. Software development

One network solution is a hierarchical topology (Fig. 1.5) with the most reliable computers at the site of the experiments dedicated to supporting the experiments. The computers at the lowest level are called level 1 computers. This is a real-time application if the level 1 computers are controlling the experiment in response to sensor output. Data are transmitted to a minicomputer at level 2. The level 2 computer consolidates and reduces data, and prepares plots and other graphic and tabular reports. A higher-level capability is provided by an off-site large mainframe computer at level 3 to compare empirical data with theoretical data generated from modeling and simulation.

With appropriate support software, it is possible to develop software for the level 1 microcomputers on the minicomputer. Otherwise, a specialized development system may be needed for software development.

1.3.3 Fast-food Service

A fast-food restaurant may require the following capabilities:

1. Customer input (i.e., touch-sensitive terminals for window ordering and menu and service feedback)
2. Pay point with bank card (real-time)
3. Environmental control, including fire and burglar alarms
4. Cooking unit control (real-time)
5. Accounting (i.e., payroll and point-of-sale records)

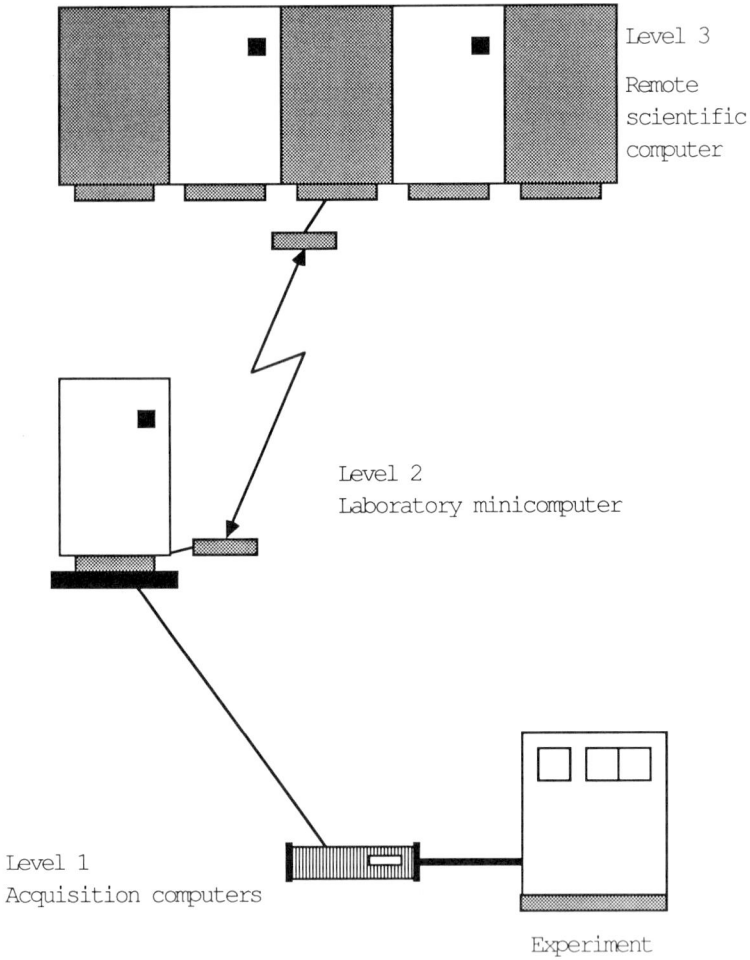

Figure 1.5   Scientific application

6. Personnel (i.e., shift schedules, worker availability schedules, and personnel data)

7. Purchasing (i.e., inventory data and delivery schedules)

The overall system topology is hierarchical. Customer input terminals, environmental control, and cooking-unit control may be performed by dedicated computers at level 1 (Fig. 1.6) because they are dedicated to well-defined tasks. They report exceptional conditions, such as fire or mechanical malfunctions, to a level 2 system in the store. The pay point interfaces to a level 2 computer and an off-site remote computer to validate the credit or automatic teller machine (ATM) card. The level 2 system also handles accounting and personnel functions. Other

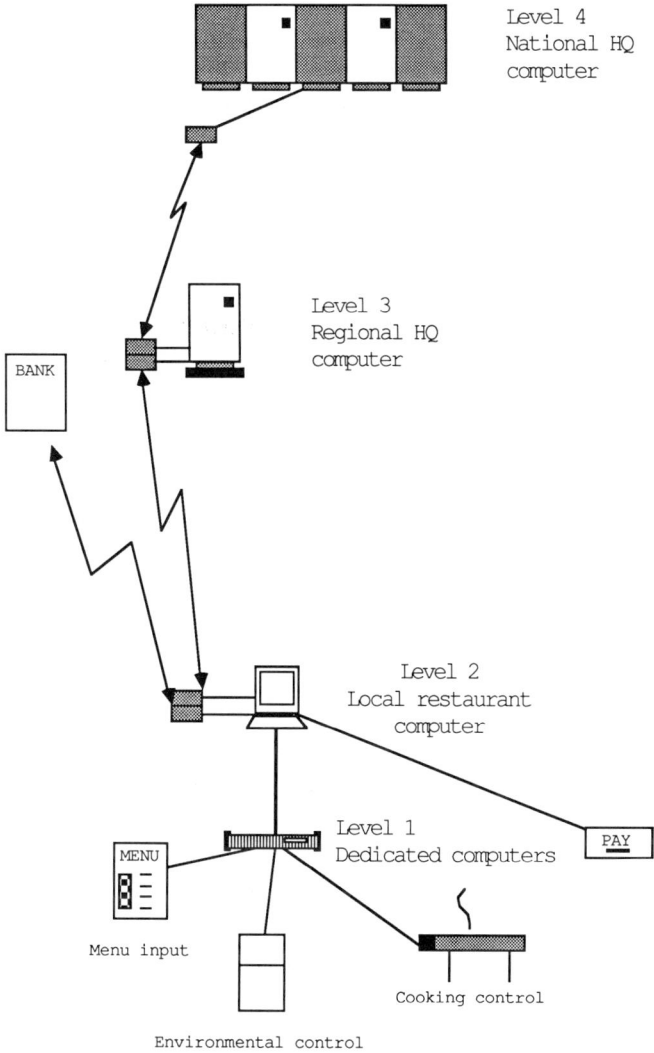

Level 4
National HQ
computer

Level 3
Regional HQ
computer

BANK

Level 2
Local restaurant
computer

Level 1
Dedicated computers

PAY

MENU

Menu input

Cooking control

Environmental control

Figure 1.6   Fast-food application

activities, such as ordering from suppliers, may be handled more effectively at the regional and corporate levels (levels 3 and 4).

1.4 SUMMARY

The number of computers, especially personal computers, is growing, and the demand for computer-to-computer communication is increasingly important. Historically, computer vendors developed proprietary protocol architectures that enabled their own line of systems to interoperate. National, military, and international protocol standards facilitate interoperability between computers from different manufacturers.

Applications are generally classed as real-time and non-real-time applications, depending on the response-time requirements. Network topology describes the connectivity and relationship between interoperable computers. Common topologies include star, ring, and bus (horizontal topologies), and hierarchical and mesh (vertical topologies).

KEY WORDS AND CONCEPTS

bus	node
hierarchical	protocol
host	ring
interoperability	star
local area network (LAN)	topology
mesh	wide area network (WAN)

PROBLEMS

1. Will a computer network supporting automobile registration at the offices of a state motor vehicle department most likely be a horizontal or vertical topology? Why?

2. Will a library interloan network be a horizontal or vertical topology? Why?

3. What limits the number of nodes participating in a star network? A bus network? A ring network?

4. What type of overall computer network architecture would you recommend for supporting manufacturing for a large manufacturer such as General Motors? Why?

5. Write an abstract of a magazine or journal article describing a computer network. Describe the major functions of the network and its topology. Show how its topology is (or is not) consistent with those functions. Would you consider it a real-time or non-real-time network?

2

DIGITAL TRANSMISSION BASICS

Digital computer-to-computer communication is much more primitive than human communication because information is limited to being transmitted in the form of binary digits (**bits**). This chapter covers binary representation of symbols and the basics of digital transmission.

2.1 SYMBOL REPRESENTATION

There is a large number of possible binary codes for representing information. Image pixel data is represented by simple binary codes. Text data is usually represented by alphanumeric codes that include the alphabet, numbers, punctuation symbols, and special control symbols. A few of the standard alphanumeric codes are discussed in this section.

The number of unique symbols that a given code can represent on a one-to-one basis is 2 raised to the power of the number of information bits available:

$$N = 2^n \tag{2.1}$$

where

$$N = \text{number of symbols}$$

$$n = \text{number of information bits available}$$

A corollary of this principle is that the number of bits required to represent N symbols is $\log_2 N$ rounded to the next higher integer.

EXAMPLE 2.1   Binary representation of symbols

There are 12 teams in the National Baseball League. What is the minimum number of bits required to represent each team with a different binary number?

$$\log_2 12 = 3.58$$

Therefore, at least 4 bits are required to represent 12 teams. The following table shows a possible assignment of codes to teams:

Binary Code	Symbol
0000	Astros
0001	Braves
0010	Cardinals
0011	Cubs
0100	Dodgers
0101	Expos
0110	Giants
0111	Mets
1000	Padres
1001	Phillies
1010	Pirates
1011	Reds

At least 36 symbols are required to represent the alphabet (all capital letters) and the numbers 0–9. If we include lowercase letters and all the punctuation symbols, the number climbs to 96. Thus, at least 7 bits are required to represent alphanumerics and punctuation symbols.

In the following sections some of the common codes for representing alphanumeric data and control characters are described.

2.1.1 ASCII Code

The 7-bit American Standard Code for Information Interchange (ASCII) (Tables 2.1 and 2.2) is the most popular communications code in the United States. It associates 7-bit codes with 128 alphanumeric control symbols. ASCII is defined by the American National Standards Institute (ANSI) in ANSI X3.4. ANSI X3.4 is the U.S. version of its international counterparts, CCITT T.50 (International Alphabet No. 5, or "IA5") and ISO 646.

In data transmission, an eighth bit is usually added in the most significant bit position for optional error detection.

TABLE 2.1   Seven-bit ASCII Code

b_7				0	0	0	0	1	1	1	1
	b_6			0	0	1	1	0	0	1	1
		b_5		0	1	0	1	0	1	0	1
b_4	b_3	b_2	b_1								
0	0	0	0	NUL	DLE	SP	0	@	P	`	p
0	0	0	1	SOH	DC1	!	1	A	Q	a	q
0	0	1	0	STX	DC2	"	2	B	R	b	r
0	0	1	1	ETX	DC3	#	3	C	S	c	s
0	1	0	0	EOT	DC4	$	4	D	T	d	t
0	1	0	1	ENQ	NAK	%	5	E	U	e	u
0	1	1	0	ACK	SYN	&	6	F	V	f	v
0	1	1	1	BEL	ETB	'	7	G	W	g	w
1	0	0	0	BS	CAN	(	8	H	X	h	x
1	0	0	1	HT	EM	)	9	I	Y	i	y
1	0	1	0	LF	SUB	*	:	J	Z	j	z
1	0	1	1	VT	ESC	+	;	K	[	k	{
1	1	0	0	FF	FS	,	‹	L	\	l	|
1	1	0	1	CR	GS	−	=	M	]	m	}
1	1	1	0	SO	RS	.	›	N	^	n	~
1	1	1	1	SI	US	/	?	O	_	o	DEL

Note: A character is represented by

$$b_7 b_6 b_5 b_4 b_3 b_2 b_1$$

For example,

$$A = 1\ 0\ 0\ 0\ 0\ 0\ 1$$

TABLE 2.2   ASCII Control Characters

ACK	Acknowledge	FF	Form feed
BEL	Bell	FS	File separator
BS	Backspace	GS	Group separator
CAN	Cancel	HT	Horizontal tabulation
CR	Carriage return	LF	Line feed
DC1	Device control one	NAK	Negative acknowledge
DC2	Device control two	NUL	Null
DC3	Device control three	RS	Record separator
DC4	Device control four	SI	Shift-in
DEL	Delete	SO	Shift-out
DLE	Data link escape	SOH	Start of heading
EM	End of medium	STX	Start of text
ENQ	Enquiry	SUB	Substitute character
EOT	End of transmission	SYN	Synchronous idle
ESC	Escape	US	Unit separator
ETB	End of transmission block	VT	Vertical tabulation
ETX	End of text		

EXAMPLE 2.2   An ASCII message

Code the message "It is 10 P.M.," and include a 0 in the eighth (parity) bit position.

```
bit→        8 7 6 5 4 3 2 1

I           0 1 0 0 1 0 0 1
t           0 1 1 1 0 1 0 0
Space       0 0 1 0 0 0 0 0
i           0 1 1 0 1 0 0 1
s           0 1 1 1 0 0 1 1
Space       0 0 1 0 0 0 0 0
1           0 0 1 1 0 0 0 1
0           0 0 1 1 0 0 0 0
Space       0 0 1 0 0 0 0 0
P           0 1 0 1 0 0 0 0
.           0 0 1 0 1 1 1 0
M           0 1 0 0 1 1 0 1
.           0 0 1 0 1 1 1 0
```

2.1.2 EBCDIC Code

Extended Binary Coded Decimal Interchange Code (EBCDIC) is a proprietary International Business Machine (IBM) character code developed in 1962 by IBM that is used on medium- and large-scale IBM computers (the IBM PC uses ASCII). It is an 8-bit code with no parity bit. The use of 8 bits permits up to 256 symbols, although only 109 are used.

Besides the normal set of alphanumeric characters, EBCDIC contains extra control characters and a few graphic symbols that are not available in ASCII.

2.2 SIGNAL TRANSMISSION

In a network, a sender's output signal seldom connects directly to the receiver. The sender usually interfaces to a transmission medium and controls some characteristic of the transmission signal that the receiver can detect. For example, in **baseband** transmission, the amplitude of the transmission signal is always proportional to the sender's output. It may be as simple as a voltage on a twisted-pair wire.

High-frequency waves such as microwaves and radio waves are called **broadband** signals, and the sender's output signal controls, or **modulates**, such wave characteristics as amplitude, frequency, and phase. Commercial radio and television communication are examples of broadband transmission.

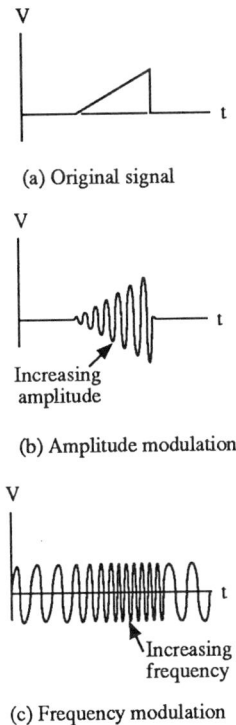

(a) Original signal

(b) Amplitude modulation

(c) Frequency modulation

Figure 2.1   Signal modulation

In *amplitude-modulated (AM)* radio transmission (Fig. 2.1b) the sender's output (for example, a speaker's voice signal) modulates the amplitude of a carrier frequency. For example, if the speaker speaks strongly, the amplitude of the carrier is greater. In *frequency-modulated (FM)* transmission (Fig. 2.1c), the sender's output signal offsets the frequency of the carrier by an amount related to the amplitude of the signal. As a result, the modulated signal covers a *band* of frequencies. FM is the basis for both radio and television communication.

Normally, communication systems such as telephone networks and radio and television are signaled by a continuous range of input voltages. This is usually called *analog* transmission. *Digital* transmission is a special form of analog transmission, where the sender's signal has *discrete*, rather than continuous, values. Because a computer processes discrete signals (i.e., logical zeros and ones) the input to the communication system between two computers are voltages that have discrete values (e.g., 0 and 5 V). Digital signals can be transmitted in baseband or broadband systems.

2.2.1 Modes of Transmission

It will be helpful if we define a few common terms that describe communication direction (Fig. 2.2).

Simplex is a mode of transmission where the transmission signal travels in one direction only, such as the commercial transmission of radio and television.

Half-duplex describes communication over a single medium but in one direction at a time. An example of half-duplex communication is radio communication between an air traffic controller and an aircraft pilot. Appropriate words, such as "over," are used by each person to indicate that the transmission in one direction is complete, and the channel is available for the other person.

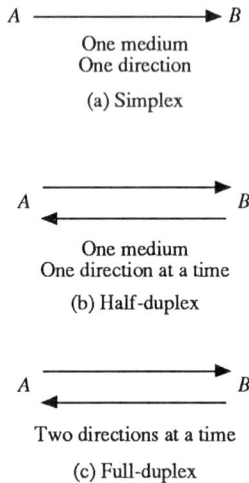

A ─────────────▶ B

One medium
One direction

(a) Simplex

A ═════════════▶ B
  ◀─────────────

One medium
One direction at a time

(b) Half-duplex

A ═════════════▶ B
  ◀─────────────

Two directions at a time

(c) Full-duplex

Figure 2.2 Modes of transmission

Full duplex, or simply *duplex*, describes transmission in two directions simultaneously.

2.2.2 Parallel Transmission

In parallel transmission, each bit in a block of bits has its own signal line, and all bits are transmitted simultaneously (Fig. 2.3). Synchronization is usually accomplished by control circuits separate from the data circuits. One control circuit may be used by the sender to indicate to the receiver that the data is ready to be transferred (a *READY/BUSY* line). Another may be used by the receiver to indicate to the sender that the data has been received and it is time to present new data on the data circuits (a *DEMAND* line).

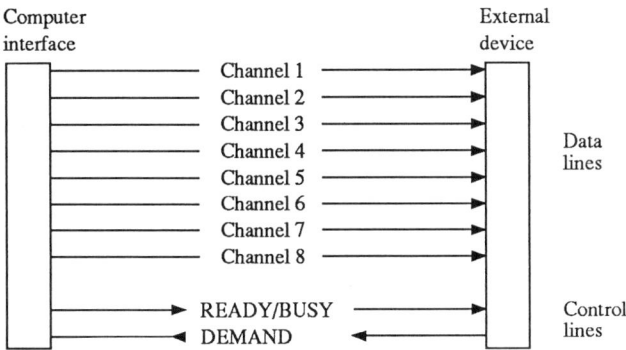

Figure 2.3   Eight-bit parallel transmission

Parallel transmission is usually limited to relatively close computer interfaces such as computer peripherals and scientific instruments. This is because the cost of multiple wires and circuits and the logistics of wiring become unmanageable as the distance increases.

2.2.3 Serial Transmission

Serial transmission involves bit-by-bit transmission of information as a function of time. The signaling rate is expressed in units of **baud.** Baud is the rate of signaling per second on a circuit.

The time of each signaling period is the reciprocal of the baud. For example, a signaling rate of 1200 baud indicates the signaling period is 1/1200 s, or 0.833 ms. The electronic circuitry must enable the voltage to change rapidly from one discrete value to another when transmitting digital data. For example, if the data is binary, the signal may jump between two discrete voltages such as 0 and 5 V or -15 and $+15$ V. Other signaling methods, such as *Manchester coding* used on Ethernet LANs (Chap. 8), are more complex but provide a better reference for timing in the circuit.

During each signaling period, there is an opportunity to transmit digital information. More than one bit may be sent in the signaling period, as we will see in Chap. 3, and thus the resulting **bits per second (bps)** can be higher than the signaling rate (baud). If the sender is simply transmitting a logical 1 or logical 0 during each signaling period, baud will be the same as bps, but be forewarned that the two terms are intended to mean different things.

2.2.3.1 Asynchronous transmission.

Asynchronous communication involves the transmission of individual symbols at arbitrary times. It is accomplished by using a start pulse on the circuit to begin clocking mechanisms that are synchronized for the duration of a single symbol. When the channel is in the *idle state* (no data being transmitted), the line is constantly transmitting logical ones (or, "marking").

Text data is usually sent between terminals and computers asynchronously. A **start bit** is sent, followed by eight data bits and one or more **stop bits**. The least significant bit (lsb) is transmitted first and the most significant bit (msb) (usually the parity bit) is transmitted last. A rule of thumb to compute the maximum character-transmission rate of an asynchronous channel, assuming one stop bit, is to simply divide the bits per second by 10. For example, a 9600-bps circuit transmits 960 characters/second.

> **EXAMPLE 2.3   Asynchronous transmission of ASCII V**
>
> Sketch the logic levels for an asynchronous communication line when it transmits ASCII V.
>
> ```
> ASCII V, with a 0 parity bit, is represented by:
> 01010110  (no parity)
> ```
>
> The circuit idles at logical 1. Transmission of a character (Fig. 2.4) begins with a transition to logical 0 (the start bit) and is followed by the data and parity bit with the lsb first and, lastly, a stop bit (logical 1).
>
>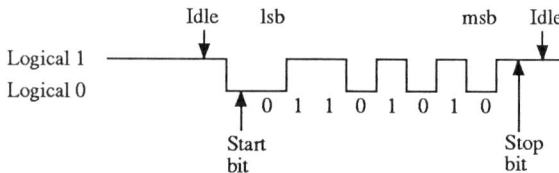
>
> **Figure 2.4**   Asynchronous transmission of ASCII V

2.2.3.2 Synchronous transmission.

In **synchronous** transmission, a large number of symbols are transmitted contiguously. For example, if the data is text, a series of 8-bit characters may run one after another. With synchronous transmission, there is a problem of synchronization so that the receiver knows when a character begins and ends. The synchronization problem is solved with a synchronizing bit pattern at the beginning of transmission of a logical block of data.

With protocols based on standard alphanumeric codes, called *character-oriented* protocols, two consecutive control characters (usually synchronous idle (SYN) characters), are used for synchronization. When the synchronizing pattern is sent by the sender, the receiver knows how to detect the start of 8-bit symbols.

Certain protocols are independent of whether the data or control symbols are standard alphanumeric codes. These *bit-oriented* protocols use a unique 8-bit pattern called a *flag* (01111110) as the initial synchronizing bit pattern. After the flag, the logical block of data has a general format (Fig. 2.5) of a header, information, and trailer. When the circuit is idling, flags are sent continuously.

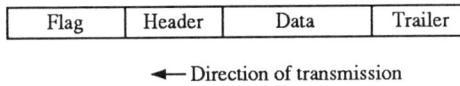

Flag	Header	Data	Trailer

◄— Direction of transmission

Figure 2.5   Example of a synchronous frame

2.3 ERROR DETECTION AND CORRECTION

The effect of noise on digital signals can be disastrous. If a sender is transmitting at 2400 bps, a simple "click" on the telephone, which may take only .01 s, can reverse up to 24 bits in succession. Most protocols permit error detection and recovery.

When an error is detected by the receiver, the most common recovery strategy is to use **automatic request-repeat (ARQ)**. With ARQ, the receiver detects the error and then requests the sender to retransmit. In Chap. 6, several WAN link protocols are discussed that use ARQ for error recovery.

An alternative common recovery strategy is for the receiver first to attempt to reconstruct the data using **forward error correction** techniques (discussed later in the chapter). If the reconstruction is unsuccessful, then the receiver requests the sender to retransmit. This is an important method if the transmission channel is costly, or short-lived or involves a significant delay between the original transmission and receipt of an acknowledgment (such as satellite communications).

2.3.1 Error-detection Methods

One non-analytical error-detection method is the technique of *echoplex*. In echoplex, a user transmits asynchronous text data from a terminal to a host computer on a full-duplex circuit, but the terminal does not print out directly what was keyed. The host computer receives the data and copies it back to the terminal. The user normally compares what he or she entered on the keyboard with what appears on the terminal. Errors in the initial transmission or in the echo will be evident in what is displayed. Incidentally, this technique is also useful for preserving security, such as password entry, because it permits sensitive data to be manually entered and transmitted but not printed on a video display terminal or hard-copy printer.

In the following sections we discuss analytical methods for detecting errors. These techniques may be implemented in software or integrated circuits.

2.3.1.1 Parity check.   A common method to detect an odd number of bit errors is to use **parity** checking. It is a simple calculation of the sum of logical ones in data. A redundant bit, called a *parity bit*, is used to ensure that the sum is an odd or even number, depending on the protocol. A parity bit is usually added to the 7-bit ASCII code in transmission for parity checking.

If *even parity* is required by the protocol and the sum of the bits in modulo 2 (no carries) is 0, the parity bit is 0. If the sum of the data bits is 1, the parity bit is set to 1. The net effect is that the sum of all the 1 bits in modulo 2, including the parity bit, is 0.

You should note that this method of error detection lets an even number of bit errors go undetected.

EXAMPLE 2.4   Code the word DOLLAR with even parity

DOLLAR is coded in Table 2.3. Notice that if it is sent with no parity, errors cannot be detected. With even (or odd) parity, an odd number of bit errors can be detected.

TABLE 2.3   Parity Calculation

Letter	ASCII with No Parity		ASCII with Even Parity	
	msb	lsb	msb	lsb
D	0 1 0 0 0 1 0 0		0 1 0 0 0 1 0 0	
O	0 1 0 0 1 1 1 1		1 1 0 0 1 1 1 1	
L	0 1 0 0 1 1 0 0		1 1 0 0 1 1 0 0	
L	0 1 0 0 1 1 0 0		1 1 0 0 1 1 0 0	
A	0 1 0 0 0 0 0 1		0 1 0 0 0 0 0 1	
R	0 1 0 1 0 0 1 0		1 1 0 1 0 0 1 0	

2.3.1.2 Longitudinal redundancy check (LRC).   An increased degree of error detection can be accomplished with a **longitudinal redundancy check (LRC)**, or *checksum*, that checks parity across all the characters in a frame (Table 2.4). The LRC may be combined with symbol parity for additional error-detection capability. The LRC is appended to the end of a data block. You should note that certain *even* bit-error patterns will go undetected (Fig. 2.6).

EXAMPLE 2.5   Compute even parity and an even LRC for the message HELLO.

Parity and the LRC are shown in Table 2.4. The characters are transmitted in character order, least significant bit first, followed by the LRC.

TABLE 2.4   LRC Calculation

Letter	ASCII with No Parity	ASCII with Even Parity
	msb lsb	msb lsb
H	0 1 0 0 1 0 0 0	0 1 0 0 1 0 0 0
E	0 1 0 0 0 1 0 1	1 1 0 0 0 1 0 1
L	0 1 0 0 1 1 0 0	1 1 0 0 1 1 0 0
L	0 1 0 0 1 1 0 0	1 1 0 0 1 1 0 0
O	0 1 0 0 1 1 1 1	1 1 0 0 1 1 1 1
LRC character:	0 1 0 0 0 0 1 0	0 1 0 0 0 0 1 0

An even number of bit errors will not be detected by parity, and an error in the same bit position on an even number of characters will go undetected by the LRC (Fig. 2.6).

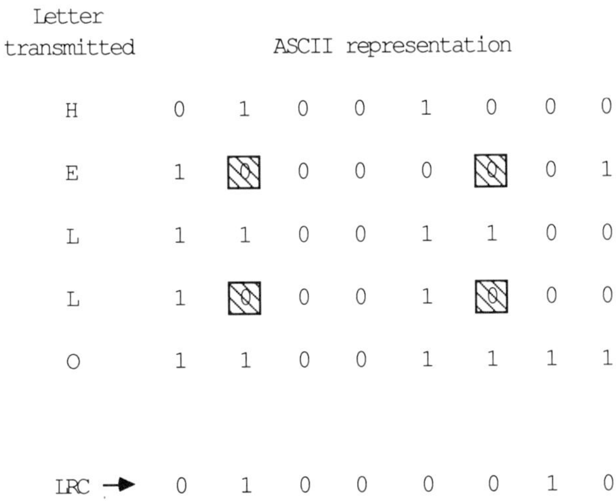

Figure 2.6   Error propagation with LRC and parity

2.3.1.3 Cyclic Redundancy Check

The **cyclic redundancy check (CRC)** is a method of checking the accuracy of a long sequence of bits received in a logical block of data. The sender computes and appends the CRC at the end of the block, and the receiver processes the data and CRC to determine if there have been any errors in transmission.

The CRC can be computed through an algorithm described in the following section either by hardware or software. The hardware implementation is very inexpensive even though the procedures to compute it appear complex.

CRC Calculation

Step 1. Represent the data as a polynomial $P(x)$ with the bits as the coefficients.

Step 2. Multiply the message polynomial P by x^p, which effectively adds p zeroes in the lower-order positions.

Step 3. The product of polynomial P and x^p is now divided by a *generating polynomial* $G(x)$ of degree p. The degree p determines the length of the CRC term. The division is done using synthetic division and modulo 2 arithmetic on the coefficients. The result is a polynomial Q and remainder R:

$$\frac{(x^p)P}{G} = Q + \frac{R}{G}$$

or

$$(x^p)P = QG + R$$

Using modulo 2 arithmetic,

$$(x^p)P + R = QG$$

Step 4. The remainder R is the CRC and is added to $P(x^p)$ for transmission.

$$T(x) = (x^p)P + R = QG \qquad (2.2)$$

EXAMPLE 2.6   A CRC-4 calculation

Compute the CRC-4 for the data 1010010111

$$P(x) = x^9 + x^7 + x^4 + x^2 + x + 1$$

where

$$G(x) = x^4 + x^2 + x + 1 \text{ (or 10111)}$$

Step 1.   Data:

$$P(x) = x^9 + x^7 + x^4 + x^2 + x + 1$$

or

$$1010010111$$

Step 2.   Multiply $P(x)$ by x^4 (add 4 zero bits):

$$(x^4)P(x) = x^{13} + x^{11} + x^8 + x^6 + x^5 + x^4$$

$$10100101110000$$

Step 3.   Take $G(x) = x^4 + x^2 + x + 1$, and calculate $\frac{(x^p)P}{G}$:

```
                1001100100
      10111)10100101110000
            10111
            11101
            10111
             10101
             10111
              10100
              10111
               1100
```

Therefore, $Q = 1001100100$, and

$$R = 1100$$

Step 4.   The remainder R, the CRC, is appended to the data as a trailer.

Step 5.   The receiver divides the received data by the same generating polynomial, $G(x)$. The remainder will be zero if there are no errors in transmission.

Limits to CRC Error Detection.   The receiver is looking for a transmitted message that is an integral multiple of $G(x)$. Therefore, an error that is a multiple of $G(x)$ will escape detection. From (2.2), $T(x) = (x^p)P + R = QG$.

If the received message is

$$QG + E(x)'$$

$E'(x)$ will go undetected if it is a product of $G(x)$:

$$E' = Q'G$$

If $G(x)$ is *even* (the degree p is an even number), such as our example, errors that propagate through are those that are a multiple of the generating polynomial, which in this case will be an even number of bit errors. Thus, a CRC calculation with an even $G(x)$ *always* detects that a block has an error when errors total an odd number of bits.

A *burst error* is a group of bits in which the first bit and the last bit are in error and the intervening bits may or may not be in error. When such an error appears as $(x^q)E(x)$, where $q < p$ and $E(x)$ is less than order p, $E(x)$ is not divisible by $G(x)$. The receiver will always detect a burst error of degree less than p by the CRC calculation.

Because the class of errors that will escape detection is so small (only even bit errors that are a multiple of $G(x)$), the CRC is often considered a very good error detector, and CRC's of degree 16 (CRC-16) are common.

EXAMPLE 2.7   DEC's data link protocol

In DEC's DDCMP data link protocol, the generating polynomial is a CRC-16:

$$x^{16} + x^{15} + x^2 + 1$$

$$1 \;\; 1 \;\; 0 \;\; 0 \;\; 0 \;\; 0 \;\; 0 \;\; 0 \;\; 0 \;\; 0 \;\; 0 \;\; 0 \;\; 0 \;\; 1 \;\; 0 \;\; 1$$

This polynomial will detect all errors that consist of a single burst error of less than 16 bits. Thus a 15-bit burst error might have as many as 15 bits or as few as 2 bits in error, and the CRC will detect them. It will also detect any odd number of bits in error in a message, since $G(x)$ is an even polynomial.

Many LAN protocols use a 32-bit *frame check sequence (FCS)* that is similar to a CRC. The additional length is inexpensive to implement in hardware and provides even greater error-detection capability.

2.3.2 Forward Error Correction

In communication systems where there may be long delays in requesting retransmission, **forward error-correction (FEC)** code may be implemented by the sender to enable error correction at the receiver. These codes are used to reconstruct the message if there is an error. Examples where FEC may be applied include satellite communications and military communications, where tactical and strategic communications systems may suffer from interference.

One of the first codes devised for forward error correction was developed by R. W. Hamming of Bell Laboratory in 1950 [35]. Depending on the number of redundant bits, **Hamming code** can detect and correct multiple errors in coded data. We will limit ourselves here to examining the simplest case, where it is possible to detect two errors and correct an error if there is only one error in the data.

If we devise a 3-bit code to represent eight characters, it could look like this:

$$
\begin{array}{cc}
000 & A \\
001 & B \\
010 & C \\
011 & D \\
100 & E \\
101 & F \\
110 & G \\
111 & H \\
\end{array}
$$

A change in one bit, perhaps caused by some electrical noise, will cause the receiver to interpret the transmitted character as different from the one that was sent. This code is said to have a Hamming distance of one. It provides no means for error detection because any error will create another valid character.

If we devise a 3-bit code to represent four characters, more bits are used than are necessary to transmit the essential information; thus, *redundancy* is designed into the code. The representation could look like this:

$$
\begin{array}{ll}
000 & A \\
011 & B \\
110 & C \\
101 & D
\end{array}
$$

Note that there is a 2-bit difference between each character; that is, it takes a change of 2 bits to create a new valid character from the original. This code has a Hamming distance of two. If 1 bit of a valid character is changed, the code indicates an obvious error condition. For example, the code 001 is not an A, B, C, or D, so it must be an error.

If we now devise a 3-bit code to represent two characters, there is even more redundancy built into the code. The following representation has a Hamming distance of three because it will take a 3-bit change to change from one character to another:

$$
\begin{array}{ll}
000 & A \\
111 & B
\end{array}
$$

In fact, it is possible at this point to tell what the original character was if there is only one 1-bit error because the code more closely resembles its original character than another.

If there are four information bits, three additional bits are required for a Hamming distance of three. This is referred to as Hamming (7, 4) code. To compute the code, even parity check bits are associated with unique combinations of information bits. For a 4-bit information code, a 7-bit *codeword* is constructed in the following sequence:

$$ C_1 \ C_2 \ I_3 \ C_4 \ I_5 \ I_6 \ I_7 $$

where I_3, I_5, I_6, and I_7 are the information bits and

$$
\begin{aligned}
C_1 &= \text{even parity check bit for } I_3, I_5, I_7 \\
C_2 &= \text{even parity check bit for } I_3, I_6, I_7 \\
C_3 &= \text{even parity check bit for } I_5, I_6, I_7
\end{aligned}
$$

If one bit is damaged, a logical comparison of the correctness of C_1, C_2, and C_3 indicates which bit is in error. For example, if C_1 and C_2 are in error, I_3, the only bit common to both of them, is incorrect.

EXAMPLE 2.8   Hamming (7, 4) code calculation

The information bits are:

$$1010$$

(a) What is the Hamming (7, 4) codeword?

ENCODED DATA C_1 C_2 I_3 C_4 I_5 I_6 I_7
$$\downarrow \qquad\qquad \downarrow \quad \downarrow \quad \downarrow$$
C_1 C_2 1 C_3 0   1   0

For even parity of the right combination of the information bits:

C_1 (even parity check bit for I_3, I_5, I_7) = 1
C_2 (even parity check bit for I_3, I_6, I_7) = 0
C_4 (even parity check bit for I_5, I_6, I_7) = 1

Therefore, the transmitted codeword is:

$$1011010$$

(b) Suppose the following codeword was received and only one 1-bit error occurred:

$$1011011$$

Observing the codeword,

C_1 = 1 and is incorrect
C_2 = 0 and is incorrect
C_4 = 1 and is incorrect

Since all these parity bits are in error, a bit was changed that is common to the calculation of all three. This can only be I_7. The original codeword was, therefore,

$$1011010$$

2.4 PERFORMANCE ON A COMMUNICATION CHANNEL

The design of a network should satisfy a number of user requirements, such as speed, accuracy, and reliability. As we discussed in Chap. 1, one of the most important requirements is the delivery speed of the data. The time to deliver a unit of data depends on both the size of the unit of data and the circuit transmission rate:

$$t = \frac{n}{R} \tag{2.3}$$

where

n = number of bits in the unit of data

R = bit transmission rate of the circuit, independent of whether or not any data bits are flowing.

An obvious measure of rate-of-transmission performance on a digital channel is the total bit *throughput*, in bits per second. The problem with the usefulness of this measure is that so much redundancy is built into typical protocols to provide services to the user that the actual number of information bits may be small compared to the total bits transferred. Additional performance measures are required that distinguish between the simple load-carrying capability of the network (R) and the rate of delivery of user data.

There are two measures of efficiency or performance that we discuss in this text to evaluate codes and protocols. They include:

1. The **code rate**, a measure of the degree of non-information (i.e., redundant) bits built into the communication code.
2. The **transfer rate of information bits (TRIB)**, a measure that allows comparisons of different communication protocols and considers all the inefficiencies in the channels due to code design, retransmission, and other protocol functions.

2.4.1 Code Rate

A measure of the coding efficiency can be computed by calculating the code rate, the ratio of the number of information bits to the total number of bits per symbol. One of the benefits of the code rate is that it helps to quantify the inefficiency due to redundant bits. The code rate, E, is then:

$$E = \frac{B_i}{B_t} \tag{2.4}$$

where

B_i = information bits per symbol

B_t = total bits per symbol (information bits plus redundant bits)

EXAMPLE 2.9   Code rate calculation

What is the coding efficiency of ASCII code with one parity bit?

$$E = \frac{B_i}{B_t}$$

L
$$= \frac{7}{8} = .875 = 87.5\%$$

2.4.2 Transfer Rate of Information Bits (TRIB)

In its sum total, the performance of a communications path must take into account the time delays in each of the following five communication phases:

Phase 1, *connection establishment*, is the time to establish the physical connection. This time is very significant with networks that use circuits that require a number of switches to be activated before the connection is complete, such as a telephone circuit (i.e., *circuit-switched networks*). With dedicated channels, this time is zero. In establishing a voice telephone call, this time is the time to dial the distant user, complete the circuit, and have the user answer the telephone.

Phase 2, *link establishment*, is the waiting time before the user can transmit data because the protocols are being initialized. In an analogous voice conversation this is the time for a greeting and for identifying the caller. In computer-to-computer communications, this is the time required to initialize a protocol, poll, or pass a token to the user. On a dedicated terminal-to-host asynchronous link, the sender can often transmit at any time without waiting for permission and therefore this time is zero.

Phase 3, *information transfer*, is the time required to send all the user's information after the communications link is established. It includes (1) time to transmit all the code; (2) time to process acknowledgments; (3) time to retransmit data because of errors; and (4) time delays, such as time-outs and encryption initialization, that may occur after the link is established.

Phase 4, *link termination*, is the time for the protocol to orderly terminate. In a voice conversation, this is the time for both parties to say good-bye. If the data link is a simple asynchronous link, this time is zero.

Phase 5, *connection clearing*, is the time for the switched circuits to clear so that the next connection can be established. Again, if dedicated circuits are used, this time is zero.

Transfer rate of information bits (TRIB) (formally described in ANSI X3.44) is one measure used to compare the efficiency of one protocol over another. This is useful when the network includes circuits of limited data transfer capacity, and alternative protocols must be evaluated.

TRIB is the rate that correct information bits are accepted by the receiving terminal during the information transfer phase (Phase 3) and is expressed in bits per second:

$$\text{TRIB} = n_{\text{info}}/t_3 \qquad (2.5)$$

where

$n_{\text{info}} = $ number of information bits

$t_3 = $ time to transfer the information bits from the sender to the receiver

In this text we generally focus on TRIB. It enables us to evaluate protocols and not be too concerned with one-time delays establishing and clearing the circuits.

The term *information bits* must be carefully defined. It is relatively simple to define information bits in asynchronous ASCII traffic — there are seven information bits that define a symbol. A redundant bit is added for possible error detection. Later, in some examples of synchronous protocols, we will assume that all the bits in the so-called information, or data, field are information bits, although in actuality, the information that the user is transmitting is buried in a message with a lot of control data. These "non-information" control bits will be identified later.

The redundant bits used for such things as control or error detection are not counted as information bits but enter into the TRIB calculation because they take time to transmit during Phase 3.

If the link has bit errors, a number of retransmissions may be required and these, too, will be reflected in the time.

Note that t_3 includes the time for transmitting the bits (t_{tot}), plus delays such as circuit delays at the receiver ($t_{interface}$), computer processing delays (t_{proc}), and propagation delays (t_{prop}) due to the finite time to transmit an electric signal from end to end.

Therefore,

$$t_3 = t_{tot} + t_{interface} + t_{proc} + t_{prop} \qquad (2.6)$$

For simplicity most of the calculation in the text will only involve t_{tot}. For example, if the link is simplex,

$$t_3 = t_{tot} = \frac{n_{tot}}{R} \qquad (2.7)$$

where

$\quad n_{tot} =$ total bits transferred from the sender to the receiver

$\quad R \quad =$ bit transmission rate of the channel

If the link is half-duplex, with receiver acknowledgments, t_{tot} is the sum of the time for bit transmission in each direction.

$$t_{tot} = \frac{n_{data} + n_{ack}}{R} \qquad (2.8)$$

where

$\quad n_{data} =$ total data bits sent from the sender
$\qquad\qquad$ to the receiver

$\quad n_{avk} =$ total acknowledgment bits returned from
$\qquad\qquad$ the receiver to the sender

$\quad R \quad =$ bit transmission rate of the channel

EXAMPLE 2.10   TRIB calculation

A 1000-character message of ASCII text is sent to a distant receiver. The receiver checks the message for errors and requests retransmission of the *entire* message if there is an error. Compute TRIB for the case of (a) an error-free circuit and (b) a circuit with a 10^{-5} bit error rate (BER) (or an average of 1 bit error in 100,000 bits).
Assume:

1. Half-duplex asynchronous link
2. 1000 ASCII-character message
3. 1200-bps circuit
4. Retransmission request is instantaneous

(a) To compute TRIB for an error-free circuit:

$$n_{info} = (7 \text{ bits/symbol})(1000 \text{ symbols}) = 7000 \text{ bits}$$

The total number of bits, including start and stop bits, is

$$(10 \text{ bits/character})(1000 \text{ characters}) = 10,000 \text{ bits}$$

Therefore,

$$t_3 = t_{tot} = 10,000 \text{ bits}/1200 \text{ bps} = 8.33 \text{ s}$$

From Eq. (2.5),

$$\text{TRIB} = \frac{7000 \text{ bits}}{8.33 \text{ s}} = 841 \text{ bps}$$

(b) To compute TRIB for a circuit with 10^{-5} BER, note that from (a), 10,000 bits are subject to being damaged. From probability theory, the probability of no errors occurring in that data is:

$$P_{no} = (1 - \text{BER})^N \tag{2.9}$$

where

$$\text{BER} = \text{bit error rate}$$

$$N = \text{number of bits in a block}$$

Therefore,

$$P_{no} = .99999^{10,000} = .905$$

Considering the need to make multiple transmissions until the message is successfully received, it can be shown from probability theory that:

$$t_3 = \frac{t_{3no}}{P_{no}}$$ (2.10)

where

t_{3no} = time to transmit a message when there are no errors

P_{no} = probability that there are no errors from Eq. 2.9

Therefore,

$$t_{3no} = 8.33 \text{ s}$$

$$t_3 = \frac{8.33}{.905} = 9.20 \text{ s}$$

and, from Eq. 2.5,

$$\text{TRIB} = \frac{7000 \text{ bits}}{9.20 \text{ s}} = 761 \text{ bps}$$

By comparing TRIB to the 1200 bps bit transmission rate, it is seen that the redundant bits necessary for signaling (start and stop bits) and error detection (parity) decrease TRIB by 30%. Noise on the circuit (incidentally, BER of 10^{-5} is typical of telephone circuits) reduces TRIB by another 10%.

2.5 SUMMARY

Symbols must be represented in binary code for computer communications. The most common code in the United States for representing alphanumeric symbols is ASCII code, which is commonly used to transmit data from interactive terminals. Data may be transmitted over parallel circuits if the sender and receiver are collocated, otherwise the transmission is usually serial. Data can be sent serially in an asynchronous mode or synchronous mode.

Interactive terminals usually communicate asynchronously because such communication permits immediate transmission of low-volume manually inputted data. Computer-to-computer communications are usually synchronous to improve efficiency because large-volume data can be sent in contiguous blocks without extra start and stop bits on each symbol. There are a number of error-detection and correction methods, including parity checking, LRC checksums, and CRC calculations. Error recovery techniques range from simple ARQ methods to forward error correction.

Protocols that are necessary for interoperability impact network performance. Code rate may be used to compare codes and TRIB may be used to compare protocols.

KEY WORDS AND CONCEPTS

American Standard Code for
  Information Interchange (ASCII)
asynchronous
automatic request-repeat (ARQ)
baseband
baud
bit
bits per second (bps)
broadband
code rate
cyclic redundancy check (CRC)
forward error correction (FEC)

full-duplex
half-duplex
Hamming code
longitudinal redundancy check (LRC)
modulate
parity
simplex
start bit
stop bit
synchronous
transfer rate of information bits (TRIB)

PROBLEMS

1. What is the reason for establishing control codes in a code set?
2. Baudot code is an old code used in teletype operations. It is a 5-bit code. How many different symbols can it transmit? (*Note*: By designating two of the characters (letters shift and figures shift) as special *escape characters*, the number of characters Baudot devices are able to send is almost doubled. When a figures shift is sent, the characters that follow are uppercase characters until a letters shift is sent, and vice versa.)
3. What advantages does an 8-bit code have over a 5-bit code?
4. What is the difference between 60 baud and 60 bps?
5. Convert your last name to its ASCII representation. Assume a zero parity bit.
6. Convert your last name to its ASCII binary representation with even parity.
7. Convert your last name to its ASCII binary representation with even parity and compute an even LRC.
8. What is the signaling time for a 75-baud line? A 2400-baud line?
9. What is the time of transmission for this sentence in ASCII? Assume the sentence is sent asynchronously on a 2400-bps line.
10. How many seconds does it take to fill a screen that is 80 characters by 25 lines from a computer at 300 baud asynchronously?
11. How many seconds does it take to fill a 356K byte diskette from a computer at 600 bps asynchronously?
12. Show that the transmitted message in Example 2.6,

$$1 \quad 0 \quad 1 \quad 0 \quad 0 \quad 1 \quad 0 \quad 1 \quad 1 \quad 1 \quad 1 \quad 1 \quad 0 \quad 0$$

has a zero remainder when divided by the generating polynomial, $G(x) = 10111$.
13. Compute the CRC for the following data:

$$1 \quad 0 \quad 0 \quad 1 \quad 1 \quad 1 \quad 0 \quad 0 \quad 0 \quad 1 \quad 1 \quad 0$$

Use CRC-3, $G = 1011$. Check the answer by computing T/G and show $R = 0$.

14. Encode 0110 with Hamming (7, 4).

15. Encode 1111 with Hamming (7, 4).

16. Encode 0000 with Hamming (7, 4).

17. Data was encoded with Hamming (7, 4) code and the following was received:

$$1 \quad 1 \quad 1 \quad 1 \quad 0 \quad 0 \quad 0$$

    (a) What codeword was sent, assuming at the most one bit error?

    (b) What were the original information bits?

18. In the following matrix, A 0 indicates that the Hamming bit arrived correct, and a 1 indicates that it arrived incorrect. Fill in the missing entries.

Parity Bit Incorrect Indicated by "1"

C4	C2	C1	Single Bit That Is In Error
0	0	0	None
0	0	1	
0	1	0	
1	0	0	
1	0	1	
1		0	
1	1	1	

19. What is the coding efficiency E when Hamming (7,4) code is used?

20. A code is needed to send uppercase letters, the numbers 0 through 9, "-", "." and ",". What is the minimum number of bits required? If ASCII characters are used, what is the coding efficiency E?

21. On a simplex link, 4000 ASCII characters with even parity are sent asynchronous over an error-free 300-bps link. What is TRIB?

22. Messages of 5000 ASCII characters are transmitted asynchronous on a 1200 bps full-duplex circuit. If there are errors, the receiver immediately notifies the sender to retransmit the entire message (similar to Example 2.10). (a) Compute TRIB for the case of no bit errors and (b) compute TRIB when BER $= 10^{-6}$.

23. Another communications performance parameter is the transfer overhead time (TOT). TOT is the sum of the time for phases 1, 2, 4, and 5 divided by n_{info} and is measured in seconds per bit.

    (a) In what situation is TOT an important measure of performance for a network designer?

    (b) Compute TOT for the data transfer in Prob. 21, where on the average, over a circuit-switched network,

$$\text{Phase 1} = 5 \text{ s}$$

$$\text{Phase 2} = .2 \text{ s}$$

$$\text{Phase 4} = .1 \text{ s}$$

$$\text{Phase 5} = 3 \text{ s}$$

3

TRANSMISSION BASICS

A communication system has three components: (1) transmitter, (2) communication medium, and (3) receiver (Fig. 3.1). The transmitter translates an input signal into a signal that can propagate on the medium. The traveling signal may be a baseband voltage signal directly proportional to the input signal or a modulated broadband radio, microwave, or light beam signal. The receiver translates the baseband or broadband signal into an output signal compatible with the user's equipment. In this chapter we discuss the physical properties of various media and the impact that the physical properties have on digital transmission.

3.1 MEDIA CHARACTERISTICS

The medium may be any material that can convey a signal between two points and may even be a perfect vacuum in the case of electromagnetic waves (for example, laser and radio signals).

One of the most common media is a pair of wires between a transmitter and receiver with the amplitude of changing voltages as the signaling method. These wires are common because so many areas and buildings have been equipped by the telephone companies with twisted-pair wiring for telephone communications.

Other media include coaxial cable, optical fibers, and free space itself, using light waves, radio waves, or microwaves.

Since the objective is to transmit digital data from one point to another, the transmitted and received signal should ideally have a clear, sharp transition from what can be called an OFF logical state to an ON state, and vice versa.

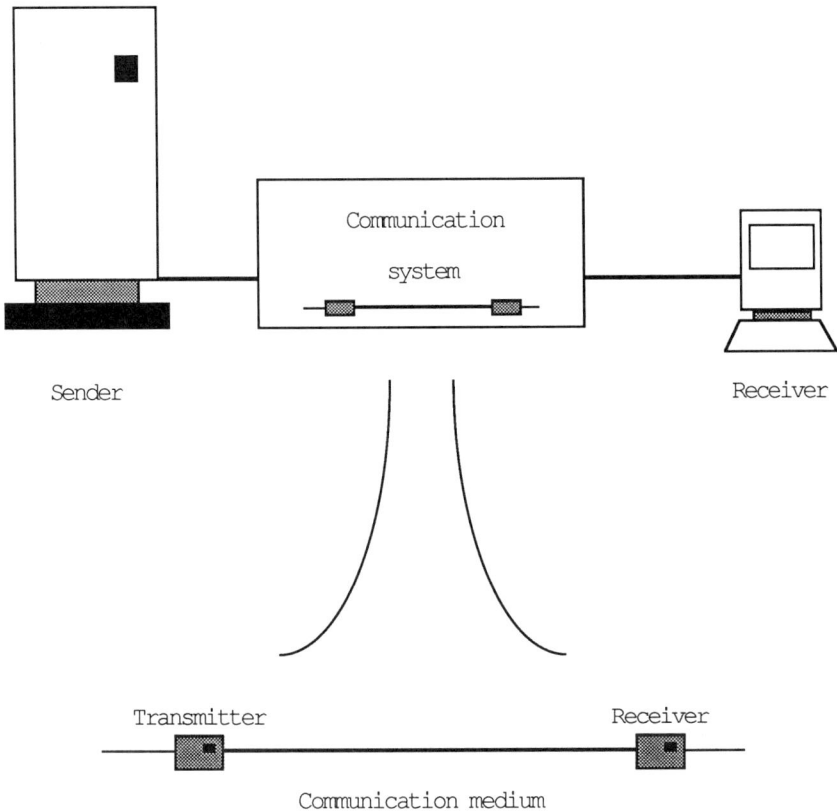

Figure 3.1   Communication components

The frequency of a signal transmitted in a medium is measured in **hertz** (**Hz**). The range of frequencies that a medium can transmit, or **bandwidth**, affects the sharpness of the transition from one state to another and limits the resulting signaling rate. The bandwidth depends on the inherent properties of the medium, such as distributed capacitance, inductance, and resistance.

The loss of signal intensity as the signal travels through the communication system is called **attenuation**. With metal wire, the signal is attenuated by the resistance of the metal and depends on the length of the circuit. Signals in optical fibers are usually attenuated by impurities in the fibers. Attenuation of waves in free space may be due to reflections and interference, normal spreading of the signal as it travels, and the presence of impurities such as rain, smoke, and haze.

3.1.1 Twisted-pair Copper Wire

Twisted pairs can transmit up to 10 Mbps (1 Mbps $= 10^6$ bps) over limited distances, assuming the full bandwidth of the twisted pair is available (no filters are installed). It is often the least expensive media for data networks within buildings when the wire has already been installed for telephone applications.

Digital repeaters are needed to regenerate the signal in amplitude and shape if the signal is to be transmitted over any substantial distance. For example, the American Telephone and Telegraph Corporation (AT&T) *T-1 digital carrier* system operates at 1.544 Mbps over wire pairs and requires regeneration and retiming at repeater intervals of about 6000 feet.

Noise is a constant problem with wire circuits. One source of noise is background thermal noise from the thermal motion of electrons, which affects the amplifiers and conductors. Other sources of noise are people-created such as heavy machinery and electrical switches in adjacent circuits.

Originally, copper lines for telegraph and telephone communications were not twisted but were strung as open-wire pairs, and they picked up *crosstalk* interference from each other. Twisted pairs reduce crosstalk because the currents are in opposite directions and the magnetic fields that are generated nearly cancel.

3.1.2 Coaxial Cable

Coaxial cable is a copper wire surrounded by a cylindrical sheath of insulation and an outer cylindrical sheath of copper mesh or foil. It can transmit frequencies that range up to 300 to 400 MHz and is generally immune to electrical interference. When used to transmit digital information, coaxial cable may carry up to 100 Mbps. Because of the high bandwidth, coaxial cable can simultaneously transmit voice, data, and video. Usually the data-only implementations are 3 to 10 Mbps; Ethernet, a LAN that operates over coaxial cable, transmits at 10 Mbps.

3.1.3 Microwave

Terrestrial microwave systems normally operate between 1.7 GHz and 23 GHz (1 GHz = 10^9 Hz) and their beams tend to follow the line of sight. Antennas to repeat and regenerate signals are spaced approximately 20 to 30 miles apart because of the curvature of the earth. The signal is attenuated because of signal path distance, interference from reflections from natural and man-made structures, and rain and snow.

Major sources of noise below 30 MHz are lightning flashes and electrostatic discharges in the atmosphere. Noise from electrical machinery is a major source of noise below 1 GHz.

3.1.4 Geosynchronous Satellite

A satellite channel consists of a satellite in orbit, an uplink from a ground station, and a downlink to another ground station. Satellites used in telecommunications are usually geostationary, in fixed orbits above the equator. There are international agreements under the auspices of the United Nations International

Telecommunications Union (ITU) about who may use which geostationary satellite orbit slots and frequencies.

In the United States, the Federal Communications Commission (FCC) has further allocated the 3.7 to 4.2 GHz (downward beams) and 5.925 to 6.425 GHz microwave frequencies (upward beams) as commercial communication satellite frequencies. This range is referred to as the 4/6 GHz band, or *C-band*. A higher band is also available to communications at 12/14 GHz (*Ku band*) that provides additional bandwidth. However, the 12/14 band is more susceptible to attenuation by rain because of reflections off raindrops, and requires more expensive equipment.

The FCC does not directly control the communications of the Department of Defense (DoD), but it does reserve certain bands of frequencies for military use. DoD then sets up its own links and allocates their use.

In 4/6-band communications, a civilian satellite is typically assigned a specific orbital position as well as upward and downward frequency by the FCC. The upward and downward links each have a 250-MHz *guardband* on the upper and lower side of the assigned frequency to prevent interference with neighboring channels, for a total bandwidth of 500 MHz.

The satellite itself contains a number of *transponders* that receive the earth signal at one frequency, amplify it, and retransmit it at the lower frequency. The lower frequency is used on the downlink because it requires less power. The 500-MHz bandwidth is divided into channels, often 36 or 40 MHz wide, with each channel handled by a separate transponder.

A geostationary orbit is approximately 22,100 miles above the surface of the earth. This distance introduces delays in communication because microwave signals travel at the speed of light at approximately 186,000 miles per second. A signal simply propagating vertically up to the satellite and down experiences a 235 ms propagation delay. Actual delays will be slightly longer (250 to 300 ms) depending on the distance between the ground stations and the elevation of the satellite above the horizon.

3.1.5 Open-air Laser

Open-air laser links are an option for distances between 2 and 4 mi. The distances are constrained by line of sight and weather disturbances, such as dense fog, severe dust, smoke, haze, and snow. Typical open-air laser links operate at 40 Mbps.

3.1.6 Optical Fiber

There are no capacitive or inductive distortions with electromagnetic radiation as there are with signals transmitted through metal wires. However, one common problem when transmitting radio waves, microwaves, and light waves in free space is that the signals attenuate rapidly simply because the energy is distributed over a wider and wider area as the beam travels farther from the source. Containing electromagnetic energy such as microwaves in a waveguide or, in the case of light, optical fibers, dramatically increases the distance that it can be transmitted.

Fiber optic technology is new, starting around 1970. A major problem was attenuation from impurities in the optical fibers, but other problems, such as making reliable semiconductor lasers, also had to be overcome. In 1977, General Telephone and Electronics (GTE) established the first commercial system with a 5.6-mi link between Long Beach, California, and Artesia, California.

Fiber optics may eventually replace terrestrial microwave and satellite links because it is impervious to noise, has high bandwidth, and has long-term reliability. It is virtually impossible to detect fiber optic signals, which makes it desirable for secure communications. The error rates are very low, as can be seen in Table 3.1.

Fiber optics can be used to transmit over distances from 4 to 5 miles. Although data rates may be over 1 Gbps, most commercial systems are from 1 to 50 Mbps. The original GTE system, just described, carried 24 voice channels at 1.544 Mbps. The Fiber Distributed Data Interface (FDDI) [12] is a fiber optic-based LAN that is planned to operate at 100 Mbps.

TABLE 3.1   Errors Expected with Various Media

Twisted pair in telephone system:	10^{-5} (1 in 100,000)
Coaxial cable:	10^{-7} (1 in 10,000,000)
Fiber optics:	10^{-12} (1 in 1,000,000,000,000)

3.2 BANDWIDTH

One of the most important terms in communications is the term *bandwidth*. As we explained earlier, it refers to the range of frequencies that can be transmitted over a given communication system, and is constrained by the characteristics of the transmitter, medium, and receiver. The telephone network (with filters at the central office) transmits frequencies between 300 and 3400 Hz; thus its bandwidth is about 3100 Hz. Bandwidth refers to the difference between the highest and lowest frequencies, not to the frequencies themselves.

3.2.1 Constraints on Signaling Rate

In order to transmit digital information, it must be possible to distinguish clearly between a logical 0 and logical 1. In 1928, Nyquist developed the maximum digital signaling rate on a noiseless circuit without incurring interference (the **Nyquist relationship**):

$$B = 2W \qquad (3.1)$$

where

$$B = \text{maximum digital signaling rate, in baud}$$

$$W = \text{bandwidth in hertz}$$

This relationship imposes no limit on the signaling rate of the sender or the transmission rate through the medium. It simply says that the receiver cannot correctly interpret any signaling rate higher than twice the bandwidth of the medium.

EXAMPLE 3.1   Maximum signaling rate on a telephone circuit

The telephone system was developed to transmit voice signals. Speech frequencies of males go up to about 8000 Hz. Although audible sounds, such as concert music, can go up to 20,000 Hz, the telephone system has been tailored to transmit the range of speech frequencies involving the most power. Thus, as a result of experimentation, the standard frequency band of a voice telephone channel was established from 300 to 3400 Hz. This is enough to make the human voice intelligible and the speaker recognizable. The bandwidth of this system from point to point is 3100 Hz. From Eq. 3.1, the maximum signaling rate is:

$$B = 2W$$

$$= 2(3100)$$

$$= 6200 \text{ baud}$$

3.2.2 Constraints on Information Rate

In 1948, C. Shannon [69] published a paper concerning encoding and decoding methods that could be employed to transmit data. In the paper, he calculated the theoretical maximum bit-rate capacity for transmitting data on a noisy analog channel of bandwidth W. **Shannon's law** is as follows:

$$C = W\log_2\left(1 + \frac{S}{N}\right) \qquad (3.2)$$

where

$$C = \text{maximum bit-rate capacity, in bits per second}$$

$$W = \text{bandwidth, in hertz}$$

$$S = \text{power of the signal}$$

$$N = \text{power of the noise}$$

What is the difference between the signaling rate computed using Nyquist's relationship and information rate using Shannon's law? Fundamentally, Nyquist is computing a signaling rate on a pure noiseless channel. However, in each signaling

period, multiple bits can be transmitted, and this total information rate is what
Shannon predicts, taking into account the effects of noise on the channel.

EXAMPLE 3.2   Maximum Information Rate on a Telephone Circuit

Compute the maximum information rate on a telephone link with bandwidth
3100 Hz. Assume the signal-to-noise ratio for the telephone system is approximately 1000.

From Eq. 3.2,

$$C = (3100 \text{ Hz})(\log_2(1 + 1000))$$

$$= 30,898 \text{ bps}$$

Comparing the maximum information rate with the maximum signaling rate
in the telephone system,

$$\frac{C}{B} = \frac{30,898}{6200} \sim 5$$

This indicates that about 5 bits must be transmitted during each signaling
period to achieve Shannon's maximum information transfer rate.

In spite of the high theoretical capacity, in practice the maximum information
data rate is only about 9600 bps on a telephone circuit that is routed through a
central office. There are several reasons for this: (a) Shannon's law was derived
for the case of random noise (e.g., thermal noise), and actual noise on telephone
lines (such as switching and crosstalk) is not random, and (b) noise on many
circuits may be higher than published figures indicate.

3.3 TELEPHONE SYSTEMS

In the United States, the primary telephone network is provided by seven regional
Bell holding companies (RBHCs) and a number of long distance carriers, including
AT&T, MCI, and Sprint. The RBHCs build, operate, and maintain extensive local
networks. They are organized around approximately 160 local access and transport
areas (LATAs) that are generally equivalent to metropolitan areas. RBHCs are
responsible for intra-LATA service and must provide equal access to long distance
carriers for inter-LATA service.

The companies that provide commercial communications services using their
own communication backbone network are called **common carriers**. Their services
and prices are described in a document called a *tariff*, which must be approved
by the Federal Communications Commission (FCC) for interstate carriers and by
state public utility commissions for intrastate traffic.

In almost all other countries the carriers are a part of the postal, telephone,
and telegraph administration (PTT) of the government. All the carriers, including
those in the United States, are coordinated internationally through a United Nations

treaty organization called the International Telecommunication Union (ITU). The members of the union are governments, and the United States is represented by the Department of State. The telephone and data communications organ of the ITU is the International Telegraph and Telephone Consultive Committee (CCITT). The CCITT formally meets every four years and makes official "recommendations" that often become U.S. standards.

The telephone network originated as a voice network, transmitting voice frequencies in the range from 300 to 3400 Hz over copper wires. Today, increasingly, many circuits transmit voice signals that have been converted to digital signals. The techniques to do this are covered later in this chapter. The trends indicate that the network will eventually be a digital network.

A local subscriber normally communicates using analog voltage signals over a twisted-pair *subscriber loop* between the home or office and the nearest *central office* switch. This circuit can be between .5 and 6 miles long.

To provide end-to-end connectivity, calls are made through a series of switches from one telephone to another for the duration of a call. At the termination of a call, the circuits are then released for the use of other callers.

In the case of a company or university, where there are a large number of telephones in a small geographic area, the telephone company may provide a *remote concentrator* or the company may install its own *private branch exchange (PBX)*, both relatively small switches, with a trunk connection to the central office.

An area code and first three digits of a telephone number uniquely specify a central office. Each office can service up to 10,000 telephone lines (−0000 to −9999). If a call is between telephones served by the same central office, it is switched at that office.

The network is configured so that local exchanges are interconnected through another switching center, called a toll office, and the toll offices are interconnected through primary, sectional, and regional switching centers. The overall telephone network is a hierarchy with five levels (Fig. 3.2). Calls are routed along the most direct path, which may vary between the centers, depending on the traffic loads between switches.

Communication beyond the central office is accomplished by grouping a number of calls on one physical medium by **multiplexing** (techniques discussed in Sec. 3.6). A twisted pair can carry 12 to 24 full-duplex voice channels over analog facilities or 24 to 96 channels using digital facilities. Coaxial cable can support the equivalent of 1800 to 10,800 voice channels. Microwave facilities can carry up to 1800 voice channels, and optic fibers carry 672 per fiber [71].

Signals on long-distance telephone connections can be masked by noise and distortion. Noise masks analog signals and introduces errors into digital signals. Two particularly important sources of noise are thermal noise and crosstalk. These, and other sources of noise, are described quite extensively in [70].

Distortion modifies transmitted analog signal. One source of distortion is attenuation that depends on the transmission frequency. For example, the inherent capacitance of wire conductors results in higher attenuation of the higher

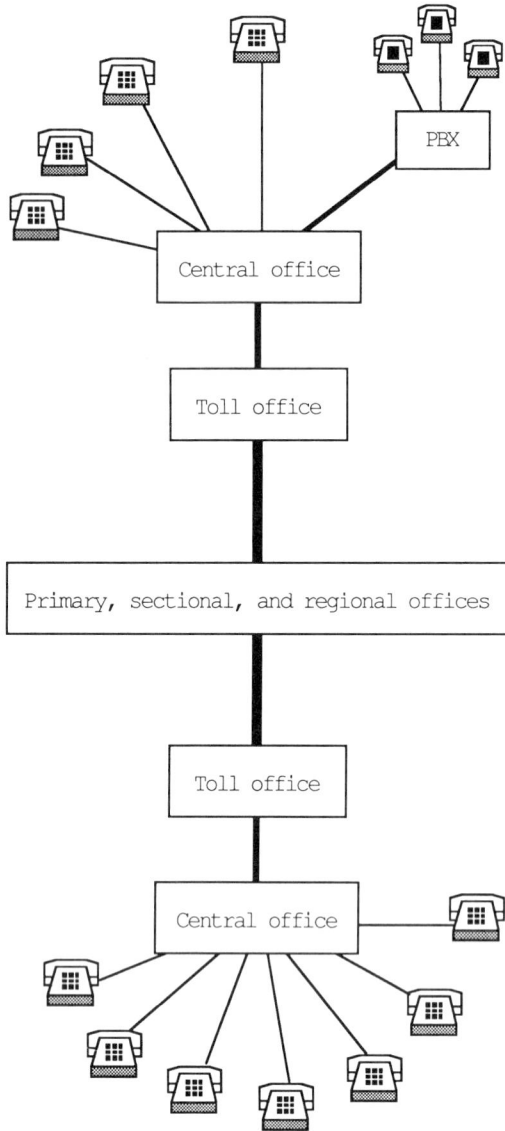

Figure 3.2   Telephone system end-to-end architecture

frequencies. This can be overcome to a large extent by adding equalizer circuits that attenuate the lower frequencies to keep the attenuation relatively constant over all the frequencies.

A major transition is being made in the telephone industry to convert circuits to carry digital voice signals. The final result will be lower cost and much higher quality transmission because of less distortion.

3.4 MODEMS

The telephone system is an obvious in-place system for transmitting data over long distances. However, as we have seen, it can transmit only those frequencies in a narrow bandwidth. In order to use the bandwidth available in the telephone system, a conversion device must be provided that can convert baseband digital information (voltages for logical ones and zeros) to signals in the voice spectrum. A modulator-demodulator for this purpose is called a **modem**.

A wave's amplitude at any moment at a given point can be represented mathematically by:

$$A = A_0 \sin(2\pi f t + B) \tag{3.3}$$

where

A_0 = amplitude of wave

f = frequency of wave

B = phase of wave relative to some reference

A, f, or B may be varied to transmit information. However, for a given communication channel, modems modulating the same variables must be used at each end.

3.4.1 Amplitude Modulation

The simplest modem converts input voltage signals into tone-on (logical 1) and tone-off (logical 0) to transmit binary data (Fig. 3.3). This is *amplitude modulation*. A major problem with this, in practice, is its susceptibility to noise interference.

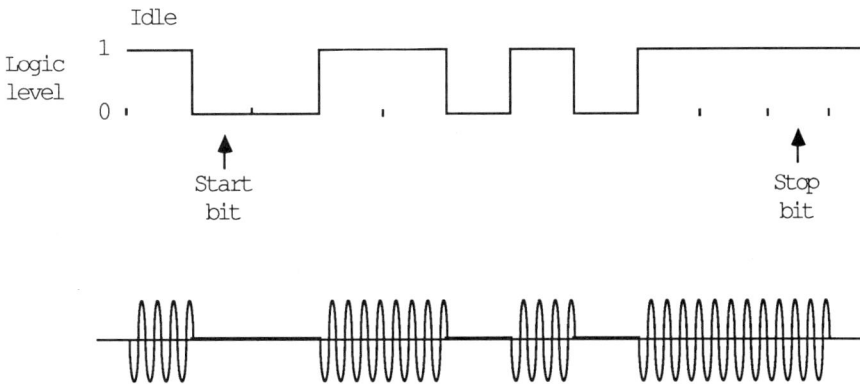

Figure 3.3 Asynchronous transmission with amplitude modulation

3.4.2 Frequency Modulation

Frequency-shift keyed (FSK) modems transmit binary data by converting input signals into low-frequency and high-frequency tones. This is the principle of almost all low-speed modems. Normal convention is for the higher frequency to represent logical 0, and the lower, logical 1 (Fig. 3.4).

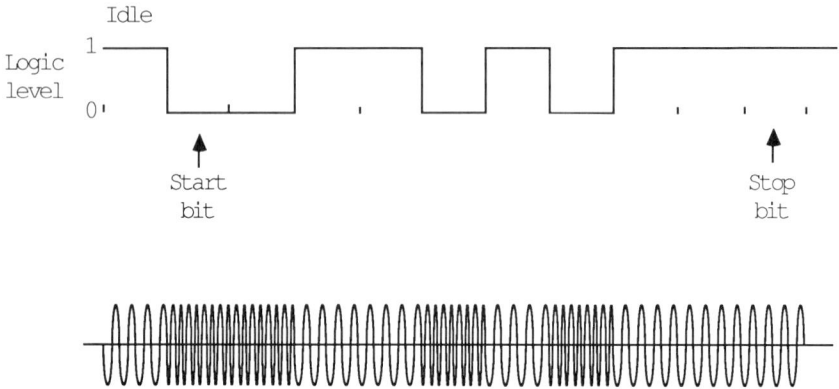

Figure 3.4   FSK asynchronous transmission

EXAMPLE 3.3   FSK modulation with AT&T 103-series modem

The AT&T 103-series modem divides the voice bandwidth into two bands for full-duplex operation with unique frequency assignments. When sending, it transmits at 1070 (logical 0) and 1270 (logical 1) Hz and when answering, 2025 (logical 0) and 2225 (logical 1) Hz. It transmits at 300 bps.

3.4.3 Phase Modulation

Phase modulation changes the phase of a wave at the transition between logical ones and zeros while keeping the frequency and amplitude constant. Modems that operate on this principle are called **phase-shift keyed (PSK)** modems.

3.4.3.1 Phase-shift keyed modem.   PSK can be conceptualized if you think of there being two signals: a reference sine wave and a second wave 180° out of phase (Fig. 3.5). Whenever a logical 1 is transmitted, the reference sine wave is transmitted, and whenever the 0 is transmitted, the out-of-phase sine wave is transmitted.

3.4.3.2 Differential phase-shift keyed modem.   An alternative method of phase-shift modulation is **differential phase-shift keying (DPSK)**. In DPSK the phase change itself—and not its absolute relationship to a reference sig-

(a) Reference signal (logical 1)

(b) 180° out-of-phase signal (logical 0)

(c) Logical 1 and 0

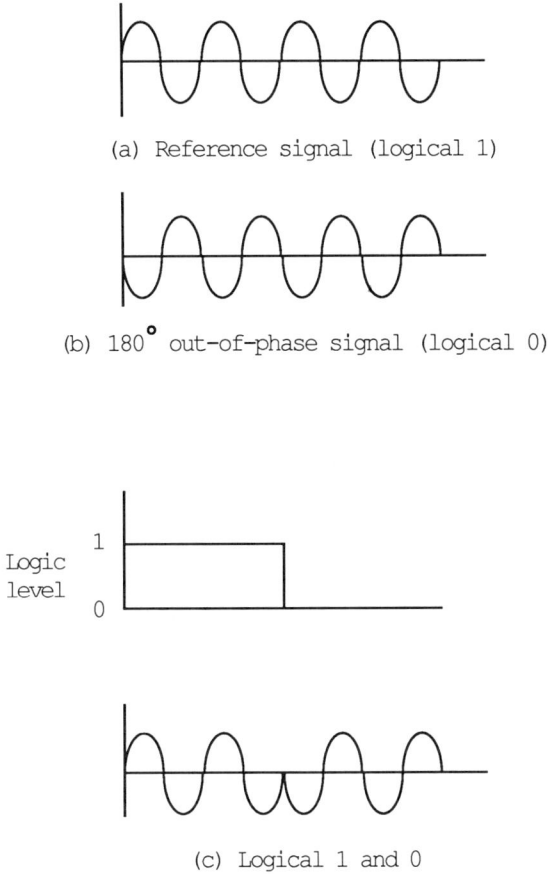

Figure 3.5   Phase-shift modulation

nal—indicates a change in the logical state. Whenever a logical 0 is transmitted in a given time interval, there is no phase change relative to the last interval; whenever a logical 1 is transmitted, there is a phase change.

With phase changes that are multiples of 90° (i.e., 0°, 90°, 180°, and 270°), four information levels can be transmitted. These units of information are called *dibits*.

```
Dibits
  00
  01
  10
  11
```

Phase changes that are multiples of 45° (i.e., 0°, 45°, 90°, and so on) provide eight levels of information. These units of information are called *tribits*.

```
Tribits
 000
 001
 010
 011
 100
 101
 110
 111
```

Another modem technique is to combine modulation methods. *Quadrature amplitude modulation (QAM)* uses four different phases and four amplitudes for a total of 16 information levels (*quadbits*). With QAM, a 2400-baud signaling rate permits a 9600-bps data rate.

EXAMPLE 3.4   DPSK modulation with AT&T 212A modem

The AT&T 212A is a dual-speed, full-duplex modem that operates from 0 to 300 bps using the FSK principle of the AT&T 103 modem (Example 3.3), or 1200 bps using DPSK to transmit dibits. It modulates dibits at 600 baud for an effective data rate of 1200 bps. At 1200 bps, in sending, it modulates a 1200-Hz tone; when answering, it modulates a 2400-Hz tone. Encoding is:

```
    Dibit               Phase Shift
     00                    +90
     01                     0
     10                    180
     11                    -90
```

3.5 DIGITAL TRANSMISSION

Analog signals, such as voice telephone signals, are converted to digital using an **analog-to-digital converter (ADC)**. The conversions are done at a specific *sampling rate* and then the digital data is transmitted over the communication system as a digital pulse train instead of fluctuating analog signals.

An ADC interprets the amplitude of the analog signal as a binary value that can be represented with the bits available to the ADC (Fig. 3.6).

The analog signal is restored through a *digital-to-analog converter (DAC)*. The digital-to-analog restoration is done at the same rate as the analog-to-digital sampling (Fig. 3.7). The output analog signal (Fig. 3.7c) is distorted because the output is a rounded-off approximation of the original signal. This disparity is called *quantization noise*.

The **Nyquist sampling theorem** states that the sampling rate must be at least twice the highest frequency in the sampled signal, otherwise the frequency

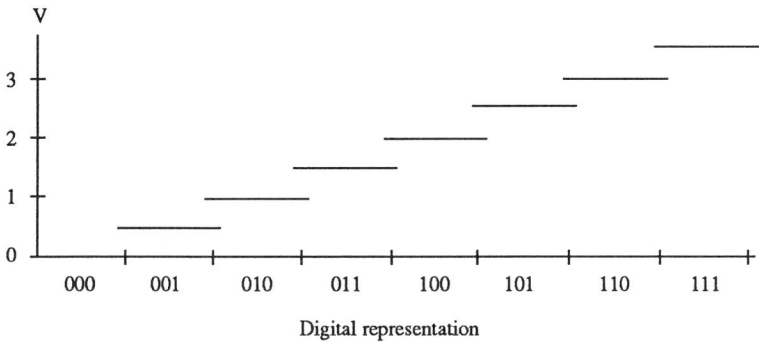

Figure 3.6 A 3-bit ADC for the range 0–3.5 V

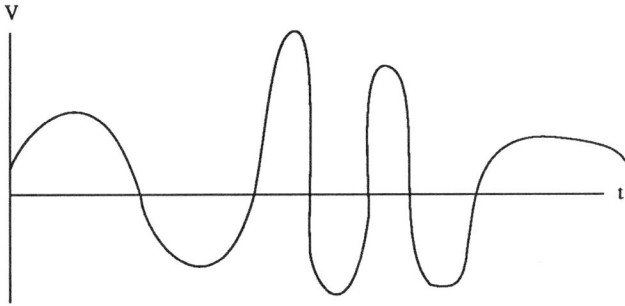

(a) An analog signal

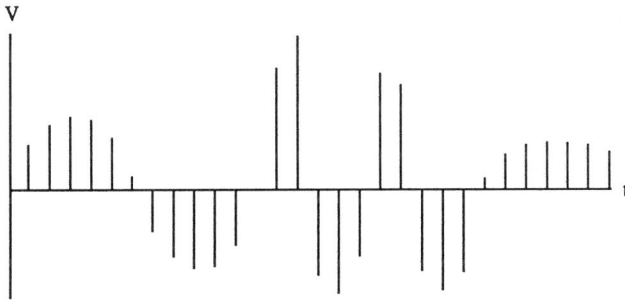

(b) Digitization of the analog signal

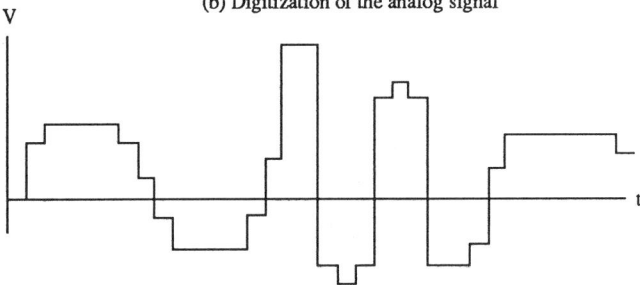

(c) Digital-to-analog restoration

Figure 3.7 Digitization of an analog signal

characteristics of the original signal cannot be recovered (Fig. 3.8). The higher-frequency components of the signal introduce errors in the restored signal called *aliasing* errors.

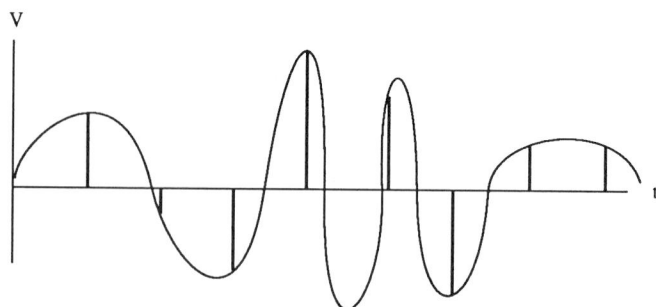

(a) Digitization of a signal at a low sampling rate

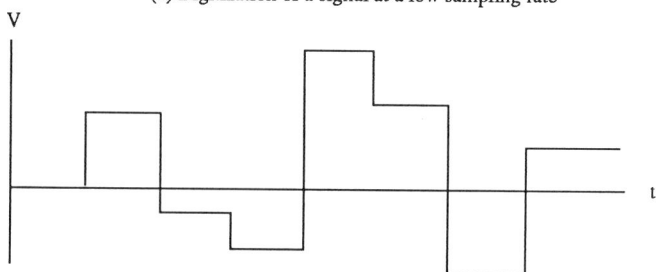

(b) Digital-to-analog restoration

Figure 3.8   Aliasing error

EXAMPLE 3.5   Digitized voice transmission

Signals in analog telephone voice signals higher than 3400 Hz do not suddenly "cut off" but rather "roll off" because of filtering at the central office. Thus, even though the voice signal should require a sampling rate of only 6600 samples per second, telephone voice digitization (**pulse-coded modulation (PCM)**) is done at 8000 samples per second to prevent aliasing.

Normally, the subscriber loop from a user to the central office is an analog loop. PCM occurs at the central office with a *codec* (coder-decoder). The digitizing is done with 7-bit ADCs, and an eighth bit is added for control. The data rate; R_{one}, for each individual channel is then:

R_{one} = (total bits per sample)(sampling rate per channel)

= (7 information bits/sample + 1 control bit/sample)(8000 samples/s)

= 64,000 bps

AT&T T-1 digital carrier channels are used in intertoll trunks and connections to high-capacity customers and represent the combination of 24 digitized voice channels. A frame is formed with information and control data from 24 voice channels and 1 synchronization bit:

$$\text{Frame} = 1 \text{ bit} + (24 \text{ channels})(8 \text{ bits/channel}) = 193 \text{ bits}$$

At a sampling rate of 8000 samples on each channel, the result is

$$R_{\text{total}} = (193 \text{ bits/frame})(8,000 \text{ samples/s}) = 1.544 \text{ Mbps}$$

3.6 MULTIPLEXING

The process of combining 24 voice channels onto one T-1 communication link is an example of *multiplexing*. Specifically, T-1 utilizes **time-division multiplexing (TDM)**, a method of giving each input channel a time interval to transmit. Most TDMs provide a specific time slot for each channel for a fixed number of bits. The output data rate equals the sum of the input data rates in a TDM multiplexer. However, this simplicity leads to inefficiency if no data is being transmitted on some of the input lines. The output, R_{muxout}, of a TDM multiplexer is

$$R_{\text{muxout}} = R_1 + R_2 + \cdots + R_N \tag{3.4}$$

where

$$R = \text{data rate, in bits per second}$$

$$N = \text{number of input channels to the multiplexer}$$

Statistical time-division multiplexing (STDM) improves the efficiency of TDM by allowing input channels to contend for the next-available time slot. STDMs have buffers that temporarily store data during peak loads because the sum of the input data may exceed the output data rate.

Frequency-division multiplexing (FDM) is a technique that divides the frequency bandwidth into smaller bands so that each user has exclusive use of a subband. For example, the AM radio band from 530 to 1210 KHz is frequency-division multiplexed into sub-bands for commercial stations. FDM is also used to increase the number of voice channels carried over a twisted-pair telephone trunk by assigning a number of channels to each sub-band. This technique is used to maximize the number of telephone channels because of the high cost of installing wire cable.

EXAMPLE 3.6   Multiplexed voice and data

By using FDM, internal telephone networks in a building can be configured to transmit voice and data simultaneously in a mode called *data-over-voice*. Filters are used to isolate the analog voice spectrum from 300 Hz to 4 KHz.

Data is simultaneously transmitted in the band from 500 KHz to 1 MHz. This higher band is also isolated by filters to prevent crosstalk. Data channels may also be time-division multiplexed on the higher band.

3.7 INTEGRATED SERVICES DIGITAL NETWORK

Since the 1950s, the voice communication system has been used increasingly for data communication. The technology has involved the use of modems to modulate digital input that is then transmitted within the frequency bandwidth of the end-to-end circuit. The increasing use of computers—in particular, personal computers—and the spread of user terminals for communication to host computers has increased the demand for data communication over the network.

If the computer interfaces directly to a digital network, higher speeds may be transmitted by routing over digital links.

In the mid-1970s, AT&T introduced direct digital interfaces for customers wishing to transmit high-speed digital data. The Dataphone Data System network provides point-to-point service between two subscribers from 2400 to 56,000 bps based on multiplexing into a T-1 trunk.

Direct access to digital circuits is an evolutionary step to an efficient *integrated digital network* that can transmit voice, data, or facsimile. Additional services such as information retrieval, banking, and electronic mail may also be added to a network such as this, at which point it can be called an **integrated services digital network (ISDN)**. International efforts are being directed through the CCITT to develop international standards for ISDN, and it is already being tested in several countries.

ISDN user access includes a combination of the following digital channels:

B channel: 64 Kbps

D channel: 16 or 64 Kbps

H channel: 384, 1536, and 1920 Kbps

The B channel is the fundamental user-access channel and is used to transmit data or digital voice (or any mix) at 64 Kbps from end to end.

The D channel carries signaling information that controls circuit-switched calls on the associated B channel. In addition, the D channel may be used for packet-switching or low-speed data transmission when the channel is not used for signaling.

The H channels are provided for higher-rate service to users. These channels may be high-speed links for data, fast facsimile, video, or multiplexed lower-rate data streams.

Two services are planned: *basic access* and *primary access*. Basic access consists of two full-duplex 64-Kbps B channels and one full-duplex 16-Kbps D channel ("2B + D"). Two B circuits are provided in the basic service anticipating that the customer will use one for voice and the other for data in a home or small office.

Primary access in the United States, Canada, and Japan is based on standard 1.544-Mbps T-1 digital service to high-capacity users. This translates to 23 B channels and one 64-Kbps D channel. However, in Europe, primary access will provide 30 B channels and one 64-Kbps D channel because their digital service is based on 2.048-Mbps trunks.

3.8 SUMMARY

Communication systems have three components: the transmitter, communications medium, and receiver. Nyquist showed that the maximum signaling rate was dependent on media bandwidth. Shannon showed that the maximum information rate also depends on media bandwidth. For digital applications optic fibers, with a very large bandwidth, provide a vast improvement in information rates and low-error transmission, compared to other media such as twisted wire, radio, and microwave.

The telephone system provides the most accessible in-place communication system. Its bandwidth is approximately 3100 Hz. Modems are used to convert digital data to signals that can be carried by this voice-oriented system. Characteristics of the signal can be modulated, including its amplitude, frequency, and phase.

Technology is moving in the direction of digital networks that transmit voice, data, facsimile images, and video. ISDN promises this capability with accessibility as common as the telephone.

KEY WORDS AND CONCEPTS

analog-to-digital converter (ADC)
attenuation
bandwidth
common carriers
differential phase-shift keyed (DPSK) modem
frequency-division multiplex (FDM)
frequency-shift keyed (FSK) modem
hertz (Hz)

integrated services digital network (ISDN)
modem
noise
Nyquist relationship
Nyquist sampling theorem
phase-shift keyed (PSK) modem
Shannon's law
time-division multiplexer (TDM)

PROBLEMS

1. Write an abstract from a recent article about one of the following communication media:
   (a) Telephone circuits
   (b) Coaxial cables

(c) Microwaves

(d) Communication satellites

(e) Open-air lasers

(f) Optical fibers

2. A certain geostationary satellite channel has a bandwidth of 36 MHz.

(a) What is the maximum signaling rate from the Nyquist relationship?

(b) What would Shannon's law predict the maximum information rate to be? Assume the signal-to-noise power ratio is 10. (*Note:* The signal-to-noise ratio for satellite communications is a function of earth-to-satellite distance, thermal noise affecting the amplifiers, and such less-predictable problems as interference from other satellite channels.)

(c) How many bits per baud are required to achieve the theoretical maximum? How many different symbols could be sent in one signaling period?

3. Name two types of electrical noise and give the causes of both.

4. What effect does noise have on channel information rates? What if there were no noise? What would the maximum capacity be?

5. Suppose a parallel modem is designed by dividing the available voice bandwidth into 8 channels, centered at 500, 900, 1300, 1700, 2100, 2500, 2900, 3300 Hz, with approximately 300 Hz per band. What is the maximum signaling rate? Compare this with a single channel modem that uses the whole band, 300 to 3400 Hz. Which would be more efficient?

6. Define baseband signal, carrier, and modulation.

7. Describe the difference between full-duplex and half-duplex modem operation.

8. Sketch frequency versus time for an FSK modem that transmits the following data (lsb first):

$$f_{\text{logical } 0} = 1200 \text{ Hz}$$

$$f_{\text{logical } 1} = 2400 \text{ Hz}$$

```
        msb              lsb
       1  0  0  1  1  0  1
```

Start with lsb here
↓

2400 Hz — f

1200 Hz —

9. Sketch frequency versus time for an FSK modem that transmits the following data in dibits (least significant dibit (lsd) first):

```
       msd                lsd
       0  0  1  0  1  0  1  1
```

(Transmit 11, 10, 10, 00)
Assume $f_1 = 00$, $f_2 = 01$, $f_3 = 10$, $f_4 = 11$.

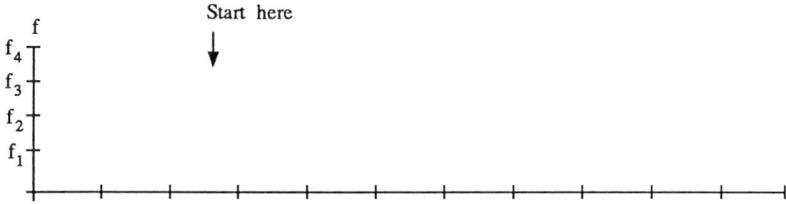

10. Sketch the waveform for a DPSK signal as it transmits the following data.

msb   lsb

Data = 0 1 0 1

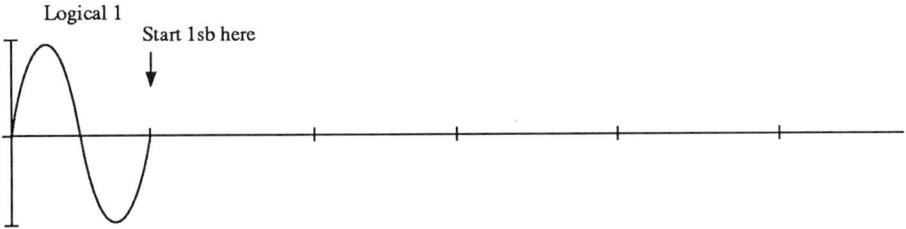

11. Sketch the waveform for a DPSK signal with four phase shifts as it transmits, in dibits:

m s d   l s d

1 0   0 1   1 1   0 0

Note: Let 00 = 0° change, 01 = 90°, 10 = 180°, and 11 = 270°.

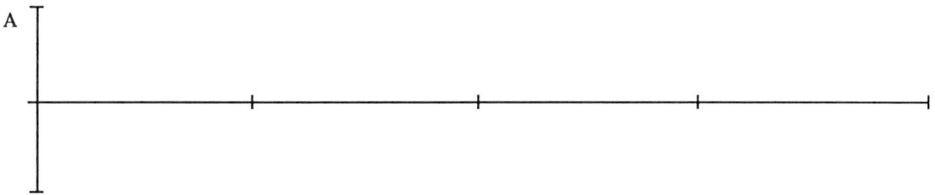

12. If 1000 ASCII symbols with parity are transmitted on a 2400-baud circuit by a modem transmitting dibits, how long will it take?

13. Does digitized voice result in a less noisy or less distorted signal? Why?

14. If you were to record concert music (20 to 20,000 Hz) digitally, from the Nyquist sampling theorem what should the minimum sampling rate be?

15. In a modern compact disk system, each of two stereo channels is sampled with 16-bit ADCs at 44,100 samples per second.
    (a) What is the minimum number of bits that must be stored on an optical disk for a 75-minute recording of Beethoven's Ninth Symphony?
    (b) In practice, 192 bits of data are encoded into 588 bits on the disk to enable error correction and control. What is the total number of bits for Beethoven's Ninth?

16. A simple incremental plotter is designed to obey the following commands:

> Pen-up
> Pen-down
> Move an increment left $(-X)$
> Move an increment right $(+X)$
> Move an increment toward top of page $(+Y)$
> Move an increment toward bottom of page $(-Y)$

   (a) How many bits are required to implement this command set?
   (b) If ASCII characters are used, what is the code rate?

17. A multiplexer is designed to accommodate input from four 300-bps lines, four 600-bps lines, and one 1200-bps line.

   (a) What should the minimum output capacity of the multiplexer be?
   (b) If two of the 600-bps lines are not being used, what is the percent utilization of the output line?

4

INTEROPERABILITY

There are usually many mutual understandings established between computers before the receiver consistently comprehends what the sender transmits. In this chapter we explore methods of classifying these understandings into protocols.

The usual way to describe a communications-related process is to describe the individual components of the system and what each of them does. Another approach, which may seem very abstract at first, is to describe the process in terms of the *functions* that are required and then, to group the functions into various **layers**. Specific services are provided through protocols in each layer and are implemented in computer hardware and software by both the sender and receiver. Looking at the communication process by the functions that are performed simplifies the task of developing protocols and achieving interoperability.

4.1 PROTOCOL LAYERING CONCEPT

Functional layering can be defined for many types of communication. In one example, aircraft pilot-to-air traffic controller conversation, we can define at least three layers (Table 4.1):

1. Physical: The means to communicate over a medium must be provided.
2. Linguistic: A language that is mutually understood must be used.
3. Cognitive: There must be a general subject to discuss. In this example it may be a pilot's request for traffic-control services.

The physical layer functions involve the physical mechanism used to

TABLE 4.1   Person-to-person communication layering

Layer	General Responsibilities of the Layer
Cognitive	Defines purpose of message exchange
Linguistic	Provides common language
Physical	Physically transmits information between users

communicate. In our example, the fundamental understanding is that the pilot and controller agree to use two-way radios at an assigned frequency in the range 118 to 135 MHz. This is the "protocol." This layer is also concerned with the mechanics of communication, such as keying the microphone for half-duplex communications and the electrical interconnections and voltages.

At the linguistic layer the information is formulated into words. In our example, this protocol is English and a published glossary of terms in the *Airman's Information Manual*.

At the cognitive level there are queries and responses related to the subject matter. There must be mutual understandings about the purpose and content of the information being discussed. There may be a procedure for initiating and terminating the conversation. A pilot calls the appropriate controller ("Coast Approach, . . ."), identifies the aircraft by its type and registration number (" . . . this is Cessna 7233-Quebec, . . ."), and states the request. General aviation pilots usually acknowledge the controller advisories or instructions by repeating the instruction and the last three digits or letters of the aircraft registration number.

It is important to emphasize that the layering model is distinct from the protocols. The layering model provides the logical framework for defining the protocols that the sender and receiver agree to use.

4.2 OPEN SYSTEMS INTERCONNECTION (OSI) REFERENCE MODEL

In 1979, ISO defined a classification scheme for communication functions, called a **reference model** for the exchange of information between computer systems. It is called the **Open Systems Interconnection (OSI)** reference model [43] and is sometimes referred to as the *seven-layer model* (Table 4.2). The reference model is not a protocol or set of rules but a layering of required functions, or services, that provides a framework with which to define protocols.

The purpose of the OSI model is to facilitate development of international computer network services. ISO initially established this framework by defining layers of services that are required in an international data communications network. The definition of layers is done in such a way that the protocols in different layers can be developed independently by teams of experts.

TABLE 4.2   OSI Layers

Layer	General Responsibilities of the Layer
Application	Performs user processes that use the lower services
Presentation	Defines the transmission format of data
Session	Organizes and synchronizes the data exchange
Transport	Provides a channel to send error-free sequential messages from one user process to another
Network	Routes data end to end over multiple computers
Data link	Transmits data error-free over circuits between adjacent computers
Physical	Physically transmits data over a circuit

Technically speaking, "open" in OSI terminology implies a mutual recognition and support of the applicable standards by the users of a network. However, the term has come to imply a commitment by the designers to use international standards.

The following discussion gives an overview of the various OSI layers. Each of the layers is covered in more detail in later chapters.

4.2.1 Physical Layer

The basic goal in digital transmission is to send bits (logical ones and zeros) across the communication system. The protocol in the physical layer ensures that when one computer electronically transmits a logical 1, it is interpreted as a logical 1 at the next computer. It is basically a computer-to-computer protocol describing the conventions of the electrical circuits and mechanical system. If the network is circuit-switched, the physical layer also includes the procedures for establishing the circuit. The following items are typical of the things that need to be specified:

- Connector cable standards, pin assignments
- Voltages
- Timing rates

EXAMPLE 4.1   Parcel service physical layer

In a parcel service, the analogy to the OSI physical layer is the function of physically carrying a parcel from one routing point to the next by hand-carry, truck, train, or aircraft.

4.2.2 Data Link Layer

The data link layer attempts to deliver data error-free over the circuit between adjacent computers established by the physical layer. Within this layer are specified such things as the following:

- Error-detection methods
- Error-recovery methods
- Error-correction methods
- Framing requirements for the data

4.2.3 Network Layer

When there are a number of computers in the network and multiple paths from the source to the destination, the network layer routes the data from computer to computer. This layer also controls congestion if the network is overloading certain computers. Within this layer are such things as these:

- Algorithms for determining the next computer to which the message must be sent
- Algorithms for determining the optimum path to reach the destination

4.2.4 Transport Layer

The transport layer is responsible for maintaining a reliable and cost-effective communications channel from a user's application software process in one computer to a user process in another. The transport layer views the intervening network as a transparent entity that is simply providing a service. The transport layer does not determine the route, but it ensures that a reliable channel exists between the computer processes.

This layer may break a long message or file into smaller segments at the source and reassemble it at the destination if it is required because of network packet-size limitations. The transport layer provides the following services:

- Addressing to a specific user process at the destination
- Message reliability
- Sequential delivery of the data
- Flow control of data between user processes

EXAMPLE 4.2   Parcel service transport layer

An analogy to illustrate the transport layer can be drawn again from a parcel service. A product manufacturing plant in Los Angeles and a purchaser's factory in New York may correspond to computers that are communicating with each other. A piece of machinery to be shipped from Los Angeles to New York corresponds to file data.

Before shipment, the manufacturer breaks down the machine for shipping, packing each subassembly separately with instructions for reassembly, and then labels each package with the final destination (plant address and office designation, such as the purchaser's receiving department). The manufacturer hands each parcel to the parcel service (analogous to the network layer) and expects the parcel service to deliver each parcel to New York. When all the parcels arrive at the office designation in New York, they are unwrapped and reassembled into the original machine. The disassembly, addressing, and reassembly process correspond to functions of the transport layer.

4.2.5 Session Layer

The session layer organizes and synchronizes a period of interactive communication between user processes. In particular, it authorizes the transport connection between user processes and maintains the continuity of the connection. For example, if the transport connection fails, the session layer provides a logical synchronization point so that the activity can be resumed. The session layer provides the following:

- Access procedures
- Rules for half-duplex or full-duplex dialogues
- Rules for recovering if the session is interrupted
- Rules for logically ending the session

EXAMPLE 4.3   Parcel service session layer

When the sales people and buyers define the terms of the contract between the manufacturer and the purchaser, they are doing a function that roughly corresponds to the function of the session layer. They negotiate such details as billing, when to deliver, and financial responsibilities of the two parties.

4.2.6 Presentation Layer

The presentation layer is responsible for the transmission format, or *syntax*, of the data. It defines how to translate the data into a suitable format for transmission. The presentation layer may define how to compact the user data to improve data transfer rates or how to encrypt it for security. The presentation layer provides the following services:

- Transmission syntax
- Message transformations and formatting
- Data encryption
- Code conversion
- Data compression

> **EXAMPLE 4:4   Parcel service presentation layer**
>
> Using our previous analogy in which a machine is dismantled and shipped via parcel service, we may say that the steps in preparation for shipping are equivalent to the functions of the presentation layer. For example, certain parts may be coated to prevent corrosion and some parts may be protected because they are fragile.

4.2.7 Application Layer

Applications, from the OSI perspective, are defined by the user and include such things as banking through automated teller machines, airline reservations, and distribution of weather forecasts. (The list is endless as we found in Chap. 1.) When the application involves cooperation between separated computers, the application layer focuses on unique communication services such as file transfer, electronic mail, and remote terminal-entry protocols. This layer provides the following:

- Unique user-oriented services
- General services available to all unique user-oriented services

4.3 OSI COMMUNICATION

Each participating network computer is viewed by OSI as a collection of subsystems with a specific layer of services mapped into each subsystem. Active elements, or **entities**, such as software programs and integrated circuits, provide the services of an OSI layer within a subsystem. Entities in the same layer on different systems are called **peer** entities.

Each entity carries on a *conversation* with its peer entity at the same layer on another machine (Fig. 4.1). For example, a file transfer entity in the application layer on one computer sends its commands to its peer file transfer entity in the application layer on another computer.

It is characteristic of OSI protocols that peer entities negotiate a connection with each other before transferring data. Figure 4.2 illustrates the concept for a typical protocol. The upper layer, which is the *service user*, commands the network protocol through a command (i.e., CONNECT.request), to establish a connection with its peer and indicate to the destination upper-layer entity that such a connection is being attempted. In the example, the destination upper-layer entity is given the option of approving the connection attempt. If it approves, the originating upper-layer entity is notified when the connection is established.

> **EXAMPLE 4.5   Postal system peer-to-peer communication**
>
> If the team of workers in Los Angeles decides to protect fragile parts before shipment, workers in New York must know that there is a specific task to unwrap

the marked parts carefully. The members of the team packing the parts expect their counterparts in New York to know how to unwrap them. There must be a mutual understanding about the function performed in that step. These teams are the equivalent of peer entities. Any discussions they have prior to delivery of the part to discuss the handling procedures are the equivalent of peer-to-peer connection-establishment procedures.

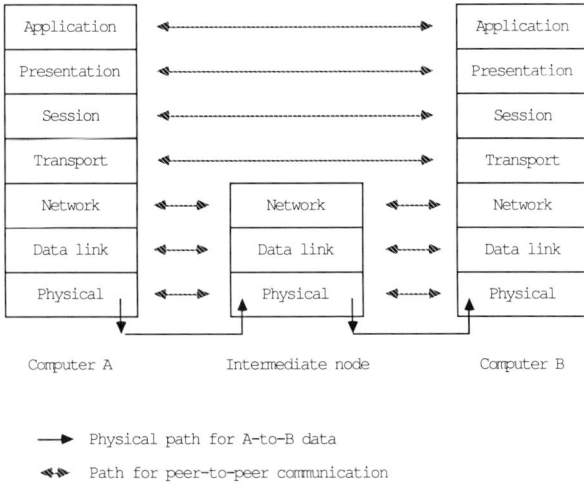

Figure 4.1   OSI layering concept

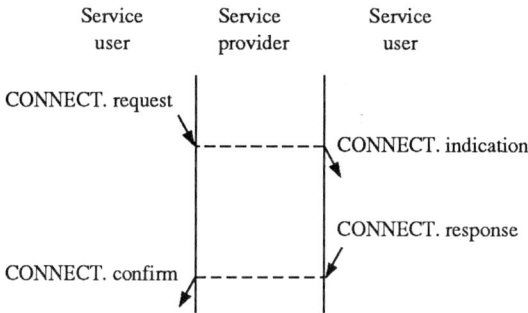

Figure 4.2   Peer-to-peer connection for an OSI network protocol

Even though the entity in each layer is maintaining a conversation with its peer in the same layer in another machine, information and control data are passed upward and downward through layers on the same system. A sender's network protocol, for example, receives segments of data from the transport layer, and passes information and control data to the link layer (Fig. 4.3). The link layer, in turn, transfers the data stream to the physical layer for delivery to the adjacent computer.

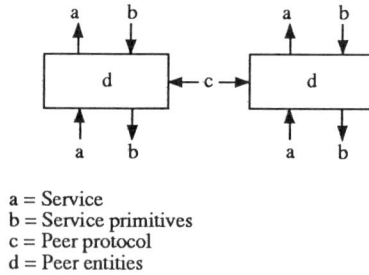

a = Service
b = Service primitives
c = Peer protocol
d = Peer entities

Figure 4.3 Summary of OSI terminology

4.4 DoD INTERNET REFERENCE MODEL

The Defense Advanced Research Projects Agency (DARPA) developed ARPANET in 1969 as the first experimental packet-switched digital network. Messages and data files were routed in small segments, called *packets*, to the final destination. The goal was to demonstrate the improved efficiency of routing small packets through fast packet-switching nodes and varying the path of data to the same destination.

ARPANET has evolved from a single, packet-switched network to the **DoD Internet**. The Internet is a collection of physically different networks (called *subnetworks*) with hosts from different manufacturers (a **heterogeneous network**) at different sites tied together by means of **gateway** computers. Gateway computers are capable of translating among different data link protocols and different network protocols.

If two hosts on different subnets wish to communicate, the source host sends packets to the appropriate gateway on its subnet. The gateway routes each packet through an appropriate connected subnet. Eventually the packets reach a gateway connected to the subnet of the destination host, where they are routed to the destination host.

A number of DoD protocols that are widely used have been developed through the program. In this section, we cover the underlying reference model behind these standards. The protocols that were developed for the Internet are generally incompatible with international protocols being developed for OSI.

The Internet architecture exists as four layers: the network, internet, service, and application layers (Table 4.3)[24].

1. *Network layer*. The network layer is concerned with host-to-subnet interface protocols and performance. The Internet is not as concerned with the subnet structure (i.e., network protocols) as much as it is with the interface of the hosts to the subnets.

2. *Internet layer*. At this layer, protocols are defined for connecting the various subnets and gateways into a system capable of delivering packets

TABLE 4.3   DoD Internet Layers

DoD Internet Layer	General Responsibilities for the Layer
Application	Performs processes that use the lower services
Service	Ensures end-to-end reliability
Internet	Routes messages between gateways and hosts
Network	Interfaces the host to the local subnet

from any source host to any destination host across the subnets. It is concerned with addressing and routing.

3. *Service layer.* The service layer provides end-to-end communication services, including mechanisms to ensure reliability and message integrity. It is concerned with the quality of service, including reliability, error rates, and delays.

4. *Application layer.* The Internet application layer provides standard application software for the user, and uses the lower layers. This layer is concerned with file transfer, electronic mail, and other fundamental applications that can be used by members of the Internet user community.

4.5 PROPRIETARY ARCHITECTURES

Major computer manufacturers such as DEC and IBM were manufacturing computers and working out networking problems a long time before ISO proposed the OSI reference model. In fact, the IBM System Network Architecture (SNA) was first announced publicly in 1974. In this section, as examples, are proprietary network architectures developed by IBM [74] and DEC [26] to provide a framework for their communications software and hardware products. Within this framework, proprietary operating systems and computers function in a **homogeneous network.**

IBM's SNA (Table 4.4) consists of seven layers that provide very similar services to the OSI layers.

DEC's DNA (Table 4.5) defines protocols, interfaces, and functions that enable the DECnet family of communications hardware and software to share data and access each other's resources, programs, and functions.

The lower SNA and DNA layers are similar to OSI layers. The major differences are at, and above, the network layer. Later in the text, several of the proprietary protocols are discussed as examples of protocols in equivalent OSI layers.

TABLE 4.4   SNA Architecture Layers

SNA Layer	General Responsibilities for the Layer
Transaction services	Provides network management services to the end user
Presentation services	Provides formatting and data compression services
Data flow control	Provides end-user control over the SNA session, such as half-duplex or duplex communication.
Transmission control	Establishes, maintains, and terminates "SNA session" (equivalent to OSI transport connection)
Path control	Creates end-to-end logical channels
Data link control	Transfers data reliably across a circuit
Physical control	Physically transmits serial and parallel data over a circuit

TABLE 4.5   DNA Layers

DNA Layer	General Responsibilities for the Layer
User	Provides system manager terminal access to lower layers
Network	Provides user control of operational parameters
Network application	Provides unique services to network users (i.e., electronic mail, file transfer, and so on)
Session control	Sends error-free sequential messages end-to-end
End communication	Performs data flow and end-to-end error control; segment and reassemble data
Routing	Routes user data; controls congestion and message lifetime
Data link	Creates communications path between adjacent computers and ensures integrity
Physical	Physically transmits data over a circuit

4.6 INTEROPERABILITY

Interoperability provides each user application program, or *user process*, access to others in the network. In the simplest form, it enables a user at one computer to send commands or data to a separate computer (and be understood), and receive, in return, the appropriate response. Interoperability is easier and less expensive if the communications architecture and associated protocols are standard throughout the network, i.e., OSI, DoD Internet, or proprietary.

Companies such as DEC and IBM achieve interoperability among their existing systems and their new hardware and software products by utilizing protocols that have been standardized within their product lines. ISO and DARPA represent user communities that are attempting to achieve interoperability between heterogeneous computers by imposing standard protocol requirements during the procurement phase of the network. Without any doubt, the trend is toward imposing the OSI architecture and international standards on suppliers of new systems.

Many large companies, including the U.S. government, that desire interoperability among systems from different manufacturers are strongly interested in supporting the OSI open systems concept and implementing international standards. However, simply imposing an OSI standard on a vendor is inadequate; it has been found that OSI standards include incompatible options.

In 1983, the U.S. government initiated a series of workshops led by the National Institute of Standards and Technology (NIST) for organizations and vendors interested in implementing OSI-related international standards [72]. The purpose of the workshops was to reach consensus on a set of implementable and interoperable agreements. Based on these agreements, vendors can presumably build equipment and software that are interoperable between vendors. Standard tests for conformance are also being developed by NIST. The resulting profile of interoperable protocols and options is called the *government OSI profile (GOSIP)*.

In subsequent chapters we examine proprietary, national, and international protocols. For teaching purposes we organize these protocols into the OSI layers, even though some of them are a part of another proprietary or public reference model, such as SNA, DNA, or DoD's Internet architecture.

4.7 SUMMARY

Many understandings must be established between computers before the receiver consistently comprehends what the sender transmits. ISO studied the functions that must be performed for computer-to-computer interoperability and grouped these into layers that form the Open Systems Interconnection (OSI) reference model. This model provides a standard layering of functions that enables development of international standard communication protocols.

Other communication architectures exist; DARPA Internet is one of the more widely known. It provides interoperability across computers from different vendors (a heterogeneous network). Major computer vendors have their own architectures that permit interoperability between computers that they manufacture (homogeneous networks).

KEY WORDS AND CONCEPTS

DoD Internet
entity
gateway
heterogeneous network
homogeneous network

layers
Open Systems Interconnection (OSI)
peer
reference model

PROBLEMS

1. Describe a postal system analogy to the network layer of the OSI model.
2. In which OSI layer do you group asynchronous or synchronous transmission requirements?
3. In which OSI layer do you specify data compression techniques?
4. In which OSI layer would the dial-up procedure be described for a telephone connection?
5. In which layer will character codes be specified in the OSI model?
6. Which subset of OSI layers is applicable if the channel between two hosts is a dedicated point-to-point link?
7. Describe a session layer protocol between two people on a telephone.
8. Describe a reference model for the typical college dating situation and give examples of protocols.

5

PHYSICAL LAYER

Computers physically connect to the transmission system at a *communications interface*. The protocols in the physical layer describe this interface and ensure that when a computer transmits a logical 1, it is interpreted by the receiving computer as a logical 1, and when a 0 is sent, it is interpreted as a 0. There are several standard interfaces that we discuss in this chapter.

The transmission system can provide either *dedicated*, or *circuit-switched*, service between its end points. A dedicated circuit is always available for transmitting data between its end points. An example is user-owned cabling between computers and terminals. A switched circuit establishes a temporary circuit between users. It is a more efficient method for creating communication channels when the circuit facilities are needed only for a relatively short period of time by a large number of users. The telephone system is the most obvious example, where a connection between users is established and, when the call is over, terminated. The use of circuit-switching requires that the physical layer describe circuit establishment and clearing procedures.

5.1 INTERCHANGE CIRCUITS

The communications interface is usually between a computer or terminal and the circuit interface equipment, such as a modem. The CCITT distinguishes between the terminal side and the circuit side of this important interface by calling the terminal or computer the **data terminal equipment (DTE)** and the circuit interface device the **data circuit-terminating equipment (DCE)** (Fig. 5.1). The circuits

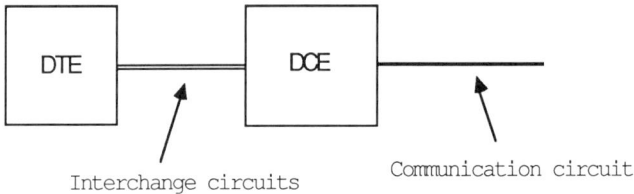

(a) DTE/DCE schematic

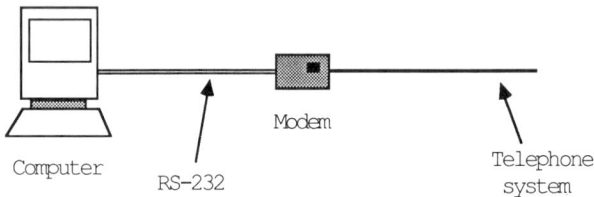

(b) Computer/modem example

Figure 5.1   DTE/DCE interface

between them are called **interchange circuits** and they may transmit data, control signals, and timing signals.

There are a number of connector and voltage standards established by the Electronic Industries Association (EIA), CCITT, and ISO for interfacing DTEs to DCEs. The most common, which we examine in detail, is EIA RS-232 [27]. RS-232 is the standard connection between DTE devices and DCEs connected to the analog telephone network.

5.2 EIA RS-232

RS-232 was approved in its latest version (EIA-232-D) by the EIA in 1986, and it conforms to international standards CCITT V.24, V.28, and ISO 2110. It is used to interface DTEs to DCEs connected to an analog telephone system. It can be used to transmit and receive asynchronous and synchronous data. RS-232 associates specific signals with specific connector pins in a D-shaped 25-pin connector (Fig. 5.2).

RS-232 circuits are an example of **unbalanced** connections because the voltages on the transmit and receive circuits are measured relative to a common-grounded return path. This common-ground circuit introduces noise and limits the RS-232 signaling rate and the length of interchange circuits. The signaling rates have a nominal 20,000 baud upper limit over a distance of 50 feet. In practice, a

SIGNAL DESIGNATION	PIN NUMBER	PIN NUMBER	SIGNAL DESIGNATION

SECONDARY TRANSMITTED DATA 14 —
DCE TRANSMITTER SIGNAL ELEMENT TIMING 15 —
SECONDARY RECEIVED DATA 16 —
RECEIVER SIGNAL ELEMENT TIMING 17 —
18 —
SECONDARY REQUEST TO SEND 19 —
DATA TERMINAL READY 20 —
SIGNAL QUALITY DETECTOR 21 —
RING INDICATOR 22 —
DATA SIGNAL RATE SELECTOR 23 —
DTE TRANSMITTER SIGNAL ELEMENT TIMING 24 —
25 —

— 1 PROTECTIVE GROUND
— 2 TRANSMITTED DATA
— 3 RECEIVED DATA
— 4 REQUEST TO SEND
— 5 CLEAR TO SEND
— 6 DATA SET READY
— 7 SIGNAL GROUND/COMMON RETURN
— 8 RECEIVED LINE SIGNAL DETECTOR
— 9 +VOLTAGE
—10 -VOLTAGE
—11
—12 SECONDARY RECEIVED LINE SIGNAL DETECTOR
—13 SECONDARY CLEAR TO SEND

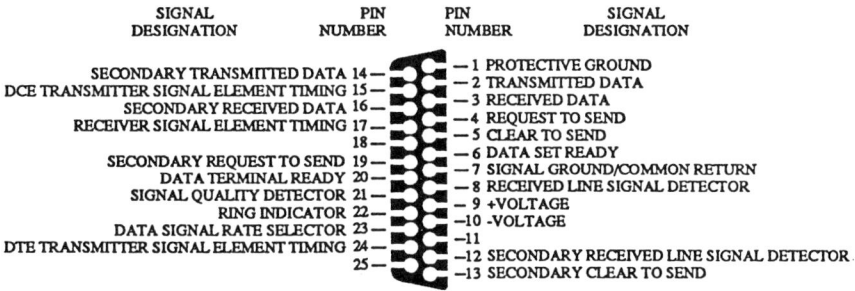

Figure 5.2   RS-232 connector

lower signaling rate is possible over a longer distance, and higher rates are possible over shorter distances.

A logical OFF on the control pins or logical 0 on a data line is a voltage between $+3$ and $+15$ V, and an ON control signal or logical 1 data signal is any voltage between -3 and -15 V. Note that the minimum transition between logic levels is 6 V.

5.2.1 RS-232 Circuit Assignments

The RS-232-D interchange circuits are listed in Table 5.1. The circuits have letter codes, where the A circuit is the ground; those starting with B, data; C, control; and D, timing. Circuit codes starting with S are secondary circuits with the same purpose as the primary circuits, only they are for secondary channels on the DCEs. The pins that are used most often are identified in the following list.

Ground.   Circuit AB (pin 7) (CCITT Equivalent 102), Signal ground: establishes the common reference potential for all voltages between the DCE and DTE.

Data.   Circuit BA (pin 2) (CCITT Equivalent 103), Transmitted data: output signals on this pin are generated by the local DTE.

Circuit BB (pin 3) (CCITT Equivalent 104), Received data: signals on this pin are generated by the DCE as a result of the signals sent from a distant DTE/DCE.

Control.   Circuit CA (pin 4) (CCITT Equivalent 105), Request to send: a pin set by the DTE to notify the local DCE to prepare for data transmission. A request-to-send signal commands the DCE (modem) to turn on its carrier. On a half-duplex channel, pin 4 controls the direction of data transmission of the local DCE.

Circuit CB (pin 5) (CCITT Equivalent 106), Clear to send: a pin set by the DCE to indicate to the DTE that its carrier is on and it is ready to accept the DTE's data.

TABLE 5.1   EIA RS-232-D Pin Assignments

Pin Number	Circuit	Description
1	—	Shield
7	AB	Signal ground/common return
2	BA	Transmitted data
3	BB	Received data
4	CA	Request to send
5	CB	Clear to send
6	CC	DCE ready
20	CD	DTE ready
22	CE	Ring indicator
8	CF	Received line signal detector
21	CG	Signal quality detector
23	CH	Data signal rate selector (DTE)
12*	CI	Data signal rate selector (DCE)
24	DA	Transmitter signal element timing (DTE)
15	DB	Transmitter signal element timing (DCE)
17	DD	Receiver signal element timing (DCE)
14	SBA	Secondary transmitted data
16	SBB	Secondary received data
19	SCA	Secondary request to send
13	SCB	Secondary clear to send
12*	SCF	Secondary received line signal detector
18	LL	Local loopback
21	RL	Remote loopback
25	TM	Test mode

* For new designs using interchange circuit SCF, interchange circuits CH and CI are assigned to pin 23. If SCF is not used, CI is assigned to pin 12.

Circuit CC (pin 6) (CCITT Equivalent 107), DCE ready: a pin set by the DCE to indicate that the DCE equipment and circuit connection is ready; for example, the local DCE is connected to an established telephone connection. If the telephone line is disconnected, the DCE-ready signal will be (logically) OFF.

Circuit CD (pin 20) (CCITT Equivalent 108.2), DTE ready: a pin set by the DTE to indicate equipment readiness.

Circuit CE (pin 22) (CCITT Equivalent 125), Ring indicator: a pin set by the DCE to indicate that a ring signal is being received on the telephone service connection.

Circuit CF (pin 8) (CCITT Equivalent 109), Received line signal detector: a pin set by the DCE when the DCE is detecting a carrier signal from the distant DCE.

Timing.   Circuit DA (pin 24) (CCITT Equivalent 113), Transmitter signal element timing (DTE source): a circuit to provide DTE bit-synchronization timing to the DCE.

Circuit DB (pin 15) (CCITT Equivalent 114), Transmitter signal element timing (DCE source): a circuit to provide DCE timing to the DTE.

Circuit DD (pin 17) (CCITT Equivalent 115), Receiver signal element timing (DCE source): a circuit to provide the DTE with received signal timing information.

5.2.2 Null Modem

A short-distance **null modem** (Fig. 5.3a) DTE-DTE connection can be built to transmit data without DCEs. For asynchronous traffic, simply cabling pins 2, 3, and 7 between two RS-232-compatible DTEs, as shown in Fig. 5.3b, will usually permit them to communicate. Sometimes additional pins at each DTE may have to be wired together to simulate a normal connection to a DCE and enable the computer's communication software to function. Synchronous null modems are more complex and require interconnecting timing signals.

For transmitting asynchronous data (Fig. 5.3b), the basic connections are the following:

- Pin 2 on DTE A is connected to pin 3 on DTE B; pin 2 on DTE B is connected to pin 3 on DTE A.
- Pin 7 on DTE A is connected to pin 7 on DTE B.

Additional pins that may have to be connected:

- Pins 6, 8, and 20 are connected together on each DTE, enabling the DTEs to function as if they were each talking to a local DCE that is connected to an established circuit with an acceptable received-signal level.
- Pins 4 and 5 are connected together so the DTEs function as if they had a clear-to-send signal from functioning DCEs.

(a) DTE-DTE connection using a null modem

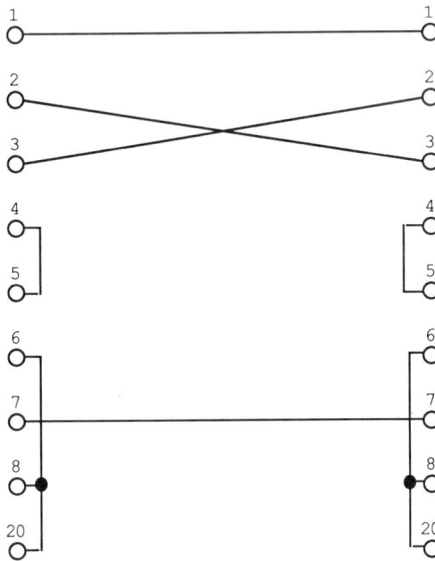

(b) RS-232 null modem for asynchronous transmission

Figure 5.3   Null modem concept

5.3 RS-449, RS-422, AND RS-423 INTERFACES

Early in the 1970s, the EIA introduced new standards to overcome the speed and distance limitations of RS-232. **RS-449** defines the mechanical, functional, and procedural characteristics of the new interface, and **RS-422A** and **RS-423A** define electrical characteristics of individual signal lines between the DTE and DCE.

As we discussed earlier, one pin (pin 7) in RS-232 is designated the signal ground pin, and all signals share this common reference. If the DTE and DCE are located far enough apart, the ground reference voltage at each site may be significantly different and create *ground loop currents* that cause noise on the signaling circuits. Both RS-422A and RS-423A circuits eliminate the problem of ground loops to gain higher data rates and longer distances, but in slightly different ways.

An RS-422A circuit provides an individual return path for each signal isolated from other grounds. This technique, called **balanced** transmission, doubles the number of wires in the cable but permits very high data rates. RS-422A achieves 10 Mbps at 12 m and drops to 100 Kbps at 1.2 km.

There is much less noise in balanced circuits because the noise signal, virtually equal on the signal line and its return path, does not affect the voltage difference between the circuits. The impact on the interface circuit is that the transition between logic levels can be small. Logical 1 is a voltage greater than $+0.2$ V and logical 0 is less than -0.2 V, a voltage difference of only 0.4 V (compared to 6 V with RS-232).

RS-423A has unbalanced circuits, as does RS-232, but it avoids ground loops. RS-423A uses a single wire as a common return path for all signals in the same direction and joins them to a common circuit ground at the sender. For example, the DTE's send-data circuit will include a signal-return path that is grounded at the DTE. Other signals generated by the DTE will also use the same ground. In an RS-423A circuit, the voltage difference between the signal line and common return must be at least 4 V, positive for logical 0 and negative for logical 1.

RS-423A operates up to 300 Kbps at a distance of 10 m and drops to 3 Kbps at 1000 m, a significant improvement over RS-232 (20 Kbps to approximately 15 m).

RS-449 (Fig. 5.4) is the mechanical specification that incorporates RS-422A and RS-423A electrical standards on its pins (Table 5.2). It provides 10 additional interchange circuits for control and testing. RS-449 involves two connectors: a 37-pin connector and a 9-pin connector. Both connectors have their own ground

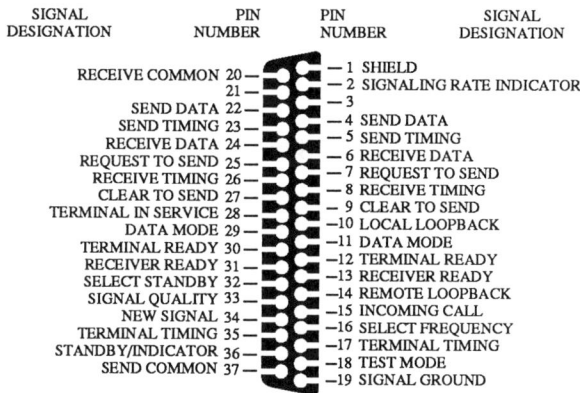

SIGNAL DESIGNATION	PIN NUMBER	PIN NUMBER	SIGNAL DESIGNATION
RECEIVE COMMON	20	1	SHIELD
	21	2	SIGNALING RATE INDICATOR
SEND DATA	22	3	
SEND TIMING	23	4	SEND DATA
RECEIVE DATA	24	5	SEND TIMING
REQUEST TO SEND	25	6	RECEIVE DATA
RECEIVE TIMING	26	7	REQUEST TO SEND
CLEAR TO SEND	27	8	RECEIVE TIMING
TERMINAL IN SERVICE	28	9	CLEAR TO SEND
DATA MODE	29	10	LOCAL LOOPBACK
TERMINAL READY	30	11	DATA MODE
RECEIVER READY	31	12	TERMINAL READY
SELECT STANDBY	32	13	RECEIVER READY
SIGNAL QUALITY	33	14	REMOTE LOOPBACK
NEW SIGNAL	34	15	INCOMING CALL
TERMINAL TIMING	35	16	SELECT FREQUENCY
STANDBY/INDICATOR	36	17	TERMINAL TIMING
SEND COMMON	37	18	TEST MODE
		19	SIGNAL GROUND

Figure 5.4   RS-232, RS-423, and RS-422 circuits

TABLE 5.2 EIA RS-449 Pin Assignments

9-Pin Connector AUX	37-Pin Connector A	B*	Circuit	Description
1	1		—	
5	19		SG	Signal ground
9	37		SC	Send common
6	20		RC	Receive common
	4	22	SD	Send data
	6	24	RD	Receive data
	7	25	RS	Request to send
	9	27	CS	Clear to send
	11	29	DM	Data mode
	12	30	TR	Terminal ready
	15		IC	Incoming call
	13	31	RR	Receiver ready
	33		SQ	Signal Quality
	16		SR	Signaling rate selector
	2		SI	Signaling rate indicator
	17	35	TT	Terminal timing
	5	23	ST	Sent timing
	8	26	RT	Receive timing
3			SSD	Secondary send data
4			SRD	Secondary receive data
7			SRS	Secondary request to send
8			SCS	Secondary clear to send
2			SRR	Secondary receiver ready
	10		LL	Local loopback
	14		RL	Remote loopback
	18		TM	Test mode
	32		SS	Select standby
	36		SB	Standby indicator
	16		SF	Select frequency
	28		IS	Terminal in service
	34		NS	New signal

*Designates the return circuit for Category I interconnection.

and common signals. Many applications do not need the smaller cable because it contains only secondary channel signals.

If desired, RS-423A circuits can be used on all RS-449 interchange circuits, and the DTE-DCE connection can be made with the minimum number of wires and the lowest cost. This is called a *category II* interconnection. However, for performance over 20 Kbps, 10 specific-circuits must be RS-422A:

> Send data
> Receive data
> Terminal timing
> Send timing
> Receive timing
> Request to send
> Clear to send
> Receiver ready
> Terminal ready
> Data mode

This high-performance combination is called a *Category I* interconnection.

5.4 CCITT X.21

In the mid-1970s it was anticipated that computers would soon be able to interface directly to DCEs associated with digital networks. Therefore, **CCITT X.21** was formulated as an international standard in 1976 for access to public data networks using synchronous data transmission. X.21 is a protocol for placing and receiving calls and for sending and receiving data using full-duplex synchronous transmission. The electrical standards are in X.26 (corresponding to RS-422) and X.27 (corresponding to RS-423A). X.21 uses a connector with only 15 pins because data and control codes travel on the same serial circuits.

There are very few networks that support X.21. The future of X.21 digital networks is being overshadowed by the prospect of ISDN, which has its own standards. However, X.21 is the recommended physical-layer protocol for terminals operating in a public X.25 packet-switched network, which we discuss in Chap. 7, and the underlying principles are important to grasp for some understanding of how ISDN operates. CCITT has recommended X.21*bis*, a standard similar to RS-232, for X.25 networks in the interim, before implementation of digital circuit-switched networks.

X.21 is fundamentally different from EIA RS-232 because it defines DTE/DCE interchange circuits for a *digital* circuit-switched system. There are fewer pins, and X.21 provides much more communication capability. For example, after a DTE "dials" a certain destination on the transmit channel with serial digital codes, a wide variety of call-progress codes are returned by the DCE on the receive channel.

5.4.1 X.21 Circuit Assignments

The X.21 pin assignments are as follows (Fig. 5.5):

T (Transmit): pin used for DTE-to-DCE data signals and call-control signals sent during call establishment and call clearing.

R (Receive): pin used for DCE-to-DTE signals in response to the data signals sent from a distant DTE/DCE and also call-control signals during call establishment and call clearing.

S (Signal element timing): pin used by the DCE to provide signal timing to the DTE.

C (Control): pin used by the DTE to indicate circuit conditions. When data is being transmitted, it is ON.

I (Indication): pin used by the DCE to send the state of the call-establishment process (ON or OFF) to the DTE.

B (Byte timing): an optional interchange circuit that may be used by the DCE to indicate to the DTE when to transmit call-control characters and may be used by the DTEs for octet synchronization.

G (Signal ground): the common signal reference potential.

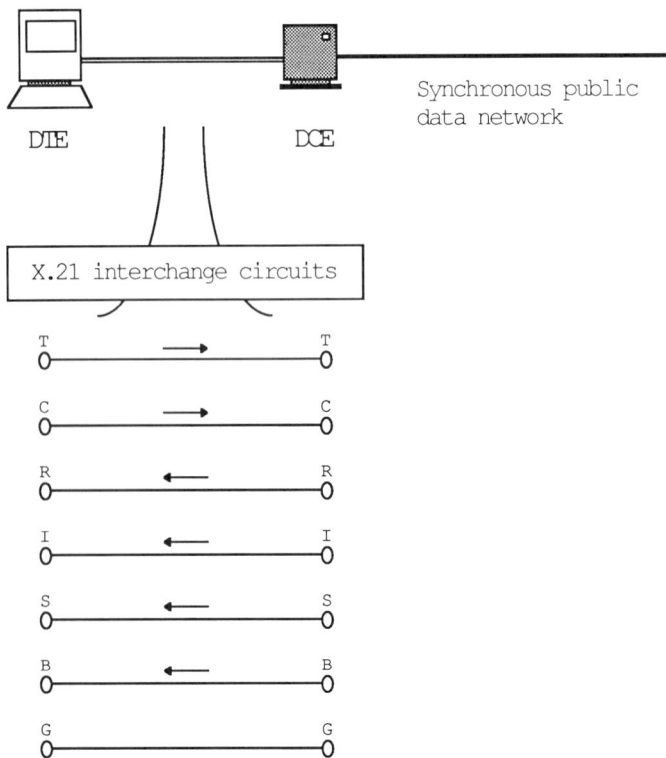

Figure 5.5   X.21 DTE/DCE interchange circuits

5.4.2 X.21 Calling Procedures

A typical procedure for establishing an X.21 connection is summarized in Table 5.3. When the DTE goes "off hook," the DCE sends a stream of ASCII plus (+) symbols to the DTE to indicate readiness. The DTE then transmits an ASCII destination address. While waiting for the connection, the DCE returns ASCII status indicators to the DTE. Typical responses may indicate such conditions as "number busy," "network congestion," or "call connected."

TABLE 5.3   Typical connection logic of X.21

DTE			DCE	
T	C	Description	R	I
$t = 1$	OFF	Ready	$r = 1$	OFF
$t = 0$	ON	Call request	$r = 1$	OFF
$t = 0$	ON	Proceed to select	$r =$ "+ + + + .."	OFF
$t =$ "ASCII address"			$r =$ "+ + + + .."	
	ON	DTE transmits address		OFF
$t = 1$	ON	Connection in progress	$r =$ call progress signals	OFF
$t = 1$	ON	Ready for data	$r = 1$	ON
$t =$ data	ON	Data transfer	$r =$ data	ON

When the connection is ready for data, the DTE sends and receives octet-oriented data over a full-duplex circuit.

5.5 SUMMARY

The protocols in the physical layer describe the DTE/DCE interface and include mechanical, electrical, and procedural specifications. They ensure that when the sender sends a logical 0 or 1 the receiver interprets it as a 0 or 1.

The most common DTE/DCE interface standard is RS-232. It is usually used to interface a DTE to a DCE connected to an analog voice network. Newer standards are RS-449, RS-422, and RS-423, which extend the cable length and bit rate of the interface.

A new standard interface is X.21, which permits a direct interconnection between a DTE and DCE connected to a digital network.

KEY WORDS AND CONCEPTS

balanced	RS-232
data circuit-terminating equipment (DCE)	RS-422A
	RS-423A
data terminal equipment (DTE)	RS-449
interchange circuits	unbalanced
null modem	X.21

PROBLEMS

1. In the following drawing. show where the RS-232 interface applies:
   (a) A and B
   (b) A and D
   (c) B and C
   (d) All of the above

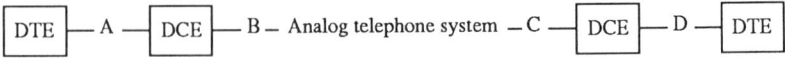

```
┌─────┐      ┌─────┐                              ┌─────┐      ┌─────┐
│ DTE │─ A ─│ DCE │─ B ─ Analog telephone system ─ C ─│ DCE │─ D ─│ DTE │
└─────┘      └─────┘                              └─────┘      └─────┘
```

2. (a) A DTE using the RS-232 standard sends the ASCII character "A" with even parity. Sketch the signal assuming 10-V logic circuits.

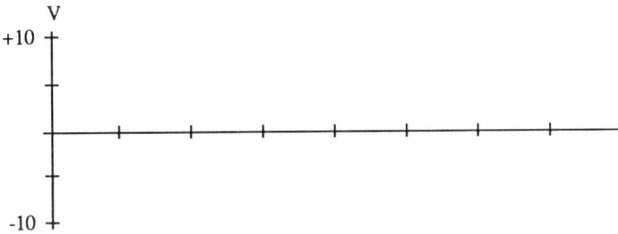

   (b) Sketch the output of an FSK modem driven by the preceding DTE. Assume logical 0 = 2200 Hz and 1 = 1200 Hz. How many cycles of the logical 1 frequency occur during each signaling period if the signaling rate is 300 baud?

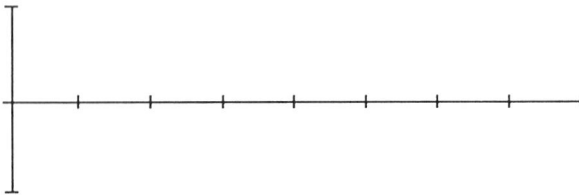

   (c) Where may the frequencies of the modem be detected?
      (i) A and B
      (ii) A and D
      (iii) B and C
      (iv) All of the above

```
┌─────┐      ┌─────┐                              ┌─────┐      ┌─────┐
│ DTE │─ A ─│ DCE │─ B ─ Analog telephone system ─ C ─│ DCE │─ D ─│ DTE │
└─────┘      └─────┘                              └─────┘      └─────┘
```

3. Describe the sequence of DTE/DCE signals when a DCE automatically answers an incoming call with RS-232 interchange circuits.

4. In X.21, why is it necessary for the DCE to give the DTE signal timing information?

5. Describe an application when a DTE may be more than 50 ft from a DCE and require something other than RS-232.

6. If the maximum bit rate is only about 9600 bps over a voice-grade telephone circuit (Example 3.2), why should a network designer be concerned over the 20-Kbps limitation of RS-232?

6

DATA LINK LAYER

In the OSI reference model, each layer provides *services* to the next higher layer by using functions performed within that layer and building on the services of the lower layer. The data link layer offers the service of a communication channel that appears free of bit errors to the network layer. To do this, it detects and corrects errors that occur on the circuits of the physical layer.

In general, the data link layer organizes data into logical blocks, or **frames**. In OSI terminology the frames are called **data link protocol data units (DLPDUs)**. The frames are transferred sequentially to the physical layer entity, which then transmits them from one computer to another. The data link layer detects transmission, format, and operational errors occurring either on the physical connection or in the procedures of the data link protocol, and then attempts to recover from those errors, notifying a higher layer entity of nonrecoverable errors.

6.1 DATA LINK SERVICES

The specific services provided by the data link layer include such things as start-up control, framing, line control, flow control, error control, and time-out control.

Start-up Control. Start-up commands initialize the protocol parameters (such as frame sequence numbers) and start the transmission of data across an established circuit.

Framing. Framing is the process of defining the beginning and end of a sequence of data for transmission. The sender provides a frame "start" indicator at the beginning of a frame and an "ending" indicator. When the receiver recognizes these indicators, the receiver can establish **frame synchronization** with multiple frames on a synchronous circuit.

Character-oriented link protocols use standard 7- or 8-bit character codes for framing. They require character, or octet, synchronization as well as frame synchronization, so that the receiver can group subsequent bits into characters. In the character-oriented protocols that we discuss in this chapter, the sender prefaces each frame with consecutive SYN (synchronous idle) symbols and sends an SOH symbol as the first character of a frame. The receiver searches for these two SYN symbols, establishes character synchronization, and then interprets for an SOH symbol.

Bit-oriented link protocols use an 8-bit **flag** (01111110) to define the start and end of a frame.

Line Control.   Line control is required on half-duplex links to designate who may transmit. Permission is granted by a line-control parameter in a specific field in each frame. The sender ends its transmission by setting the line-control parameter in the last frame as a signal to the receiver that it may enter the transmit mode.

Flow Control.   To keep from being overrun, software in the receiver may control the rate at which it receives frames through a "handshaking" process with the sender. Handshaking acknowledges that the data has been received and that the receiver is ready for more.

Error Control.   A major responsibility of the data link layer is to detect and correct errors. The protocols we discuss in this chapter use LRC-, CRC-, or CRC-equivalent algorithms to detect errors.

Time-out Control.   If a communication channel is noisy, handshaking for error and flow control may be disrupted because acknowledgments from the receiver never return. To solve this problem, time limits may be imposed on events that should occur in a reasonable amount of time. For example, after the sender transmits a data frame, a timer may be started while waiting for an acknowledgment. After a predetermined period of time, the sender may assume the worst (the data frame never made it to the receiver) and retransmit the same data frame.

EXAMPLE 6.1   Telephone conversation

A telephone conversation provides the following analogies to the functions of the data link layer:

FUNCTION	TELEPHONE ANALOGY
Start-up control	"Hello"
	"Hello, this is . . . "
	"Oh, hi!"

Framing	Careful use of pauses:
	(pause) "How are you?" (pause)
Line control	Careful use of pauses:
	"How are you?" (pause) "Fine"
Flow control	"Slow down, I can't understand you!"
Error control	"What? Please repeat what you said!"
Time-out control	"Are you still there?"

6.2 DATA LINK PROTOCOLS

6.2.1 Ideal Error-free Link Protocol

In an ideal situation where the computers have unlimited buffer space and
the circuit is error-free, the link protocol is very simple—the sender continuously
frames the data and transmits (Fig. 6.1). The sender has no need to be concerned
about the receiver's ability to keep up or recover from bit errors.

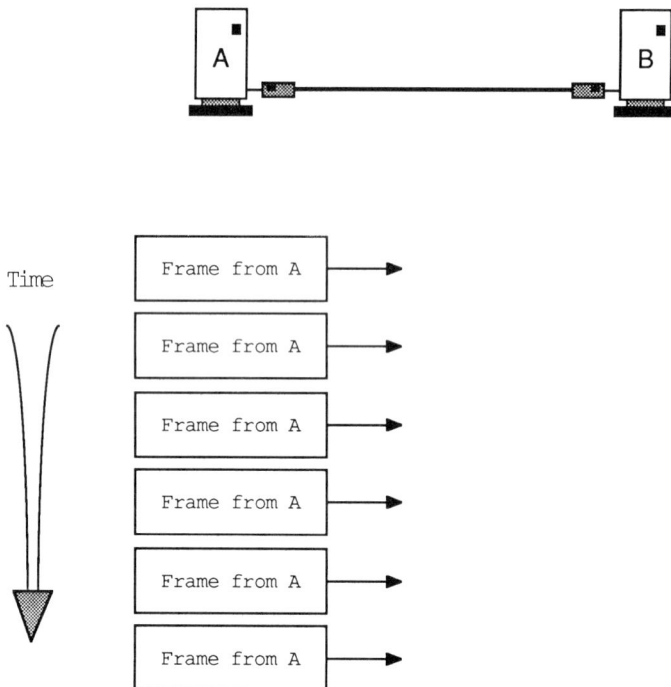

Figure 6.1   Ideal error-free transmission

6.2.2 Stop-and-Wait Protocol

If the receiver cannot keep up with the sender, there is a need to restrict the flow of frames. This can be done through the use of acknowledgments from the receiver back to the sender to acknowledge that each frame has been received without error (Fig. 6.2). After the sender has transmitted a frame, it must receive an acknowledgment before proceeding to send the next frame. This is a **stop-and-wait** protocol. The acknowledgment can be a simple dummy frame or character.

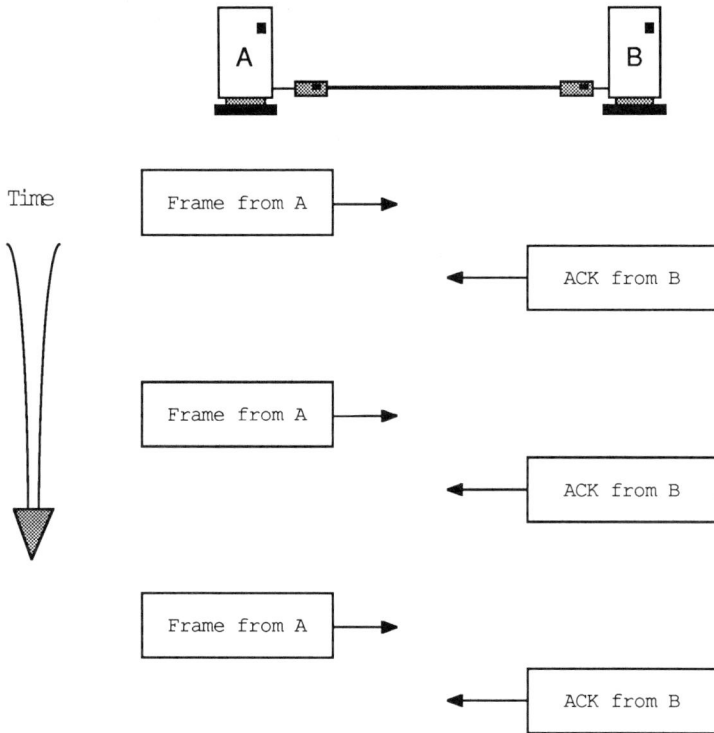

Figure 6.2   Flow control with a stop-and-wait protocol

One of the problems with a noisy channel is that acknowledgments may be lost or delayed. If that happens, the sender may time out and resend the original data. If the earlier acknowledgment was simply delayed, it may not be known for which data frame it was meant. The result is a lot of confusion. To eliminate this problem, sequence numbers are assigned to each frame, and the acknowledgment includes the number of the received data frame (Fig. 6.3).

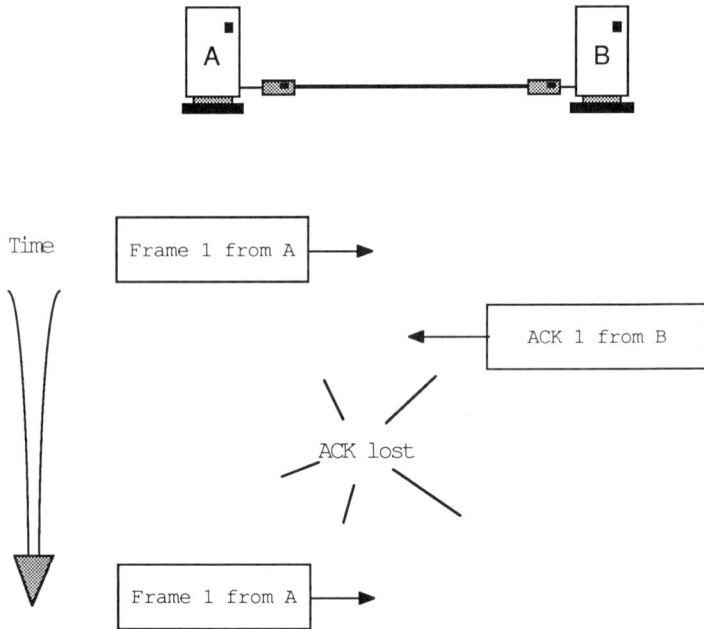

Figure 6.3   Stop-and-wait transmission with numbered frames

6.2.3 Piggybacking

Some protocols reserve a field in the frame header for an acknowledgment. When computer A sends a frame successfully to computer B, a returning frame from B to A will include the frame number of the successfully received frame in its header as an acknowledgment (Fig. 6.4). This **piggybacking** procedure prevents tying up the link with a lot of acknowledgment frames. If no data exists to be sent from computer B to computer A, eventually B will time out and send an acknowledgment in a short control frame.

EXAMPLE 6.2   Piggybacking (See Fig. 6.5)

Computer A sends the first frame of the exchange, a data frame labeled A1, to computer B. Computer A leaves the ACK field initialized at 0. Next, B sends a data frame (B1) to A and includes an ACK for A's A1 data frame. Computer A then sends a final data frame A2. Since B has no more data, it times out and sends A an acknowledgment frame for A2.

6.2.4 Windows

Stop-and-wait protocols require that each frame be acknowledged before the next frame is transmitted. In some situations, such as in satellite communications,

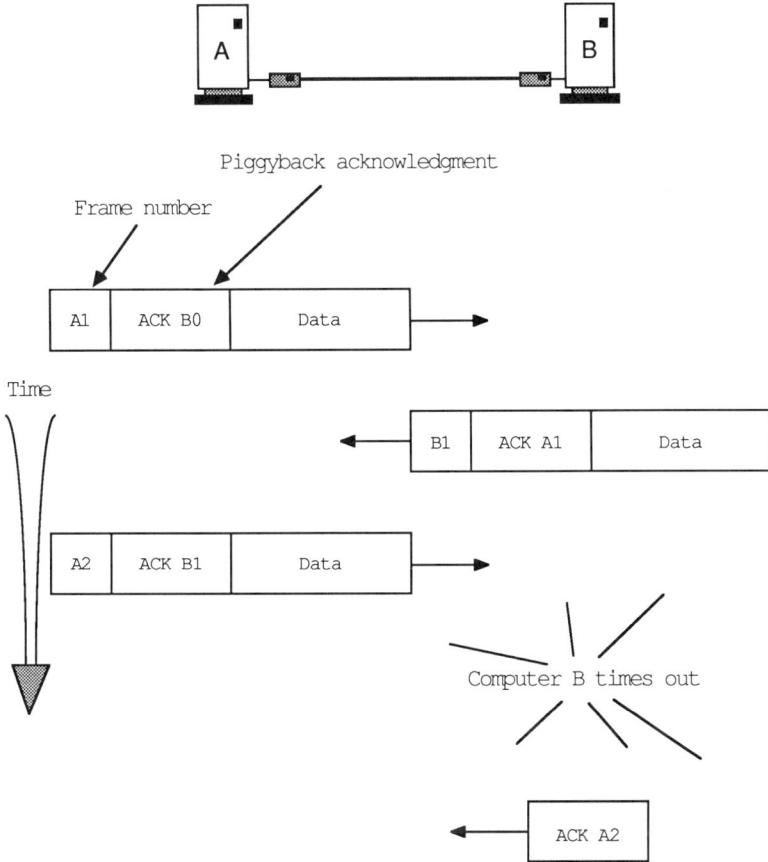

Figure 6.4   Acknowledgment piggybacking

this limits the maximum information rate because of lengthy transmission delays. The concept of **windows** opens the possibility of increased efficiency by defining a *range* of frame numbers that may be legally transmitted or received. The range of consecutive sequence numbers that may be sent before an acknowledgment is required is called the *sender's window*. The range of sequence numbers that the receiver may accept is the *receiver's window* (Fig. 6.5).

The stop-and-wait protocol that we discussed earlier has a sender and receiver window of 1. The sender may send only one frame; then it must receive an acknowledgment before continuing. Likewise, the receiver may acknowledge only the next sequential frame.

When the window size is greater than 1, **pipelining** can be accomplished; that is, more frames, up to a network-specified maximum, may be transmitted by the sender before an acknowledgment is required (Fig. 6.6), and the maximum information rate can be greatly increased.

Computer A
(send)

| 0 | 1 | 2 | 3 | 4 | 5 | 6 | 7 | 0 | 1 | 2 | 3 | 4 | 5 | 6 | 7 | 0 | 1 | ...

Moving window
indicates range of
frames that can be sent

Computer B
(receive)

| 0 | 1 | 2 | 3 | 4 | 5 | 6 | 7 | 0 | 1 | 2 | 3 | 4 | 5 | 6 | 7 | 0 | 1 | ...

Moving window
indicates range of
frames that can be received

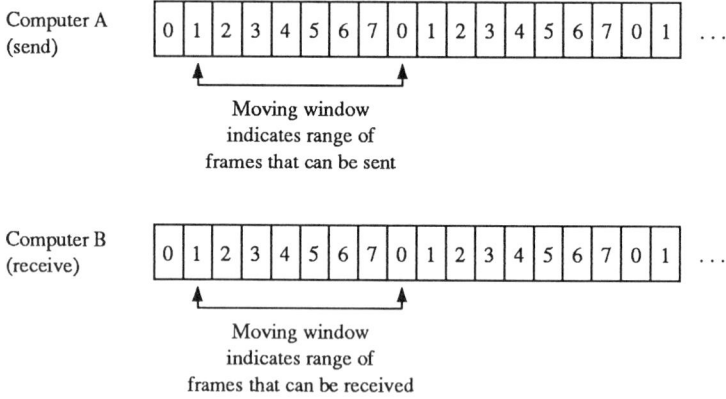

(a) Sender (computer A) transmits frames 1 & 2 to computer B

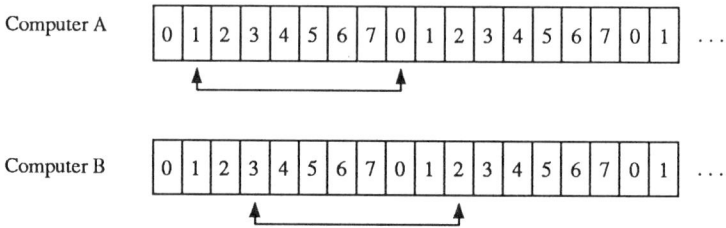

Computer A

| 0 | 1 | 2 | 3 | 4 | 5 | 6 | 7 | 0 | 1 | 2 | 3 | 4 | 5 | 6 | 7 | 0 | 1 | ...

Computer B

| 0 | 1 | 2 | 3 | 4 | 5 | 6 | 7 | 0 | 1 | 2 | 3 | 4 | 5 | 6 | 7 | 0 | 1 | ...

(b) Computer B acknowledges frame 2 and updates receiver's window

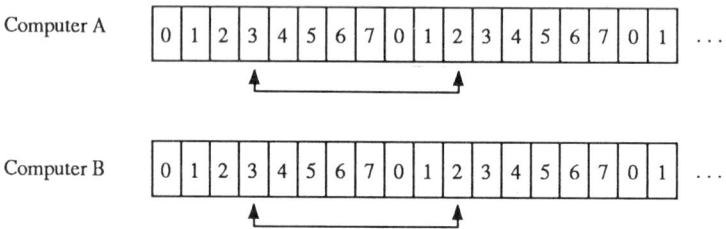

Computer A

| 0 | 1 | 2 | 3 | 4 | 5 | 6 | 7 | 0 | 1 | 2 | 3 | 4 | 5 | 6 | 7 | 0 | 1 | ...

Computer B

| 0 | 1 | 2 | 3 | 4 | 5 | 6 | 7 | 0 | 1 | 2 | 3 | 4 | 5 | 6 | 7 | 0 | 1 | ...

(c) Computer A receives acknowledgment and updates sliding window

Figure 6.5   Pipelining with window size of 7

(a) Computer A sends frame A1 to computer B

Time

(b) Computer A sends frame A2 to computer B and waits

(c) Computer B sends frame B1 to A with piggyback
indicating last successful receipt from A (A2)

(d) The pointer for computer A may be advanced once its table has been updated,
and then it sends A3 with B1's acknowledgement

(e) Computer B has no more data to send to A, times out,
and sends an ACK control frame for receipt of A3

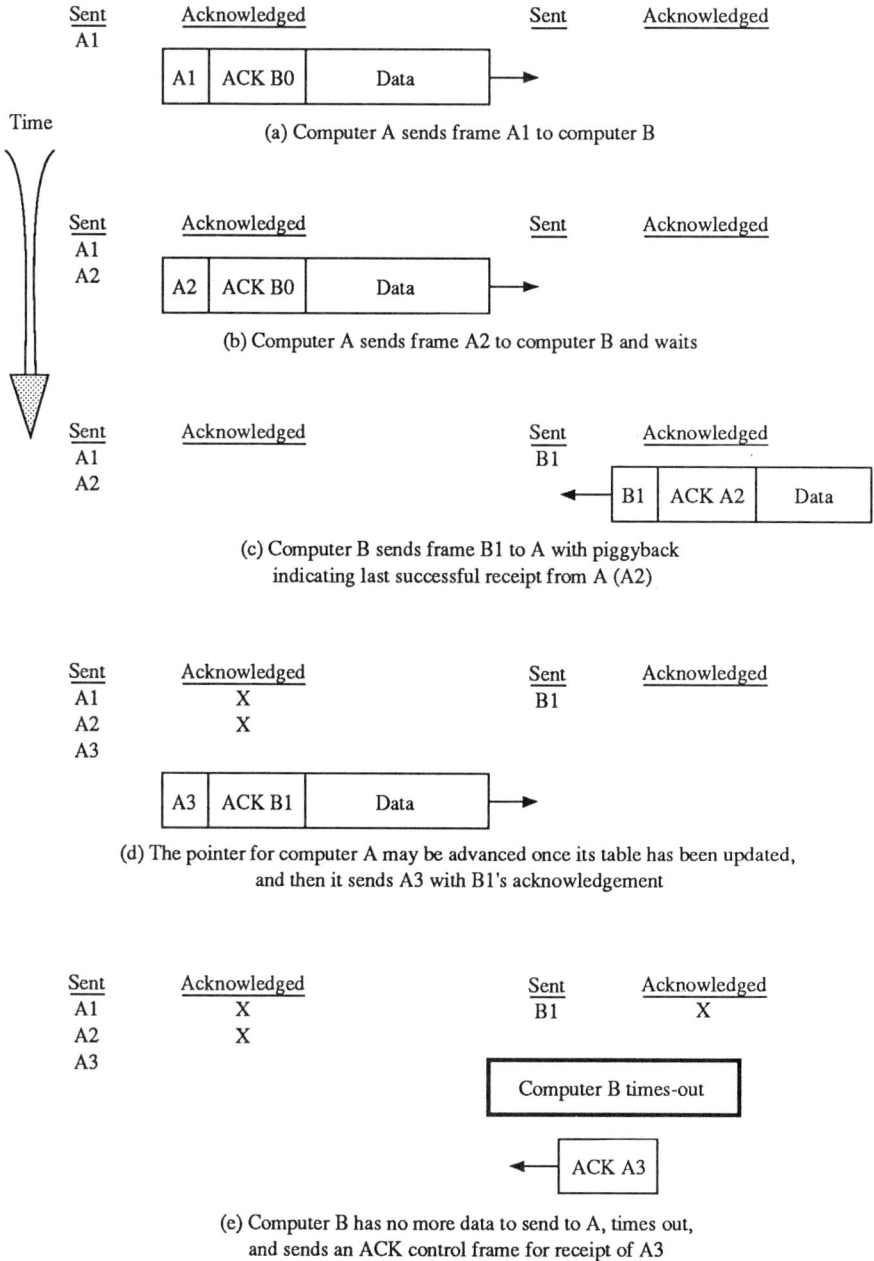

Figure 6.6   Frame pipelining with a window of 2

The sender maintains a table that records the outgoing frame number and indicates if it has been acknowledged or not. As the lowest-numbered frame is acknowledged, a pointer moves, keeping a running indication of the next expected acknowledgment. The pointer also shifts to permit the next sequential frame to be sent.

The length of the frame number field limits the window size. Otherwise, the frame numbers of the most recent transmissions would overlap the numbers of frames already transmitted but waiting for acknowledgment.

Depending on the protocol, an acknowledgment may be required for each frame or only for the last frame of a series that was sent since the last acknowledgment. In the case of errors, the receiver may request that the specific frame that was in error be retransmitted or that the faulty frame and all the subsequent frames be retransmitted.

6.3 EXAMPLES OF LINK PROTOCOLS

Link-level protocols are usually either character-oriented or bit-oriented, depending on how they maintain frame synchronization. Each type of protocol has its own method of identifying the length of the information field of the frame. In character-oriented protocols, ASCII or EBCDIC symbols are often used to delineate the information field of the frame. In a variation, called a *byte-count-oriented* protocol, the frame header contains a field that specifies the length of the information field so that the receiver can compute the location of the end of the information field and not depend on control characters. Bit-oriented protocols use a flag to terminate frames of variable length.

In the next section, an example of a simple character-oriented protocol and a byte-count-oriented protocol will be examined, and then an international standard bit-oriented protocol.

6.3.1 Binary Synchronous Communications

Binary Synchronous Communications (BSC) protocol was created by IBM in 1966 for computer-to-terminal and computer-to-computer communications and is still in common use. It is a character-oriented, half-duplex protocol that uses special characters for frame synchronization, character synchronization, and control of frame transmission. In the following section we discuss its frame format and link procedures.

6.3.1.1 BSC frame format.   The format of a typical BSC frame is illustrated in Fig. 6.7. The dual SYN characters are used for frame and character synchronization.

The SOH and STX characters are special control characters found in both ASCII and EBCDIC codes. The contents of the header are specified by the user except for particular status and test request frames.

Bits →	8	Network option	8	User option	8	8/16*
	SOH	Header	STX	Data	ETX or ETB	BCC

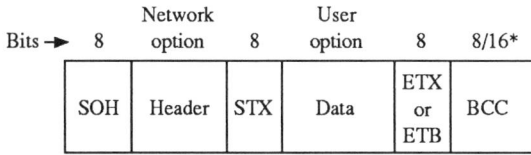

SYN = Synchronous idle
SOH = Start of heading
STX = Start of text
ETX = End of text
ETB = End of transmission block
BCC = Block check character*

*BCC = 8-bit LRC for ASCII or 16-bit CRC for EBCDIC code

Figure 6.7   BSC frame format

With character data, an STX indicates the start of the text field and an ETB indicates the end of the frame when there are more frames to follow. ETX is used to terminate the last frame of a text message. The data portion is variable in length, but an integral number of octets. Sometimes a frame may be used to transmit binary data that is not character-oriented, but the binary data must be a multiple of eight bits.

A link-control problem will arise if eight consecutive bits in an octet position in the information field inadvertently look like an ETX or ETB symbol. A technique is needed for **data transparency** such that symbols in the information field that resemble link control characters are not interpreted as protocol control characters. BCS provides *transparent mode* operation with *character stuffing*, where a DLE symbol is inserted by the sender before the STX, ETX, and ETB link-control symbols. In this mode, BSC requires the receiver to detect a 16-bit pattern (e.g., DLE and ETB) before taking action on the link. If, by chance, the symbol code for a DLE is in the information field, the sender inserts an extra DLE before it is transmitted. In the transparent mode, the receiver will interpret two DLEs as one DLE.

To detect and correct errors occurring during transmission, BSC uses either a combination of parity and LRC (ASCII) or a CRC (EBCDIC). The *block check character (BCC)* is computed from the initial SOH through the ETX or ETB.

When a transmitted BCC matches the block check calculated at the receiver, the receiver sends a positive acknowledgment. When errors are detected, a negative acknowledgment is returned for ARQ error correction.

6.3.1.2 BSC line discipline.
Link establishment begins with the transmission of an ENQ from the sender; the receiver acknowledges with an ACK. When all the messages are transmitted and the sender wishes to terminate the link or relinquish control to the distant end, the sender transmits an EOT. In general, the line-discipline protocol operates as illustrated in Fig. 6.8.

Link establishment

Computer A   Computer B

ENQ ─────────────▶

                          ◀───────────── ACK

Information transfer

Send data block ─────────────▶

                          ◀───────────── If error,
                                          NAK

Retransmit ─────────────▶

                          ◀───────────── If no error,
                                          ACK

Send next block, etc. ─────────────▶

Link termination

EOT ─────────────▶

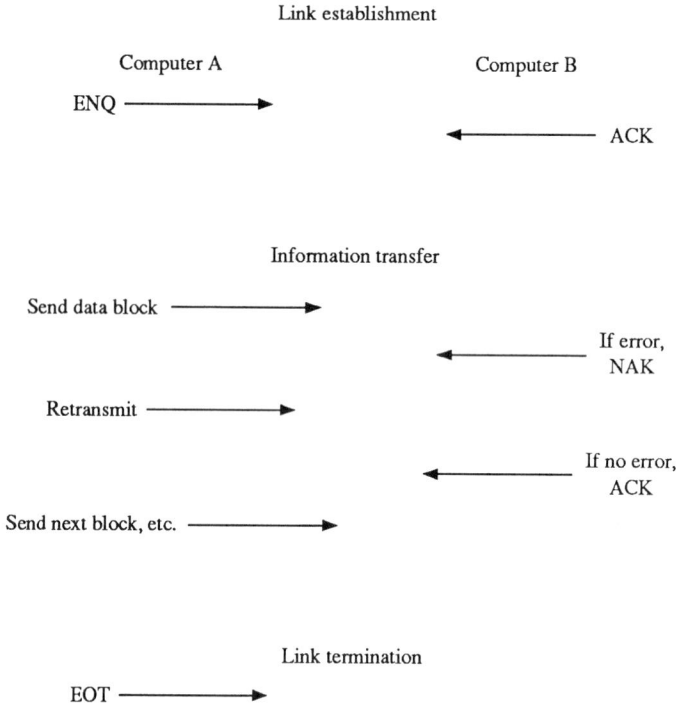

Figure 6.8 BSC line-control protocol

6.3.2 Digital Data Communications Message Protocol

DEC developed the Digital Data Communications Message Protocol (DDCMP) in 1974 for the data link layer of DNA. In contrast to BSC, DDCMP protocol can be used in a half-duplex or full-duplex mode. DDCMP may also be used on synchronous or asynchronous links.

DDCMP is a byte-count-oriented protocol, where the length of the information field (in octets) is stored in the header and the end of each frame is computed by software, rather than by detection of control characters. This technique guarantees data transparency for all 8-bit binary codes.

6.3.2.1 DDCMP frame format.

Each DDCMP frame is numbered, and a CRC-16 is used for error detection. Error correction is through an ARQ technique. The protocol allows information fields of up to 16,383 octets; however, with noise on the channel, much smaller frames are desirable because if an error is detected, the entire frame must be retransmitted.

Because each frame is numbered within an 8-bit field, pipelining for up to 255 outstanding frames is possible. If an error occurs, the sender retransmits all messages back to the last sequential correct frame, thereby losing any pipelining in effect on the link.

Three kinds of frames are exchanged: data, control, and maintenance. Data frames contain the user information. Control frames include commands to maintain the link and recover from errors. Maintenance frames are used in an off-line mode for testing and debugging and are not discussed here.

The type of frame is specified by the *special character* in the header (Fig. 6.9). You should note that the header is the same length for each type of frame. The header contains important parameters for controlling the link and has its own CRC-16.

The data field is an integral number of octets followed by its own CRC-16.

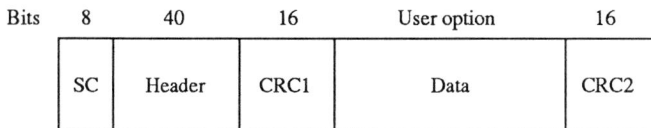

Bits	8	40	16	User option	16
	SC	Header	CRC1	Data	CRC2

SC = Special character
CRC1 = CRC-16 for the header
CRC2 = CRC-16 for the data

Figure 6.9   DDCMP general frame format

Data Frames.   The data frame header (Fig. 6.10) starts with an SOH character and includes a *count* field for the number of information octets in the frame. The *flags* field is used for line control of half-duplex lines and other functions.

The *response* is used in piggybacking and pipelining; it is the number of the last consecutive correctly received frame from the other computer. The next field, *number*, is the sequence number of this data frame. The *address* of tributary stations, when DDCMP is being used on multipoint links, follows the number field. Since potentially long frames can be sent, the header has its own CRC to ensure that the receiver can compute the end of the information field. This is vital to the control of the link.

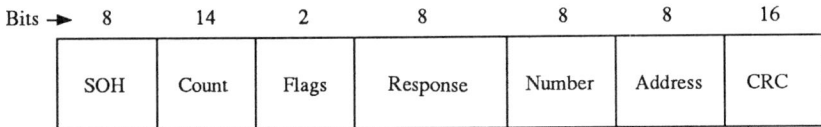

Bits ➤	8	14	2	8	8	8	16
	SOH	Count	Flags	Response	Number	Address	CRC

Figure 6.10   DDCMP data frame header

Control Frames.   Control frames (Fig. 6.11) are distinguished by the control character ENQ in the beginning of the header. The control frames are unnumbered.

A parameter in the *type* field denotes each type of control frame:

1. Acknowledge message (ACK) (type = 1). You should note that an ACK control frame is not the same as an ACK symbol in standard ASCII or EBCDIC code.
2. Negative acknowledge message (NAK) (type = 2).
3. Reply to message number (REP) (type = 3). This is the message used to request frame status from the receiver.
4. Start message (STRT) (type = 6). This is the message used to establish initial contact and synchronization on a link.
5. Start acknowledge message (STACK) (type = 7). This is the message that the receiver sends to the sender in response to a STRT.

The *subtype* field provides additional information for some frame types, such as the reason for rejection by a NAK.

The *receiver* field is used in certain control frames to pass specific information from the receiver back to the sender—for example, the number of the last successfully received data frame. The *sender* field is used to pass specific information from the sender on to the receiver, such as the number of the last data frame sent by the sender.

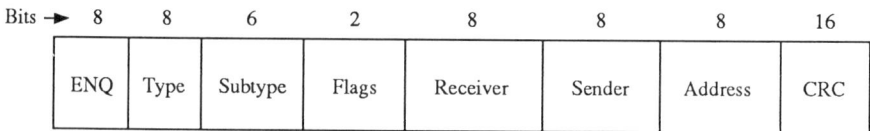

Bits ➤ 8   8   6   2   8   8   8   16

| ENQ | Type | Subtype | Flags | Receiver | Sender | Address | CRC |

Figure 6.11   DDCMP control frame

An acknowledge message is a typical control frame. It may be sent to indicate frame status (in response to a REP control frame) or when the node owes an acknowledgment but has no more data to send.

Maintenance Frames.   The maintenance class of frames is used in an off-line mode for basic diagnostic testing. A DLE is used as the special leading character in the header to distinguish them from the data and control frames.

6.3.2.2 DDCMP line discipline.   The STRT control frame is used to establish initial contact and synchronization on a link. Whichever end receives a STRT responds with a STACK when the frame numbering is reset. An ACK is sent following STACK to indicate that the computer is ready to transmit data.

The line discipline from this point depends on the mode of communication. If it is full-duplex, each party may begin to transmit. If the mode is half-duplex (Fig. 6.12), the FLAGS field in each header is used to transfer link control from one node to another. To be specific, the select bit (SEL) is the least significant bit of the FLAG field; it indicates control on the half-duplex link. When SEL is set to 1, the frame invites the other party to send data.

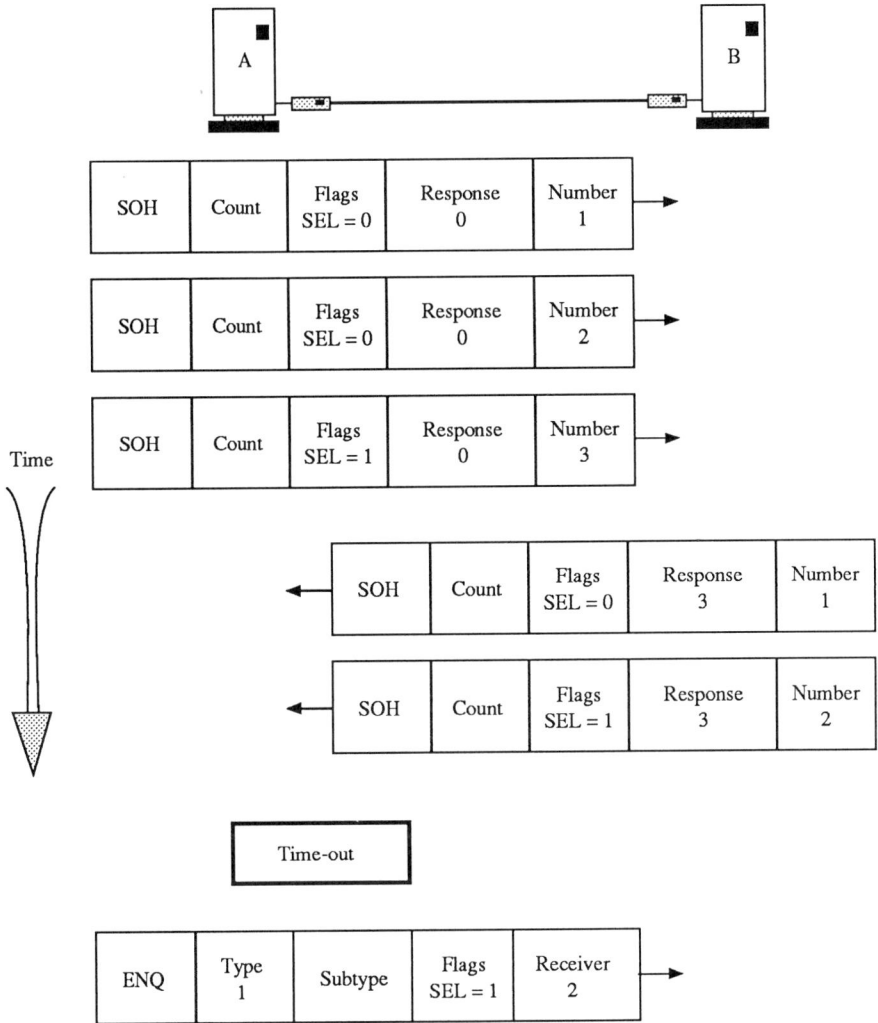

| SOH | Count | Flags SEL = 0 | Response 0 | Number 1 | → |

| SOH | Count | Flags SEL = 0 | Response 0 | Number 2 | → |

Time

| SOH | Count | Flags SEL = 1 | Response 0 | Number 3 | → |

| ← | SOH | Count | Flags SEL = 0 | Response 3 | Number 1 |

| ← | SOH | Count | Flags SEL = 1 | Response 3 | Number 2 |

| Time-out |

| ENQ | Type 1 | Subtype | Flags SEL = 1 | Receiver 2 | → |

Figure 6.12   DDCMP half-duplex line protocol (simplified)

6.3.2.3 DDCMP TRIB.   A TRIB estimate for a DDCMP link provides a baseline with which to compare performance with other link protocols and give insight to trade-offs between the character-oriented and bit-oriented protocols. In Example 6.3 (a), we assume an error-free circuit. In (b) and (c) we show that the length of DDCMP is a strong factor in its efficiency on a noisy link. For the sake of simplicity, we ignore SYN characters and assume that propagation, processing, and circuit interface delays are zero.

EXAMPLE 6.3   DDCMP TRIB calculation

Calculate TRIB for a 2400-bps DDCMP link with a window of 1. A file of 65,500 octets is to be transferred. Compute TRIB for a link with (a) no bit errors and a short 131-octet information field (the reason for this odd number will become obvious when we compare DDCMP later with X.25 LAPB); (b) BER of 10^{-5} with the same short frame; and (c) BER of 10^{-5} with a long (16,375 octet) information field.

The total number of information bits is

$$n_{info} = (8 \text{ bits/octet})(65,500 \text{ octets}) = 524,000 \text{ bits}$$

The number of short frames is

$$N_{shortframes} = \frac{(65,500 \text{ octets})}{(131 \text{ octets/frame})} = 500 \text{ frames}$$

The number of long frames is

$$N_{longframes} = \frac{(65,500 \text{ octets})}{(16,375 \text{ octets/frame})} = 4 \text{ frames}$$

(a) Compute TRIB with BER = 0. The number of bits per frame includes the data header, data field, and CRC:

$$n_{frame} = 64 \text{ bits} + (8 \text{ bits/octet})(131 \text{ octets}) + 16 \text{ bits} = 1128 \text{ bits}$$

Therefore, the time to transmit one frame is

$$t_{oneframe} = \frac{n_{frame}}{R} = \frac{(1128 \text{ bits})}{(2400 \text{ bps})} = .470 \text{ s}$$

The time to send an ACK (or NAK) is

$$t_{ACK} = \frac{(64 \text{ bits})}{(2400 \text{ bps})} = .027 \text{ s}$$

The total time for the information transfer period (t_3) is

$$t_3 = (t_{oneframe} + t_{ACK})N_{shortframes}$$

$$= (.470 \text{ s/frame} + .027 \text{ s/frame})(500 \text{ frames})$$

$$= 248 \text{ s}$$

Therefore, from Eq. 2.4,

$$TRIB = \frac{n_{info}}{t_3}$$

$$= \frac{(524,000 \text{ bits})}{(248 \text{ s})} = 2113 \text{ bps}$$

(b) Compute TRIB and assume BER $= 10^{-5}$ and use the same length information field.

Any detected error will require a negative acknowledgement and retransmission of the entire frame. There may be multiple retransmissions. We can use the results of Eqs. 2.8 and 2.9 to compute the time for information transfer.

For a data frame, the probability of a frame arriving at the receiver and being acknowledged (1128 bits $+$ 64 bits) with no errors is

$$P_{no} = .99999^{1192} = .988$$

Therefore, the time to transmit one frame successfully, on the average, is

$$t_{oneframe} = \frac{(.470 \text{ s} + .027 \text{ s})}{.988} = .503 \text{ s}$$

and

$$t_3 = (.503 \text{ s/frame})(500 \text{ frames}) = 251 \text{ s}$$

Therefore,

$$\text{TRIB} = \frac{(524,000 \text{ bits})}{(251 \text{ s})} = 2088 \text{ bps}$$

(c) Compute TRIB, assuming BER $= 10^{-5}$, and use long information fields.

$$n_{frame} = 64 \text{ bits} + (8 \text{ bits/octet})(16,375 \text{ octets}) + 16 \text{ bits}$$

$$= 131,080 \text{ bits}$$

$$P_{no} = .99999^{131,144} = .269$$

Therefore,

$$t_{oneframe} = \frac{(131,080 \text{ bits} + 64 \text{ bits})}{(2400 \text{ bps})/(.269 \text{ s})} = 203 \text{ s}$$

and,

$$t_3 = (203 \text{ s/frame})(4 \text{ frames}) = 812 \text{ s}$$

Therefore,

$$\text{TRIB} = \frac{(524,000 \text{ bits})}{(812 \text{ s})} = 645 \text{ bps}$$

This is only 31% of the TRIB in (b) because the probability that a frame will incur an error has increased and there are time delays retransmitting the long frames.

6.3.3 X.25 Link Access Procedures Balanced

CCITT X.25 provides international standards for the physical, data link, and network protocols for packet-switched public data networks. X.25 was originally approved in 1976 and was modified in 1980 and 1984. We covered the physical layer (X.21) in Chap. 5. In this chapter we discuss the data link layer protocol, **Link Access Procedures Balanced (LAPB)**. In Chap. 7 we cover the network layer protocol.

As far as the computer interface is concerned, this layer specifies the link access procedures that are used between the local DTE and local DCE. In a basic X.25 network environment, an LAPB frame is normally a maximum 135 octets and the information field within the frame contains a network packet.

LAPB is a derivative of IBM's Synchronous Data Link Control (SDLC) protocol that is the link protocol in SNA. SDLC derivatives that share the same principles are the ANSI X.66-1979 Advanced Data Communication Control Procedures (ADCCP) and ISO High-level Data Link Control (HDLC). LAPB is a specific implementation of HDLC. LAPB is not only OSI-oriented, but by studying LAPB we will see the underlying principles of all these bit-oriented, synchronous, full-duplex protocols.

The frame format and procedures described here are for the *basic mode*. The *extended mode* permits a longer information field. We examine the protocol for single link operation.

LAPB has the following features:

1. Frame sequencing, which permits up to seven outstanding frames for pipelining in the basic operation.
2. Error detection with a 16-bit frame check sequence (FCS) similar to a CRC-16, with correction by positive acknowledgment and retransmission (PAR). If an error occurs, the receiver discards the frame and the sender re-transmits after a timeout period.

6.3.3.1 LAPB frame formats.   In LAPB, a flag is used as the synchronizing bit pattern at the beginning of a frame and as a frame terminator. A single flag may be used as both the closing flag for one frame and the opening flag for the next frame.

The *address* field (Fig. 6.13) identifies a frame as either the command or a response. A command from a sender (such as an information frame) is followed by a response by the receiver (for example, an acknowledgment). A command frame contains the address of the DCE or DTE to which the command is being sent, and a response frame contains the address of the DCE or DTE sending the frame.

The *control* field contains the command or a response and sequence number when applicable. There are three types of control field formats: (1) numbered information transfer; (2) numbered supervisory functions; and (3) unnumbered control functions. The *information* field is discussed in the next section.

Bits ➔   8   8   8   User option   16

| Flag | Address | Control | Information | FCS |

(a) I frame

Bits ➔   8   8   8   16

| Flag | Address | Control | FCS |

(b) S and U frames

Figure 6.13   LAPB frame formats (Reprinted by permission)

The *frame check sequence FCS* is a minor variation of a CRC.

Information (I) Frame.   The control field of an I frame contains the frame sequence number, polling bit, and a frame acknowledgment number (Fig. 6.14). $N(S)$ is the sequence number of the transmitted information frame. $N(R)$ is the sequence number (bit 6 = lsb) of the next in-sequence information frame expected to be received by the receiver (in other words, the last successfully transmitted frame was $N(R) - 1$).

Bit order of transmission	1	2	3	4	5	6	7	8
Information command format	0	N (S)			P	N (R)		

Figure 6.14   Information (I) frame control field

P is the *poll* bit. The poll bit is set to 1 by the sender in a command to solicit (poll) a response. When used in the information frame, it solicits a supervisory frame. The response may be an indication of readiness on the part of the receiver or acknowledgment. The final bit is set to 1 in the supervisory response to indicate that the frame is a result of the poll.

6.3.3.2 Bit stuffing.   Data transparency, which is needed to avoid data in the frame being confused with a flag, is accomplished by **bit stuffing**. When five consecutive ones occur in the frame, a 0 is automatically inserted by the sender. The receiver automatically deletes a 0 following five consecutive ones. The procedure is analogous to the character stuffing that takes place in BSC to ensure information data does not become confused with line control characters.

EXAMPLE 6.4   Bit stuffing

```
Data              0 1 1 1 1 1 1 1 1 0 0 1 1 1 1 1 1 1 1 1
```

```
Transmitted            *                    *         *
bits          0 1 1 1 1 0 1 1 1 1 0 0 1 1 1 1 0 1 1 1 1 0

 * Denotes bit stuffing
```

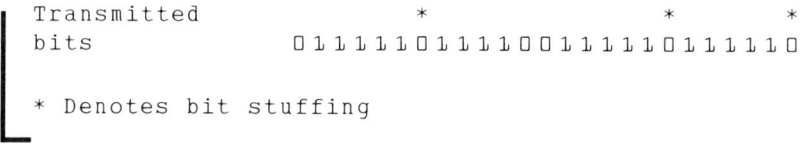

Supervisory (S) Frames. The S frames are used to perform control functions such as acknowledging I frames, requesting retransmission of I frames, and temporarily suspending transmission of I frames. The command field is shown in Fig. 6.15.

Bit order of transmission	1	2	3	4	5	6	7	8
Supervisory command format	1	0	S	S	P/F	N (R)		

S's are the supervisory function bits:

	Bit position	3	4
Receive ready (RR)		0	0
Receive not ready (RNR)		1	0
Reject (REJ)		0	1

Figure 6.15 Supervisory (S) frame control field (Reprinted with permission)

The 2-bit *supervisory function* field has three commands. Receive ready (RR) indicates that the sender is ready to receive an I frame and to acknowledge that it is ready for an I frame numbered $N(R)$. Receive not ready (RNR) indicates a busy condition. The reject (REJ) command is used by the DCE or DTE to request retransmission of I frames starting with $N(R)$.

P/F is the poll/final bit and is used in the same way as P/F in the I frame.

Unnumbered Command (U) Frames. The unnumbered commands (Fig. 6.16) perform additional data link functions such as reinitiating transmission after a busy period and varying command/control field length. SABM and DISC are two of the unnumbered commands whose functions are as follows.

1. SABM (set asynchronous balanced mode) establishes a full-duplex link between nodes that take equal responsibility for link control. The normal response to an SABM is an unnumbered acknowledgment (UA).
2. DISC (disconnect) terminates a link.

6.3.3.3 LAPB line discipline. The DCE initially indicates that it is able to set up the data link by transmitting contiguous flags to the DTE (this is the active

Bit order of transmission	1	2	3	4	5	6	7	8
SABM command format	1	1	1	1	P	1	0	0

(a) SABM command field that establishes a link

Bit order of transmission	1	2	3	4	5	6	7	8
UA response format	1	1	0	0	F	1	1	0

(b) UA control field in response to the previous SABM

Figure 6.16   Unnumbered command (U) frame command fields (Reprinted with permission)

channel state). The DTE initiates link setup by transmitting an SABM command to the DCE. When the command is correctly received, the DCE confirms that it can transfer information, returns a UA to the DTE, and resets its state variables $N(R)$ and $N(S)$ to zero.

The DTE or DCE may terminate the mode by transmitting a DISC command. The receiver acknowledges the command by transmitting a UA response. The DTE or DCE enters the disconnected phase after receiving the UA.

6.3.3.4 LAPB TRIB.   To estimate TRIB for a LAPB link, we assume that the degree of bit stuffing in each frame is represented by the factor

$$F_{\text{bitstuff}} = \frac{B_{\text{after}}}{B_{\text{before}}} \tag{6.1}$$

where

$$B_{\text{after}} = \text{average number of bits in frame} \\ \text{after bit stuffing}$$

$$B_{\text{before}} = \text{average number of bits in frame} \\ \text{before bit stuffing}$$

This factor will be included in the calculation of time to transmit one frame.

EXAMPLE 6.5   LAPB TRIB calculation

Calculate TRIB when a file of 65,500 octets is to be transferred over an error-free 2400-bps LAPB link with a window of 1. The frames have 131-octet information fields. Assume:

1. $F_{\text{bitstuff}} = 1.02$
2. One flag per frame

The number of frames is

$$N_{\text{frames}} = \frac{(65,500 \text{ octets})}{(131 \text{ octets/frame})}$$

$$= 500 \text{ frames}$$

The total number of information bits is

$$n_{\text{info}} = (8 \text{ bits/octet})(65,500 \text{ octets}) = 524,000 \text{ bits}$$

The number of bits per frame includes the flag, plus the address, control, information, and FCS fields times the bit-stuff factor.

$$n_{\text{frame}} = 8 \text{ bits} + (16 \text{ bits}$$

$$+ (8 \text{ bits/octet})(131 \text{ octets}) + 16 \text{ bits})1.02$$

$$= 1110 \text{ bits}$$

Therefore, the time to transmit one frame is

$$t_{\text{oneframe}} = \frac{(1110 \text{ bits})}{(2400 \text{ bps})}$$

$$= .462 \text{ s}$$

The time to send an RR (ACK) or REJ (NAK) is:

$$t_{\text{ACK}} = \frac{(40 \text{ bits})}{(2400 \text{ bps})}$$

$$= .017 \text{ s}$$

The total time for the information transfer period is

$$t_3 = (t_{\text{oneframe}} + t_{\text{ACK}})N_{\text{frames}}$$

$$= (.462 \text{ s} + .017 \text{ s})(500 \text{ frames}) = 240 \text{ s}$$

$$\text{TRIB} = \frac{n_{\text{info}}}{t_3}$$

$$= \frac{(524,000 \text{ bits})}{(240 \text{ s})}$$

$$= 2183 \text{ s}$$

This is not much better than DDCMP (2088 bps) under similar conditions, despite DDCMP's longer header, due to LAPB bit stuffing. The 1.02 bit-stuff factor is representative of text data, and can be larger or smaller, depending on the actual user data in the application.

6.4 SUMMARY

The data link layer provides higher OSI layers with the services of a point-to-point link that appears free of errors. The protocols organize data into frames and provide error detection and correction. IBM's BSC and DEC's DDCMP link protocols are character-oriented, and CCITT X.25 LAPB is bit-oriented. A major protocol design issue is keeping the protocol from confusing data with control symbols (transparency); bit-oriented protocols solve the problem by using the technique of bit stuffing.

TRIB performance depends on the length of the headers and trailers and the error-correction technique. The more sophisticated protocols detect errors with a CRC and improve performance with piggyback acknowledgments and pipelining.

KEY WORDS AND CONCEPTS

bit stuffing
data link protocol data unit (DLPDU)
data transparency
flag
frame
frame synchronization

Link Access Procedures Balanced
    (LAPB)
piggybacking
pipelining
stop-and-wait
window

PROBLEMS

1. Why is character synchronization important in character-oriented link protocols?

2. Why does pipelining give better performance than a stop-and-wait protocol?

3. For what are synchronous idle (SYN) characters used in synchronous transmission?

4. Assume that in a given BSC network, the BSC header is an SOH symbol plus a one-octet field used to store the frame number. In an ASCII system, for a frame number of (decimal) 47 and information field of "DATA," show the parts of a whole frame. Assume odd parity and odd LRC.
   (a) Header field
   (b) Data field
   (c) BCC field

5. For the frame in Prob. 4, describe at least two events that must happen for the frame to be transmitted successfully.

6. Eight bits of user data are going to be sent in one frame via BSC. Assume the data is simply 1001 0111 (an ETB character). Show the BSC data field. Assume ASCII with odd parity.

7. How many bits are required for the sequence number field of a frame if pipelining is used and up to 15 frames can be outstanding? If 63 frames can be outstanding?

8. A data frame with an information field of COLLEGE GRADES is sent on a point-to-point DDCMP link. It is the 206th frame and the sender just received the 180th frame

correctly from the other end. Give the following header parameters in binary: COUNT, RESP, and NUM.

9. If the last successfully received frame on an LAPB link was (decimal) 5, what is in the $N(R)$ field in the response (in binary)?

10. **(a)** Apply bit stuffing to

$$0110111110011111010111110$$

   (b) Compute $F_{bitstuff}$ for the data in (a).

11. Suppose the following bit string is received. Remove the stuffed bits and show the actual flag.

$$01111101111101010111100011111101$$

$$111100110001111110101111010$$

12. In the following problem, we analyze DUNKLINK. DUNKLINK is the data link protocol for DUNKNET, a student-devised network protocol.
DUNKLINK has the following frame structure:

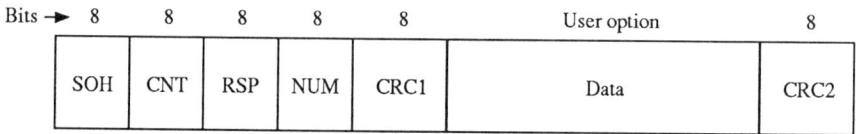

Bits → 8	8	8	8	8	User option	8
SOH	CNT	RSP	NUM	CRC1	Data	CRC2

Each field is one (1) octet except for the data field

SOH	=	Start of heading symbol
CNT	=	number of octets contained in the following data field
RSP	=	number of the last consecutive correctly-received frame
NUM	=	number of this data frame
CRC1	=	a CRC-8 on the header (only)
Data	=	integral number of octets
CRC2	=	CRC-8 on the data field (only)

An ACK frame has the following structure:

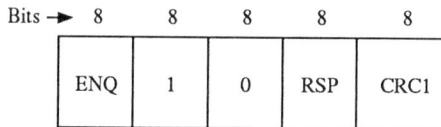

Bits → 8	8	8	8	8
ENQ	1	0	RSP	CRC1

(a) DUNKLINK is what kind of protocol?

(b) Assume that the data field is 50 octets. The DUNKNET frame is the fourteenth frame sent by the sender. The other 13 have been successfully received and acknowledged.

The receiver has not sent back any data frames. Describe contents of the following fields of the data frame: CNT, RSP, and NUM.

(c) The receiver sends back an acknowledge frame rather than piggybacking an acknowledgment. Describe what is in the RSP field.

13. Compute TRIB for an error-free 2400-bps DUNKLINK from Prob. 12. Assume a window of 1. A file of 65,500 octets is to be transferred in 500 frames. Compare your result with Example 6.3 and explain why it is significantly different.

14. In the following problem, we analyze PACLINK, the data link protocol for PACNET, a student-developed packet network. PACLINK has the following frame and flag structure:

Flag	Control	Information	FCS
01110	5 bits	N bits	3 bits

$$N \;=\; \text{a network-defined number of bits}$$

$$FCS \;=\; \text{field check sequence}$$

The PACLINK control field is:

Bit order of transmission	1	2	3	4	5
	0	S		R	

0 = indicator that this is an I frame

S = sequence number of this frame (bit 2 is lsb)

R = sequence number of the *next* information frame expected (bit 4 is lsb)

(a) The flag is 01110. This will require the frame to be bit-stuffed when it is transmitted, to avoid confusion with the flag. One student devised a bit-stuffing algorithm requiring two 1s and a 0 to avoid three 1s in succession. Bit-stuff the following information with the "two 1s and a 0" algorithm:

1 0 1 1 1 1 1 1 0 0 1 1 1 0 0 0 1 1 1 1

← Direction of transmission

(b) If this frame is number 3, what will be in the R field of the returning frame to indicate that this was successfully received?

(c) If we want to use pipelining, what will be the maximum number of outstanding frames possible?

(d) The following stream of bits was received by computer A (be careful: *PACLINK* bit stuffing was used):

☐1110001010011001101100011001101000111☐

← Direction of transmission

Find the following: the buried PACLINK frame, the frame sequence number, the next information frame that node A is expected to send, and the information that was originally sent.

15. Calculate TRIB for a 1200-bps DDCMP link with BER $= 10^{-4}$. Assume an ASCII file of 32,750 octets. The length of each information field is 131 octets.

16. Calculate TRIB for an error-free 2400-bps dedicated LAPB link transmitting 500 frames, each with 131 octets of information. Assume $F_{bitstuff} = 1.05$.

7

NETWORK LAYER

Software and procedures in the data link layer provide error detection, error correction, and flow control over a physical circuit between computers. However, if there are multiple paths to each destination through a number of computers, another layer of software is needed to route the data from one computer to the next and to control potential congestion. These are the primary functions of the network layer.

The network software organizes control information and data into **packets**. In OSI, the basic units for transit are called **network protocol data units (NPDUs)**. Software manages routing from one network entity to another and reports nonrecoverable errors to the transport layer. It is the first layer that we encounter that has responsibility for end-to-end communications. It is expected to provide services to the transport layer at a known financial cost and quality of service (QOS). If there are intermediate networks, called subnetworks, involved in the transmission of data from end to end, the network layer software manages the internetworking so that all the details of the end-to-end connection appear transparent to the transport layer, even if the underlying subnets have incompatible network and data link protocols.

The usual operation is for the sender's network layer software to append a network header to the data (Fig. 7.1a) to indicate its source, final destination, and control parameters. The information field is called a *network service data unit* because the packet is delivering the data in this field as a service to the transport layer. The resulting packet is transferred to the data link layer with an indication of the physical connection that will enable it to reach the next computer. The software in the data link layer wraps it with a link header and trailer (Fig. 7.1b)

Network service
data unit

Network header	Data

(a) Network protocol data unit

Data link service data unit

Data link header	Network header	Data	Data link trailer

(b) Data link protocol data unit

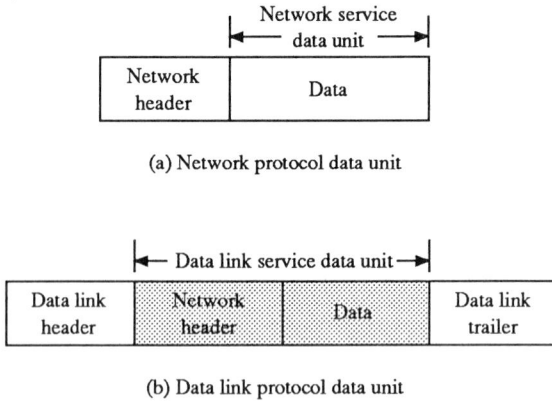

Figure 7.1 Wrapping of data in the OSI data link and network layers

for transmission by the physical layer. The physical layer then transfers the bits in the complete frame to an adjacent computer over the indicated communications circuit.

At the next computer, data link layer software examines the frame for errors, and when they are corrected, passes the packet to the network software. Here the network software decides, based on the network address, if the data is destined for itself or for yet another computer farther along in the network and routes it accordingly. If the packet is destined for another computer, the network software will pass it down to the link software with information on what the physical circuit should be, and the process is repeated.

Initially in the chapter we discuss routing concepts and examine two network protocols used in wide area networks. We assume that the host computers are supporting user functions and the networking function is done by dedicated nodes. Local area networks, which do not need routing algorithms because of predetermined communication circuits among computers, are covered in Chap. 8. Two protocols for internetwork communication are examined later in this chapter.

7.1 NETWORK ROUTING CONCEPTS

There are basically two network routing concepts. The first concept establishes a complete path between end nodes before passing the first data packet from the sender to the receiver. It is **connection-oriented**, a concept analogous to a circuit-switched physical network such as the telephone system, where the path is established over a switching system before any conversation occurs. Once established, the users have a routing path that lasts for the duration of the "call." Because of the analogy, it is often referred to as a **virtual circuit** network model. The second network concept routes the data over a path that is selected as the data arrives at each node. It is **connectionless** and, in fact, sequential data can be routed over different paths. This is called a **datagram** network model.

The virtual circuit model uses an initial *call request* packet to establish a path. The packet notifies the software at each intermediate computer to insert an entry for that virtual circuit. The data is then transmitted as if there were a dedicated line between the network end points. Each intermediate computer recognizes the virtual circuit number in the control field of incoming data packets and immediately associates a specific physical link to that circuit. When there is no more data, *call termination* packets clear the routing tables. By the virtual circuit's very nature, all the packets are delivered in sequence and there are no flow-control problems.

In contrast, the datagram network passes data packets from one intermediate point to the next, and a routing algorithm makes the routing decision for each datagram individually. The datagram model is analogous to the postal service. As we will see later, connectionless networks are very flexible in overcoming congestion and broken links, but the penalty is that datagrams can be delivered out of sequence or can even be lost.

7.1.1 Connection-Oriented Networks

In a connection-oriented network, the sender associates a *virtual channel number* with each call request. During call establishment, the local DCE and subsequent nodes update a table with one entry per virtual circuit and an incoming and outgoing circuit designation. It is not necessary that the virtual circuit number be the same through the whole path of a packet. In fact, it may change at each node. The data packets contain a field for the virtual circuit number rather than a full destination address.

Connection-oriented networks usually have relatively short headers on the data packets because the destination and source addresses are not necessary. For this reason, they are usually more efficient for transferring large files of data.

The virtual circuit mode of operation is vulnerable because if one node crashes, all virtual circuits going through it are aborted. All the packets on the path at that moment are lost. Recovery steps are required to reestablish the calls. These procedures are the responsibility of the transport layer.

7.1.2 Connectionless Networks

A connectionless network accepts data from the transport layer and attempts to deliver each datagram as an isolated unit. The physical links may be pre-established, but the decision as to which one will be used to move the datagram toward its final destination is made when the datagram arrives. Each datagram must have a control field that includes its final destination. Datagrams may arrive out of sequence or not at all. When messages are relatively short, datagram operation is usually more efficient than virtual circuit operation. The time to establish a virtual circuit often outweighs any benefits in shorter headers. Datagram networks are not as vulnerable as virtual circuit networks because the path for each datagram can be changed quickly; however, additional software and protocol overhead is required in the transport layer to guarantee reliable service to the upper OSI layers.

7.2 ROUTING ALGORITHMS

Each network node utilizes a routing algorithm to relate each final destination with a link to an adjacent node. The routing algorithm prioritizes links according to criteria established by the network designers.

For virtual circuit operation, tables resulting from the routing algorithm are referenced once, during call setup. For datagrams, a reference is made on the spot for each arriving datagram.

An important design issue is this: What should be optimized in the routing algorithm? In the case of first-class mail delivered by the post office, the criteria may simply be, how can this mail be delivered to its destination in the shortest period of time? In the case of digital transmission, minimum transit time, transit costs, maximum network throughput (which may involve bypassing congested areas), and quality of service may all be factors in the algorithm.

In the following section, three classes of routing methods are discussed: (1) flood-search algorithms, (2) static algorithms, and (3) dynamic algorithms.

7.2.1 Flood-Search Routing Algorithms

In **flood-search** algorithms, the sender transmits the same call request packet or datagram on a large number of outgoing circuits. The adjacent nodes that receive the packet then send the packet out on a large number of their outgoing circuits, excluding the circuit it came in on. Note that if this is for a virtual circuit network, the result will be a network connection over a route with minimum number of hops. This algorithm provides a very survivable network because computers that are malfunctioning are omitted from the path. A drawback is the large number of redundant packets that the system must tolerate.

There are a number of options to increase the efficiency of flood-search algorithms. For example, the algorithm may send out packets to all the adjacent computers or only to a selected subset, for example, those in the general direction of the destination. Tailoring the number of packets to those that are heading in the right direction limits the congestion on the network.

7.2.2 Static Routing Algorithms

Static routing tables are defined by the routing algorithm before the network is operational and then are updated periodically. For example, if the criterion for calculating the best route to a final destination is the minimum transit time, the tables may be computed ahead of time based on the individual link rates. A transit time is then associated with each link, and the routing algorithm computes the least time from the source to each possible destination. A routing table is then developed for each node that relates every possible destination with a circuit to a nearest neighbor. Several circuits may be specified and prioritized for each destination so that if specific links are congested, alternate paths can be utilized.

EXAMPLE 7.1   Static routing algorithm

The following algorithm [27] is useful for developing the routing table from a source to each destination when the link *cost* is known for each link and the goal is to minimize cost from end to end. The cost may be anything the network designer chooses, such as the financial cost or time to transit. We will work through the network shown in Fig. 7.2.

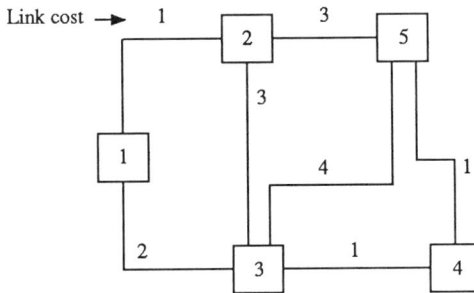

Figure 7.2   Static routing example

Step 1.   Let $l(i, j)$ be the cost of a link between node i and node j. If there is no direct connection, $l(i, j)$ is infinite. For example, in our hypothetical network,

$l(1,2) = 1$	$l(2,1) = 1$	$l(3,1) = 2$	$l(4,3) = 1$	$l(5,2) = 3$
$l(1,3) = 2$	$l(2,3) = 3$	$l(3,2) = 3$	$l(4,5) = 1$	$l(5,3) = 4$
	$l(2,5) = 3$	$l(3,4) = 1$		$l(5,4) = 1$
		$l(3,5) = 4$		

All the other link weights are infinite since there is no direct connection between the computers.

Step 2.   Let $D(v)$ be the distance (sum of link weights along a given path) from node 1 to node v. Starting with set $N\{1\}$ for each node v not in N, let $D(v) = l(1, v)$.

	D(2)	Path	D(3)	Path	D(4)	Path	D(5)	Path
$N\{1\}$	1	1–2	2	1–3	∞	–	∞	–

Step 3. Find a node w not in N for which $D(w)$ is a minimum, and add node w to the set N. In our example, the distance to node 2, $D(2) = 1$, is the minimum, so we add node 2 to the set of N: $N\{1, 2\}$.

Step 4. Update the distance $D(v)$ to all the nodes not in set N with the minimum of either the current distance to $D(v)$ or the current distance to the added node plus the distance from the added node to node v. Mathematically,

$$D(v) \leftarrow \min[D(v), D(w) + l(w, v)] \tag{7.1}$$

We compute, for example,

$$D(3) \leftarrow \min[D(3), \ D(2) + (2, 3)]$$

$$D(3) \leftarrow \min[2, (1 + 3)]$$

$$D(3) \leftarrow 2$$

Repeating for $D(4)$ and $D(5)$:

	$D(2)$	Path	$D(3)$	Path	$D(4)$	Path	$D(5)$	Path
$N\{1\}$	1	1–2	2	1–3	∞	–	∞	–
$N\{1, 2\}$	1	1–2	2	1–3	∞	–	4	1–2–5

Step 5. Now note that $D(3)$ is the minimum of the remaining computers, and repeat steps 3 and 4 until all nodes have been evaluated:

	$D(2)$	Path	$D(3)$	Path	$D(4)$	Path	$D(5)$	Path
$N\{1\}$	1	1–2	2	1–3	∞	–	∞	–
$N\{1, 2\}$	1	1–2	2	1–3	∞	–	4	1–2–5
$N\{1, 2, 3\}$	1	1–2	2	1–3	3	1–3–4	4	1–2–5
$N\{1, 2, 3, 4\}$	1	1–2	2	1–3	3	1–3–4	4	1–2–5

By noting the paths, the following schematic may be constructed.

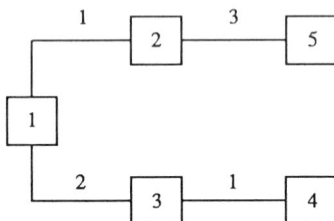

The routing table for node 1 is:

DESTINATION	NEXT COMPUTER
2	2
3	3
4	3
5	2

7.2.3 Dynamic Routing Algorithms

Dynamic routing tables are updated from once per second to once every 10 minutes. The adaptive nature of the tables helps to alleviate temporary congestion problems. Network maintenance packets keep network-control nodes informed of congestion and other delays on certain routes so that this data can be utilized by the algorithm. In a network with **central control**, a single network-control node takes the input from the maintenance packets, runs the algorithm, and informs each network node of its new routing tables.

In a network with **distributed control**, individual nodes run algorithms based on maintenance packets only from neighboring nodes. Because of the time lapse between sending and receiving maintenance packets among different regions of the network, a node may modify its table based on information that is slightly out of date, with the result that adjustments may be out of phase with the actual conditions. These algorithms help the network adapt to congestion and malfunctioning circuits, but the algorithms take time to converge because they try to adjust routing paths under changing conditions; they are always trying to hit a moving target.

7.3 DNA ROUTING LAYER

Under DEC's network architecture, routing of data over multiple nodes is done within the DNA *routing layer*. The protocol routes frames through the network in a datagram mode, deciding at each node what the next intermediate destination should be. Routing is a layer in the DNA reference model and thus does not necessarily provide all the services of the OSI network layer, although they are comparable.

7.3.1 DNA Routing Layer Operational Philosophy

The building block of the DEC architecture is the DDCMP data link protocol that we discussed in Chap. 6. DDCMP is responsible for maintaining the integrity and sequence of data sent over a single communication channel.

The DEC routing protocol provides connectionless service. This implies that packets may or may not be delivered in sequence, and some may not be delivered at all. DNA has a higher layer (*end communication* layer), which corresponds to the OSI transport layer, to ensure reliable end-to-end service.

The routing layer performs three tasks: routing, congestion control, and message lifetime control.

Routing.   Routing supports dynamic, distributed routing through the network over the most "cost-effective" path.

Cost, the performance measure, is defined by the network implementor, but DEC suggests that the cost of each link be inversely proportional to the link capacity. Cost may also be based on line-quality characteristics such as delay, throughput, or error rate.

In DNA, the logical distance from one node to the next is a *hop*, and the distance between a sender and receiver is the *path length*, measured in hops.

Each network node maintains a matrix with both a path length and cost to each destination in the network. Routing is determined by least cost, even if this is not the path with the fewest hops. If the costs of all links that lead to the destination are set to the same value, the routing algorithm will choose the outbound link that permits the message to reach the destination with the minimum number of hops.

Whenever an event occurs that impacts the throughput, such as when a circuit is disabled or enabled, the local node notifies its immediate neighbors that its paths have changed. When a change occurs, the new information is passed on to the immediate neighbors with a network maintenance message. The changes are then propagated throughout the network with subsequent messages.

Congestion Control.   When the length of an output queue on a link exceeds a specified threshold, frames generated by the local host to be sent out on that link are delayed, and incoming messages for that link are discarded.

Packet Lifetime Control.   The maximum number of hops permitted by DNA is 63. When the number of hops in the network header field exceeds this parameter, the frame is discarded. This eliminates the problem of looping of packets because of address or routing problems.

7.3.2 DNA Routing Layer Datagram Format

Fig. 7.3 illustrates the structure of the routing protocol header.

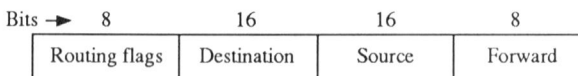

Bits ➤	8	16	16	8
	Routing flags	Destination	Source	Forward

Figure 7.3   DNA routing layer header

The 8-bit *routing flags* field contains information for directing the nodes how to handle the packet. For example, when the *return request* bit within this field is set by the sender, the node returns this packet to the source if it is not deliverable.

A *choke* bit is set in a returning packet to indicate that the queue length and utilization of the line required to transmit the packet farther have been exceeded. Each sender keeps a record of the number of messages sent to a particular destination, and cuts down the number of further packets to that destination when it gets a choke response. This is a means of congestion control.

The *destination* field contains the address of the final destination and the *source* field contains the sender's address. The *forward* field keeps a record of the number of hops the frame has encountered after leaving the source. Every time the frame is forwarded, the counter is incremented by one.

The DNA routing protocol has a series of its own maintenance messages, called *routing control* messages, that are used between peer entities to control the network. In particular, routing messages provide information that is necessary for updating the routing tables of neighboring nodes. The routing message contains updates to path cost and path length for a set of destinations.

7.4 OSI NETWORK SERVICES

OSI network services that are available to the transport layer are defined in ISO 8348. They are defined in terms of protocol **primitives** similar to operating system commands. As far as the transport layer is concerned, when it interfaces to a connection-oriented network, it sees the network establishing a virtual circuit as illustrated in Fig. 7.4. The transport layer makes an N-CONNECT.request to the network layer, and the destination transport entity is presented with an N-CONNECT.indication. The distant transport entity, if agreeable to a connection, responds with an N-CONNECT.response that is delivered to the original requester as an N-CONNECT.confirmation.

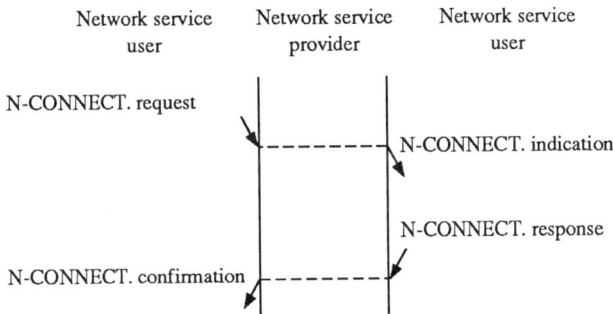

Figure 7.4   Schematic of connection-oriented operation

The total list of connection-oriented network services to the OSI transport layer is summarized by the primitives in Table 7.1.

7.5 CCITT X.25

X.25 defines a connection-oriented packet-switching network that conforms to the ISO 8348 network service definition. Establishing a connection, such as an X.25 virtual circuit, is characteristic of all the OSI architecture-related protocols.

The intent of packet-switched networks is to have a relatively short packet length so that routing decisions can be made while the packet resides in main memory of the node, instead of in mass storage. The original ARPANET had a maximum user data field of 128 octets, which is also the basic maximum X.25 information field. However, packet-switching nodes are available that can process

TABLE 7.1   ISO 8348 Network Service Primitives and Parameters

N-CONNECT	Request	Called address
		Calling address
	Indication	Receipt confirmation selection
		Expedited data selection
		QOS parameter set
		User data
N-CONNECT	Response	Responding address
		Receipt confirmation selection
	Confirmation	Expedited data selection
		QOS parameter set
		User data
N-DATA	Request	User data
	Indication	Confirmation request
N-DATA-ACKNOWLEDGE	Request	
	Indication	
N-EXPEDITED-DATA	Request	User data
	Indication	
N-RESET	Request	Originator
		Reason
	Indication	
N-RESET	Response	
	Confirmation	
N-DISCONNECT	Request	Originator
	Indication	Reason
		User data
		Responding address

QOS - quality of service

X.25 packets with extended information fields up to 4096 octets. The goal is to move the packet to the next computer within milliseconds, thus eliminating processing delays at each node and improving TRIB.

CCITT Recommendation X.25 defines an interface between a local DTE and its DCE rather than peer network software modules. The DCE is basically the network node (Fig. 7.5). X.25 was first published in 1976 and has been amended every four years since then. It is an integrated set of three levels of protocols, two of which we have already discussed:

1. X.21 and X.25 *bis*, physical layer protocols that specify the physical DTE/DCE interface.
2. LAPB, the data link access procedure between the DTE and DCE.

X.25 provides two types of connections. One is a normal virtual circuit established with a call request packet and terminated with a clear request packet. A limited number of *permanent virtual circuits* may also be established by the network manager, to avoid call-establishment delays to certain destinations.

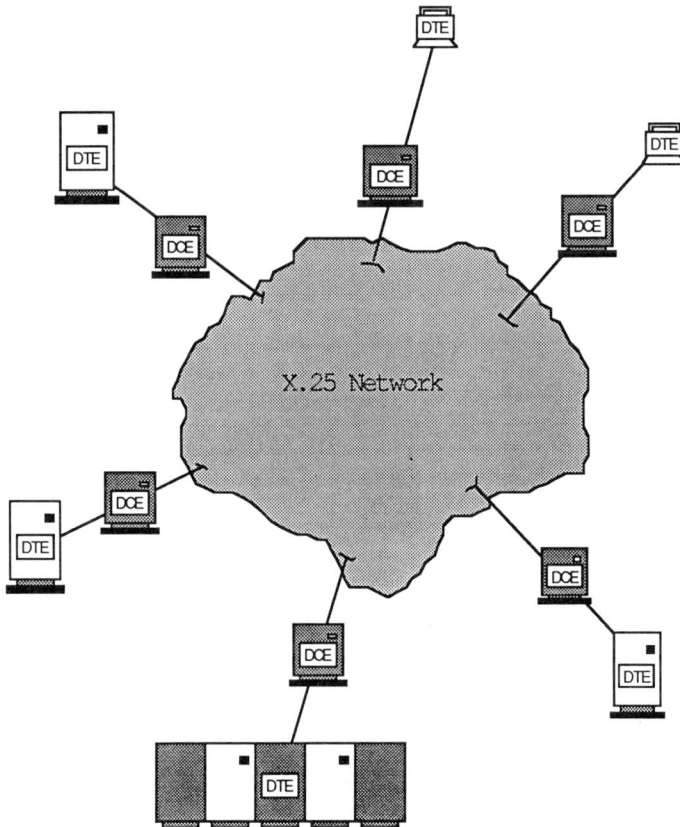

Figure 7.5   X.25 network concept

7.5.1 X.25 Packet Types

The X.25 packet types are listed in Table 7.2.

TABLE 7.2   X.25 Packet

From DCE to DTE	From DTE to DCE
Call Setup and Clearing	
Incoming call	Call request
Call connected	Call accepted
Clear indication	Clear request
DCE clear confirmation	DTE clear confirmation
Data and Interrupt	
DCE data	DTE data
DCE interrupt	DTE interrupt
DCE interrupt confirmation	DTE interrupt confirmation
Flow Control and Reset	
DCE RR (modulo 8)	DTE RR (modulo 8)
DCE RR (modulo 128)	DTE RR (modulo 128)
DCE RNR (modulo 8)	DTE RNR (modulo 8)
DCE RNR (modulo 128)	DTE RNR (modulo 128)
	DTE REJ (modulo 8)
	DTE REJ (modulo 128)
Reset indication	Reset request
DCE reset confirmation	DTE reset confirmation
Diagnostic	
Diagnostic	
Registration	
Registration confirmation	Registration request

(Reprinted with permission)

7.5.2 X.25 Data Packet Structure

The X.25 data packet structure is shown in Fig. 7.6. The packet is transmitted octet 1 first, then octet 2, and so on. Each octet is transmitted least significant bit first.

The *qualifier* bit (Q) is an optional bit available to the sender that may be used to distinguish between two types of user information.

The *delivery confirmation* bit (D) is used to indicate if the source DTE wishes to receive an end-to-end acknowledgment for the data it is transmitting. If set, the

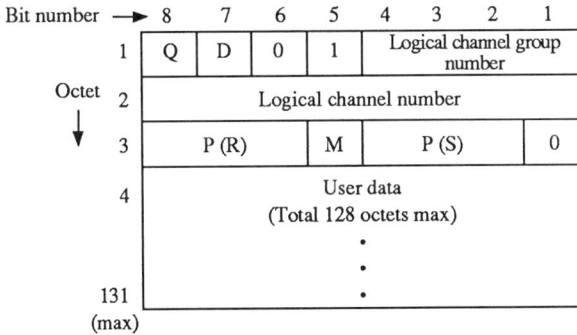

Figure 7.6   X.25 data packet

receiver will acknowledge by piggybacking in the *receive sequence number P(R)* field.

Logical channel group numbers and *logical channel* numbers, assigned during call setup, are virtual circuit assignments. *P(S)* is the *packet sequence number*.

The *More data* bit (M) indicates that more data is to follow. The bit is used when the packet must carry a network service data unit longer than the network permits.

P(R) is the *receive sequence* number with the same function as *N(R)* in LAPB, only it is an *end-to-end* confirmation, in contrast to a link-level confirmation. *P(R)* is the sequence number of the next in-sequence information frame expected to be received by the receiver. When pipelining, P(R) permits up to seven outstanding packets between the sending and receiving DTEs. Note that LAPB permits up to seven outstanding frames between the local DTE and DCE.

7.5.3 X.25 Control Packet Format

Fig. 7.7 shows the structure of the call request packet, one of the control packets.

The *delivery confirmation* bit in octet 1 is used in the same way as in an information packet.

Logical channel group numbers and logical channel numbers in octets 1 and 2 are assigned during call setup.

Octet 3 is the *packet type* identifier, in this case, call request. The four lower-order bits in octet 4 specify the field length of the address of the called DTE. The upper four bits specify the field length of the calling DTE address. The subsequent address is then coded in *binary coded decimal* format with two digits per octet. The addressing scheme is described in X.121.

The *facility field length* and *facility* field are involved only when the DTE is using optional user services (such as reverse charging).

There may be a 128-octet user data field in a call-request packet when the sender chooses *fast select*. The fast-select option permits the sender to transmit a small amount of data during call establishment. With this option, the receiver can respond with data in the call accepted packet.

Bit number →	8	7	6	5	4	3	2	1
Octet 1	0	D	0	1	Logical channel group number			
2	Logical channel number							
3	0	0	0	0	1	0	1	1
4	Calling DTE field length				Called DTE field length			
	Called address							
	Calling address							
					0	0	0	0
	Facility field length							
	Facilities							
	User data*							

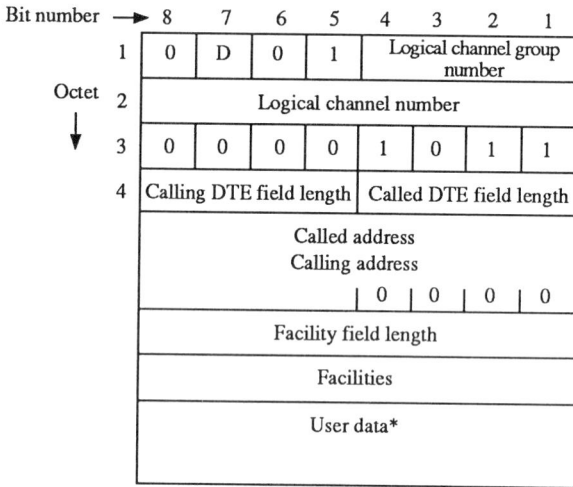

* Up to 128 octets of user data when "fast select" facility used.

Figure 7.7   X.25 call request packet

7.5.4 Virtual Circuit Channel Control

Control packets are required for call setup, call clearing, and other control functions. We describe here the exchange of packets required to set up a virtual circuit between the source and destination computers.

A single DTE may set up virtual circuits to more than one destination. The DTE assigns a logical channel number for each virtual circuit from itself to a particular destination. The network implementor establishes the range of channel numbers for a given DTE/DCE. The DTE will initiate calls with numbers at the high end of the range, and the DCE will assign a number for incoming call requests from the low end of the range to avoid *call collisions*.

To establish a virtual circuit (Fig. 7.8), the DTE first transmits a call request packet to the DCE. The logical channel is then in the waiting state.

The DCE notes the incoming physical circuit number and also the channel number in the packet. It assigns a new channel number and changes the channel number in the packet header accordingly. It also determines the outgoing physical link to the next node in the path to the destination using a routing algorithm provided by the network designer. X.25 does not address the problems of routing algorithms; they are implementation-specific.

The DCE at the receiving end indicates to its DTE that there is an incoming call by transferring an incoming call packet to the DTE on the lowest-numbered channel available. The receiver's DTE indicates its acceptance of the call by returning a call accepted packet with the same channel number as that of the incoming-call packet. This places the destination logical channel in the data transfer state.

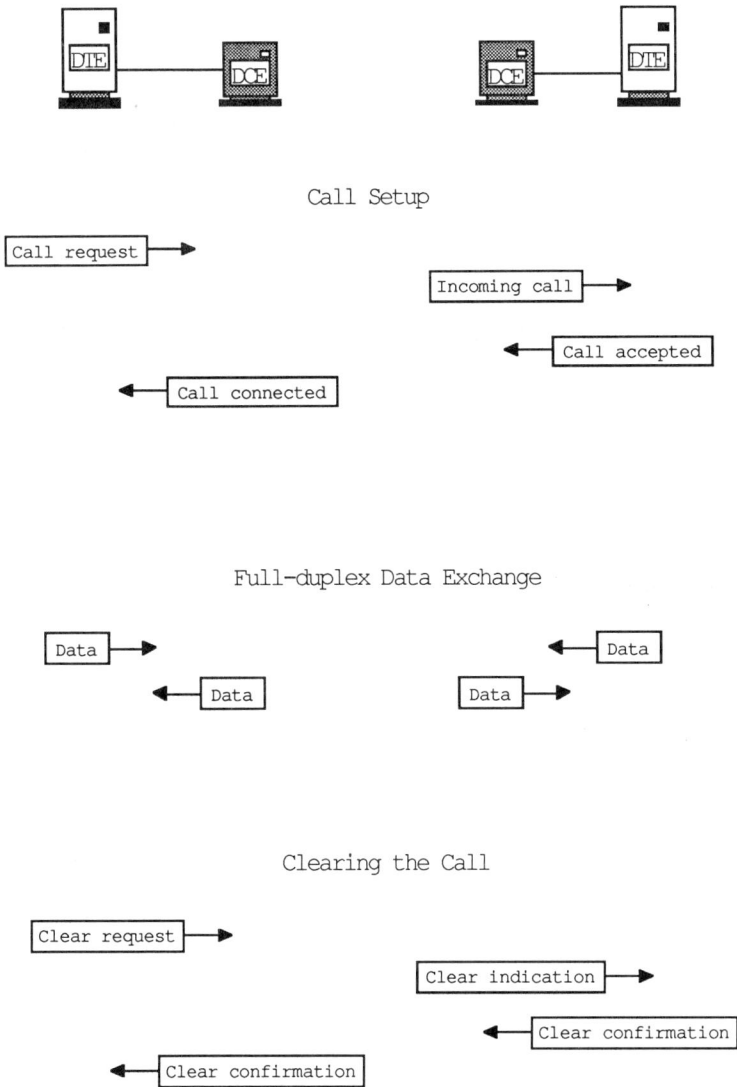

Call Setup

Call request →

Incoming call →

← Call accepted

← Call connected

Full-duplex Data Exchange

Data →   ← Data

← Data   Data →

Clearing the Call

Clear request →

Clear indication →

← Clear confirmation

← Clear confirmation

Figure 7.8   X.25 virtual circuit establishment and clearing

When the call-accepted packet is received by the original DCE, it transmits a *call connected* packet to the originating DTE. This places the call originator's channel in the data transfer state.

There are similar exchanges with *clear request* and *clear confirmation* packets to clear the virtual call. The DTE that initiated the clear request is given a clear confirmation by its local DCE.

7.5.5 Packet Assembler/Disassembler

Packet assembler/disassemblers (PADs) are terminal interface units associated with X.25 networks and are worth a brief description. The devices provide an interface between an asynchronous DTE, such as a user terminal, to an X.25 public network. They are specified in CCITT X.3, X.28, and X.29. CCITT X.3 describes the functions of the PAD and the parameters used to control its operation.

The terminal connected to a PAD sends asynchronous characters that are buffered within the PAD and converted into X.25 packets sent synchronously using X.25 protocol. The DCE may return X.25 information packets that the PAD disassembles into asynchronous characters and delivers at the appropriate speed to the user terminal.

In summary, its functions include asynchronous communication with the terminal, assembly of characters into packets for outgoing data, disassembly of incoming packets, handling of virtual call setup and clearing, and resetting and interrupt procedures.

7.6 INTERNETWORKING

Data networks are often formed by joining different physical subnetworks. The subnetworks, or subnets, may be either public networks or privately owned networks. The OSI reference model gives the network layer the responsibility of managing routing through the subnets and making the network connections transparent to higher layers. Subnets are connected by special gateway computers. Software is required at each gateway to accept packets from a link on one subnet and make them compatible with physical, data link, and network characteristics of the next subnet. The gateway must have special routing tables to handle internetwork addressing. If the subnets have different length restrictions on the packet sizes, the software must sometimes break larger packets into smaller pieces and send them through the subnet as individual fragments.

There are various ways to implement internetworks. One method is to provide a subnet-specific protocol that can bridge homogeneous subnets. An example is CCITT X.75, which bridges X.25 (only) subnets.

Another approach is to provide a subnet-independent protocol that resides in the host computers and gateways, and that can internetwork sets of heterogeneous or homogeneous subnets. Examples of this approach are ISO's connectionless-mode network protocol **(ISO 8473)** and DoD's **Internet Protocol (IP)**. They may be used to communicate among computers on LANs and WANs. They both provide datagram service. Because they are connectionless, a higher-layer protocol at the transport layer is required to ensure reliability.

Address administration is a key problem when internetworking because there are both subnets and local computers to identify. ISO 8473 requires the destinations to have X.25-like addresses. In DOD's IP, each host is located by a 32-bit combination of subnet number and host address.

7.6.1 ISO 8473 Connectionless-Mode Network Protocol

ISO 8473 lies in the internetwork sublayer of the OSI network layer and provides connectionless service to the transport layer. The maximum user information field in the protocol data unit is 64,512 octets.

When a transport layer protocol uses the services of the network layer, one of the initial requests is for a specific **quality of service (QOS)**. In the case of the connectionless mode, this includes such parameters as transit delay, cost, and the probability of losing, duplicating, or damaging packets. The subnetworks must be able to indicate these parameters back to the higher-layer protocol, so that if alternatives are available, the transport layer can choose the subnetwork that provides the best QOS.

If the PDU is longer than the maximum information field of intervening networks, ISO 8473 will segment the PDU into smaller PDUs and reassemble it at the destination. It is assumed by ISO 8073 that the underlying subnetworks support a user information field of 512 octets. If the subnet is a basic X.25 subnet with a 128-octet information field, an additional software module *(IP-to-X.25 subnetwork dependent convergence protocol)* that conforms to ISO 8473/DAD1 is required in the host to manage the virtual circuit and use the X.25 *M* bit to transfer the potentially long datagram.

7.6.1.1 ISO 8473 operation. The relatively simple ISO 8473 network service primitives are shown in Table 7.3.

TABLE 7.3   ISO 8473 Connectionless-mode Network Primitives

Primitives		Parameters
N-UNITDATA	Request Indication	Source address Destination address Quality of service User data

The transport layer protocol uses the primitives in Table 7.3 to transmit a datagram from sender to receiver, as shown in Fig 7.9.

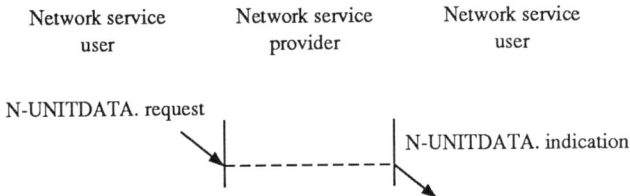

Figure 7.9   Schematic of connectionless-mode operation

7.6.1.2 ISO 8473 PDUs. The ISO 8473 PDU has a 4-part header with a fixed part, address part, segmentation part, and options part (Fig. 7.10).

Fixed Part. The *network layer protocol identifier* field identifies this protocol as ISO 8473. The *version* in octet 3 describes which version of this protocol is being used. The *length indicator* describes the length of the header in octets and has a maximum value of 254. Since this is a datagram, the *lifetime* field indicates the remaining lifetime of the datagram in units of 500 ms to purge lost datagrams from the system.

There are several 1-bit flags in the next part of the header. The first, *segmentation permitted (SP)*, permits gateways to segment the datagram to fit in networks that have a user information field less than the PDU length. *More segments (MS)* notifies the receiving ISO 8473 entity that segmentation has occurred and more segments are following. The *error* flag notifies the receiving entity either to discard this datagram if an error has occurred or to follow a prescribed error-reporting procedure.

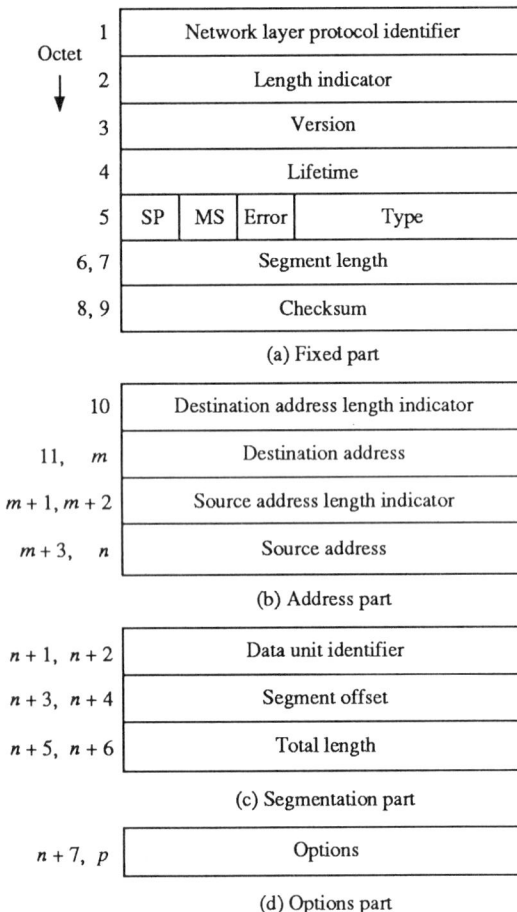

Octet			
1	Network layer protocol identifier		
2	Length indicator		
3	Version		
4	Lifetime		
5	SP	MS	Error	Type
6, 7	Segment length		
8, 9	Checksum		

(a) Fixed part

10	Destination address length indicator
11, *m*	Destination address
m + 1, *m* + 2	Source address length indicator
m + 3, *n*	Source address

(b) Address part

n + 1, *n* + 2	Data unit identifier
n + 3, *n* + 4	Segment offset
n + 5, *n* + 6	Total length

(c) Segmentation part

n + 7, *p*	Options

(d) Options part

Figure 7.10 ISO 8473 Transport protocol header (Reprinted with permission)

The *type* field indicates if the datagram is a data PDU or error report PDU (these are the only types). The 2-byte *segment length* indicates the length of the PDU, including both header and data, in octets. The 2-octet checksum is an LRC-like calculation on the header.

Address Part.   The *destination* and *source* addresses immediately follow the fixed part of the header and have a variable length. The *length indicators* provide the length, in octets. The maximum address length is 20 octets and its structure is given in ISO 8348/DAD2.

Segmentation Part.   If the SP flag is set in the fixed part, a 6-octet *segmentation* part is included in the header. A 2-byte *data unit identifier* is the sequence number of the original PDU. The *segment offset* contains the relative position of the segment contained in the data field relative to the start of the data field in the original PDU. The *total length* is the length of the original PDU and is included in every segment.

Options Part.   The options part includes optional fields that may be used for such functions as security, routing preferences, quality of service, and precedence.

If the PDU is a Data PDU, the header will be followed by the user data field. If the PDU is an Error Report PDU, the header is followed by fields that describe the reason for discard and the header of the discarded PDU.

7.6.2 DoD Internet Protocol

Initially, Internet   was one network and offered virtual circuit service. Internet   capability expanded by interconnecting additional subnets, including datagram-based subnets. This required a protocol to deal with two possibilities: that data might be lost or delivered out of sequence, and that network and link protocols might be incompatible. The result was the development of a strong transport layer protocol to ensure reliability and an internet protocol to enable communication across subnets.

7.6.2.1 IP operation.   Very similar to ISO 8473, IP packages data as an internet datagram and transfers it across the local subnet (Fig. 7.11). If the destination is on the local subnet, the data goes directly to that subnet computer. If the destination is a "foreign subnet," IP sends the datagram to the local gateway computer. The gateway must have subnet-routing tables, analogous to network-routing tables, to route the internet datagram to the appropriate adjacent subnet. The gateway, in turn, sends the datagram through the adjacent subnet on its way to the destination computer or to another subnet or gateway.

IP contains a fragmentation algorithm for breaking a large datagram into smaller fragments. This is used to make a transition across subnets with varying limits on packet size. Normally, fragmentation is performed only by the IP modules in gateways. The module divides the data portion of the datagram into two or more pieces on octet boundaries and provides a datagram header for each fragment. Each

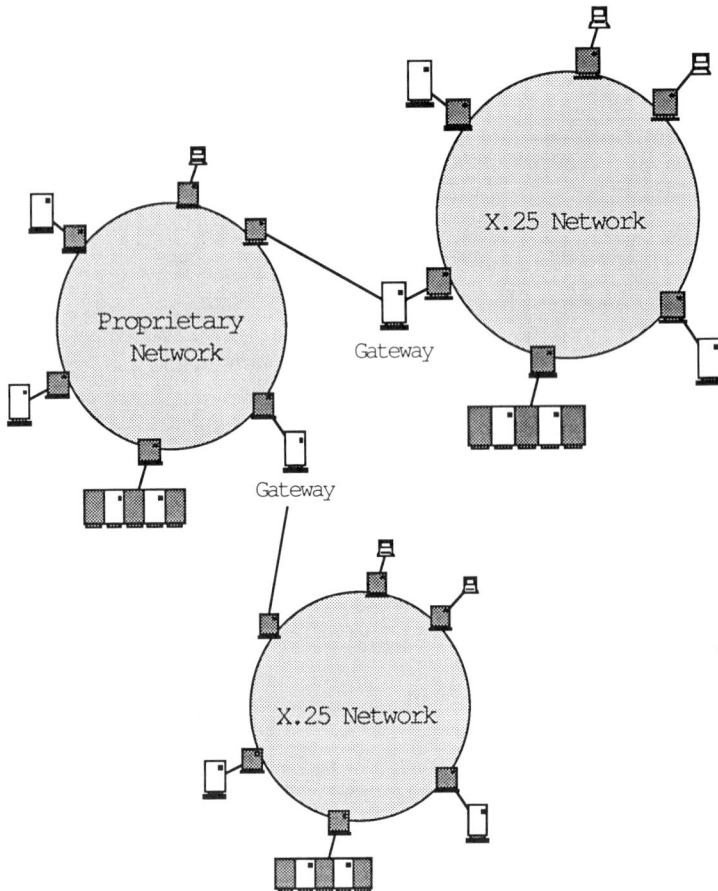

Figure 7.11   Example of internet operation

fragment is handled independently until the destination IP module is reached. They are reassembled based on the identification, source address, destination address, security, and protocol.

Because the subnet may be unreliable, some fragments making up a complete datagram may be lost. IP uses the arrival of a fragment to reset a reassembly timer. If the timer expires before all the fragments have been collected, IP discards the partially reassembled datagram.

7.6.2.2 IP datagram structure.   Fig. 7.12 shows the structure of the IP header specified in MIL-STD-1777. It is at least 20 octets, or longer, if options are selected.

Version indicates which version of IP is being used by the datagram. The *internet header length (IHL)* defines the length of the IP header in 32-bit words.

Bits ➤   4   4   8   16

Version	IHL	Type of service	Total length
Identification		Flags	Fragment offset
TTL		Protocol	Header checksum
Source address			
Destination address			
Options			Padding

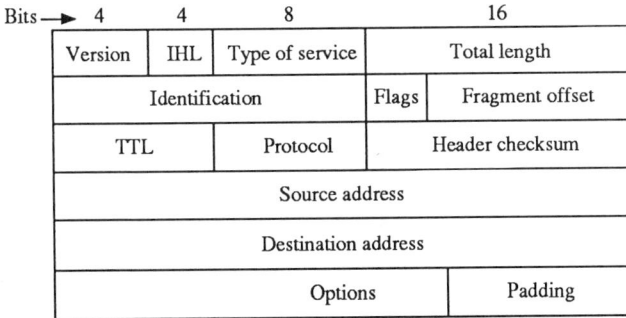

Figure 7.12 DoD IP header

The *type of service* field contains the IP parameters describing the quality of service for this datagram. For MIL-STD-1777 (Version 4):

Precedence (3 bits) (i.e., priority of this datagram)
Delay (1 bit) normal or low
Throughput (1 bit) normal or high
Reliability (1 bit) normal or high

Total length is the length of the fragment measured in octets, including headers and data.

The *identification field* is used to associate fragments of a datagram. *Flags* is a 3-bit field that contains a "don't fragment" indicator and an indicator that there are more fragments in the sequence. The 13-bit *fragment offset* field indicates the position of the fragment's data relative to the beginning of the data carried in the original datagram.

Time to live (TTL) ranges from 0 to 255 s. TTL indicates the maximum time the datagram is allowed to remain in transit. Every gateway on the internet route reduces TTL by either 1 s or the elapsed time since the last gateway processed it (if known by a time stamp option). If it drops to zero, the datagram is discarded. The *protocol* field indicates which next higher protocol is to receive the datagram. *Header checksum* is the 16-bit 1's complement of the 1's complement sum of all 16-bit words in the header, not including the checksum.

The *source* and *destination* addresses are fixed 32-bit addresses. An internet address begins with an 8-bit subnet address followed by a 24-bit local address. There is a variable-length *option* field for use between participating subnets. This may include such things as a security classification or timestamp. Extra bits, or *padding*, are used to fill out the options field to 32 bits.

In summary, ISO 8473 and IP are very similar in function and design. (In fact, ISO 8473 was derived from IP.) They are both datagram-oriented and require a higher-level protocol to ensure reliability. The major difference is that ISO 8473 may have a variable address field while IP has a fixed 32-bit address field. Also, to use ISO 8473, the minimum information field of each subnetwork protocol must be 512 octets; otherwise additional convergence software protocol is needed.

7.7 SUMMARY

The network layer is responsible for routing data packets from a sender to a receiver across multiple nodes. The service may be either connection-oriented, where routing decisions are made at the time of call setup, or connectionless, where decisions are made for each individual datagram. Connection-oriented networks such as X.25 generally deliver packets reliably and in sequence. Connectionless networks such as DEC's DNA and DoD's Internet deliver packets on a best-effort basis. Datagrams may be delivered out of sequence and they may even be lost. A connectionless network requires the services of a strong transport layer protocol to ensure reliable service to higher OSI layers.

KEY WORDS AND CONCEPTS

central control
connectionless service
connection-oriented service
datagram model
distributed control
dynamic routing table
flood search
Internet Protocol (IP)
ISO 8473 connectionless-mode
   network protocol

network protocol data unit (NPDU)
packet
packet assembler/disassembler (PAD)
primitive
quality of service (QOS)
static routing table
virtual circuit model
X. 25

PROBLEMS

1. (a) Explain the difference between a physical circuit and a virtual circuit.
   (b) Can there be more than one virtual circuit on a physical circuit? Explain.
2. Develop a static routing table for node 2 in Example 7.1 using the algorithm given there.
3. Develop a static routing table for node 1 in the following network minimizing the transit times between nodes. Use the algorithm in Example 7.1.

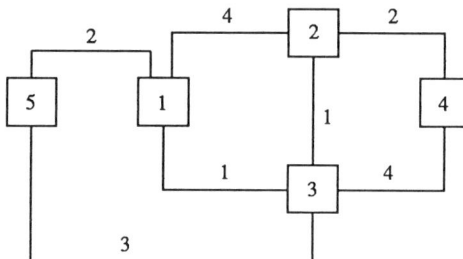

4. Set up a routing table for each node in the following figure by inspection. List the final destinations under the "To" column and the next node under "Next." Minimize the transmission times noted on the links between the nodes. If there are equal times, minimize the number of hops.

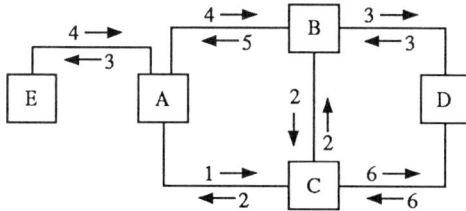

Node A		Node B		Node C		Node D		Node E	
To	Next	To	Next	To	Next	To	Next	To	Next

5. DEC's routing algorithm is sometimes implemented to find the least-cost path from end to end, where cost is a metric proportional to the inverse of bit transmission rate R. In what way is this the "best" path? When might this not be the best path?

6. DUNKNET is a student-developed protocol (see Chap. 6, Prob. 12). It provides datagram service. A DUNKNET packet has the following structure:

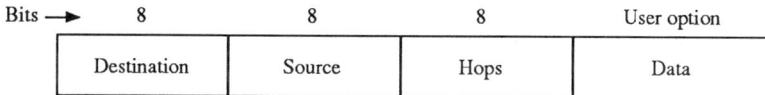

(a) As a datagram service, DUNKNET provides which of the following?
  (i) Guaranteed delivery
  (ii) Best-effort delivery
  (iii) In-sequence delivery
  (iv) Possible out-of-sequence delivery
  (v) Virtual circuit service

(b) A student communications analyst is analyzing the network requirements for SPORTSCORES. SPORTSCORES has 100 computers in its network.
  (i) What is the minimum number of bits required for the address field of the network protocol?
  (ii) How many destinations are actually possible with DUNKNET?

(c) On a mythical network, an average DUNKNET datagram has 200 octets of user data. Using the DUNKLINK frame structure from Chap. 6, Prob. 12.
  (i) If the data rate is 1200 bps over AB and 2400 bps over BC, how long will the datagram take to travel from A to C via ABC?

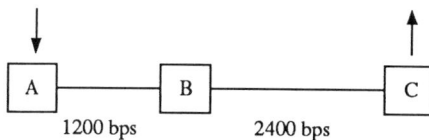

(ii) A DUNKLINK acknowledgment is 7 octets. Will node A get its link acknowledgment from B first or will node B get a link acknowledgment from C first?

7. PACNET is a student-developed connection-oriented network. The PACLINK data link protocol was given in Chap.6, Prob. 14. PACNET's network header is:

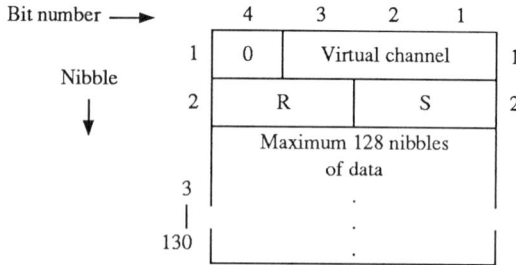

Nibble = 4 bits

Nibble 1, bit 4 = 0 indicates that this is an information packet

Nibble 2, bits 1,2 (S) = sequence number of this packet

Nibble 2, bits 3,4 (R) = sequence number of the next expected packet

(a) What is the difference between the PACNET packet and the PACLINK frame in terms of their destination and function?

(b) If a PACNET packet has a total of 52 bits of user data, how long will the PACLINK frame be before bit stuffing?

(c) In a mythical virtual circuit network, an average PACLINK frame is 200 bits long (ignoring flags) and has 20% additional bits due to bit stuffing.

(i) If the data rate is 1200 bps between AB and 300 bps over BC, how long will the packet take to travel from A to C via ABC? Ignore the flags.

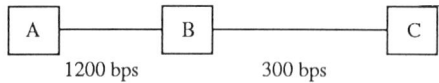

(ii) Assume a packet end-to-end acknowledgment is 8 bits and its PACLINK frame also has an average 20% additional bits after bit stuffing. How long will it take for a packet acknowledgment to return?

(iii) What is the total time for a successful packet transmission, assuming error-free channels?

8

LOCAL AREA NETWORKS

Many organizations are installing LANs within the bounds of their premises to improve communication between people doing related functions. Typically the users exchange data and share computing and peripheral resources. The number of these networks has grown sharply because of the proliferation of personal computers. LANs usually have the following characteristics:

- They exist within a geographic area under 2 km.
- Their circuit signaling rates exceed 1 Mbps.
- The physical circuits are privately owned.
- They often share the same medium and require an access procedure so each computer has a turn to transmit.

Media access procedures can be generally classified into two categories: *centralized*, for networks with a single network computer that controls access (e.g., polling), and *distributed*, for networks that require a media access control strategy for each participating computer. For the most part, the LANs that we examine in this chapter have distributed access control.

We discuss each of the standard LANs and adapt the ANSI concept of TRIB to evaluate LAN performance. With a LAN, the computer must gain access to the medium to transmit each frame. In a strict sense, ANSI TRIB is defined for point-to-point networks that have an information transfer phase distinct from link establishment and link termination. However, a picture of LAN performance from the perspective of an *average single user* is possible if we define $TRIB_{LAN}$ to mean the transfer rate of information bits over a period of time that includes media access, information transfer, and media release phases.

If we adapt Eq. 2.4 for a LAN:

$$\text{TRIB}_{\text{LAN}} = \frac{n_{\text{info}}}{t_3} \qquad (8.1)$$

where, for one frame,

$$n_{\text{info}} = \text{the information content of one frame}$$

and

$$t_3 = t_{\text{access}} + t_{\text{oneframe}} + t_{\text{release}} \qquad (8.2)$$

where

t_{access} = time to gain access to the medium

t_{oneframe} = time to transmit an average-length frame

t_{release} = time to release control of the medium to another computer on the LAN

Note that TRIB is useful for comparing impacts on an average user, but not the impact on overall network performance from the point of view of *medium utilization*. For example, the LAN's medium may be utilized, or busy, 100% of the time; however, if one user is dominating control and the others are idle, waiting for their turn because of a poor access procedure, TRIB suffers. As an analogy, in a human conversation on a ham-radio frequency, if one person dominates, but many people have information to share, the transfer rate of information by the average person is low even though the airwaves are utilized most of the time.

8.1 RELATIONSHIP OF LAN PROTOCOLS TO OSI

Since LANs transmit information over a physical medium with no intermediate routing, only the physical and data link layers need to be specified. The physical layer specifies the usual electrical and mechanical characteristics such as timing, voltages, and the signaling method. The data link layer is concerned with frame format, error control, flow control, and media access control.

In the OSI environment, the LAN data link layer is divided into two sublayers: (1) **media access control (MAC),** a unique sublayer that defines frame formats and media access strategy, and (2), **the logical link control (LLC)** sublayer, which provides a non-media-dependent protocol for interfacing to peer entities and the network layer.

The Institute of Electrical and Electronics Engineers (IEEE), through its *802 Committee*, developed a number of LAN standards that have been adopted as national standards. They are each highlighted in this chapter. The reader should reference the individual specifications for specific details ([37]-[40]).

The IEEE 802 MAC standards include the following:

1. *Carrier-sense multiple-access with collision detect (CSMA/CD) LANs* such as Ethernet, specified in IEEE 802.3;

2. *Token-passing buses,* as specified in IEEE 802.4 and used in the Manufacturing Automation Protocol (MAP);

3. *Token rings* such as the LAN that IBM specifies for its personal computers, specified in IEEE 802.5.

IEEE 802.2 is the LLC standard that provides a common interface for all the lower MAC protocols to the higher network layer. It is discussed towards the end of the chapter. The relationship of the MAC and LLC protocols to the OSI reference model is shown in Fig. 8.1.

D a t a	LLC	Logical link control 802.2				
l i n k	MAC	CSMA/CD 802.3		Token bus 802.4		Token ring 802.5
P h y s i c a l		Baseband coaxial cable 10 Mbps	Shielded twisted pair wire 1 Mbps	Single-channel broadband coaxial cable 1, 5, 10 Mbps	Broadband coaxial cable 1, 5, 10 Mbps	Shielded twisted pair wire 1, 4 Mbps

Figure 8.1   IEEE 802 local area network standards

8.1.1 MAC Sublayer Services

The MAC sublayer provides connectionless service. MAC services include framing and deframing of LLC PDUs, error checking, and acquiring the right to use the underlying physical medium. The MAC primitives are listed in Table 8.1. A schematic of MAC connectionless service (datagram delivery) is shown in Fig. 8.2.

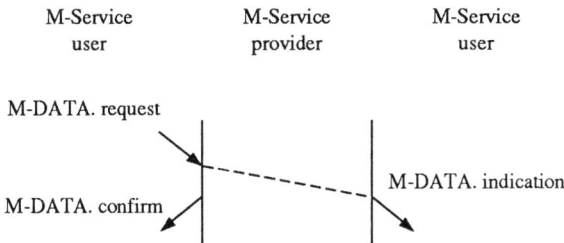

Figure 8.2   Time sequence of MAC service primitives

TABLE 8.1   Summary of MAC Service Primitives and Parameters

Primitives		Parameters
MA-DATA	Request	Destination address
		MS data unit
		Service class
	Indication	Destination address
		Source address
		MS data unit
		Reception status
	Confirm	Transmission status

MS - media access control service

8.1.2 LLC Sublayer Service

The LLC sublayer uses the MAC-layer services to provide either connection-oriented or unacknowledged connectionless service to the network layer. If the service is connection-oriented, LLC sets up a virtual connection between its peer entities and provides sequencing, flow control, and error recovery. If the service is connectionless, it simply provides the means for point-to-point, multicast, or broadcast message delivery. The LLC primitives are listed in Table 8.2.

TABLE 8.2   Summary of 802.2 LLC Service Primitives and Parameters

Primitives		Parameters
	Unacknowledged Connectionless Service	
L-DATA	Request	Local address
		Remote address
		Data units
		Service class
	Indication	Local address
		Remote address
		Data units
		Service class
	Connection-oriented Service	
L-CONNECT	Request	Local address
		Remote address
		Service class

TABLE 8.2 (continued)   Summary of 802.2 LLC Service Primitives and Parameters

Primitives		Parameters
	Indication	Local address Remote address Status Service class
	Confirm	Local address Remote address Status Service class
L-DATA- CONNECT	Request	Local address Remote address Data unit
	Indication	Local address Remote address Data unit
	Confirm	Local address Remote address Status
L-DISCONNECT	Request	Local address Remote address
	Indication	Local address Remote address Reason
	Confirm	Local address Remote address Status
L-RESET	Request	Local address Remote address
	Indication	Local address Remote address Reason
	Confirm	Local address Remote address Reason
L-FLOW CONTROL	Request	Local address Remote address Amount
	Indication	Local address Remote address Amount

8.2 CSMA/CD LAN

Xerox initially developed the Ethernet concept based on the results of broadcast radio network experiments at the University of Hawaii (the ALOHA network). Xerox, DEC, and INTEL collaborated to produce the original Ethernet specification in 1976. The principles are embodied in the IEEE 802.3 national standard. The CSMA/CD concept allows multiple transmitters to share a common communication channel, such as a radio frequency band or, in the case of IEEE 802.3, the bandwidth of a passive coaxial cable.

The 802.3 protocol enables computers to transmit and receive data over 500 m coaxial cable segments at 10 Mbps. Up to 100 media access units (MAUs) may be attached to a 500 m segment. Up to five segments may be joined using *repeaters* (for a maximum separation between MAUs of 2500 m). Figure 8.3 illustrates the most common implementation with taps in the coaxial cable. An implementation with thinner coaxial cable is available that provides computer interfaces to the cable with BNC T-connectors. A third option is to use a twisted pair, but that implementation is limited to 1 Mbps.

The *interface station* (basically a card in a computer) interfaces to a media access unit, in this case a *transceiver*, and *tap* attached to the cable. The transceiver can simultaneously transmit and receive. If the medium is quiet, with no other stations broadcasting, a station proceeds to broadcast connectionless packets. Although all stations hear the broadcast, the destination station is the only station that copies the packet to its host computer. Simultaneous attempts to transmit from multiple stations are expected. Once transmission is started, if interference, or a "collision," with other packets is detected, transmission ceases and is rescheduled after a random time interval. If the medium then appears quiet, the station attempts to retransmit.

IEEE 802.3 provides unacknowledged connectionless service. The LLC entity at the destination computer, if implemented, will be notified of frame errors based on a 32-bit FCS check.

For an 802.3 coaxial cable implementation, with a 10-Mbps transmission rate, the packet size ranges from 64 octets to 1518 octets.

8.2.1 CSMA/CD Physical Layer

At the physical layer, 802.3 topology is a passive-shared bus. The coaxial cable signal is a baseband signal; that is, there is no modulation of a high-frequency carrier.

An 802.3 MAU uses **Manchester-coded** signaling (Fig. 8.4). Recall that RS-232 signaling assigned a specific voltage to correspond with logical 0 and logical 1. With RS-232 coding, a steady stream of zeros or ones appears as a steady voltage. However, with Manchester coding, there is a voltage transition at the midpoint of every bit. The slope of the transition is positive for a logical 1 and negative for logical 0. Thus with Manchester coding, a steady stream of zeros, ones, or

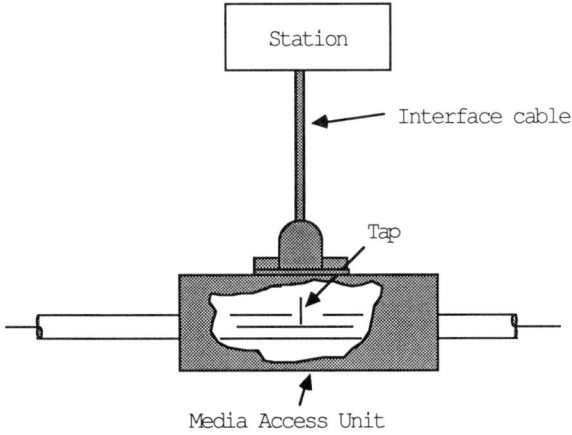

(a) Coaxial cable connection

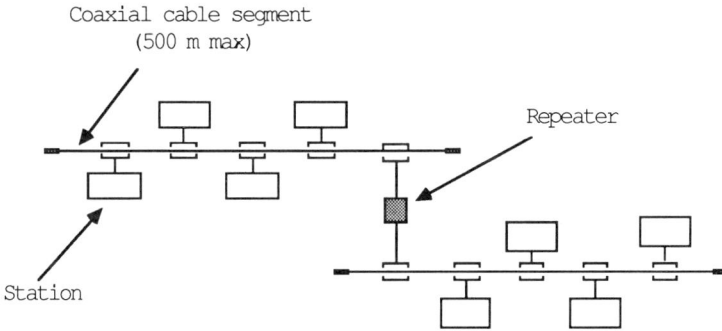

(b) CSMA/CD network

Figure 8.3 CSMA/CD bus interface

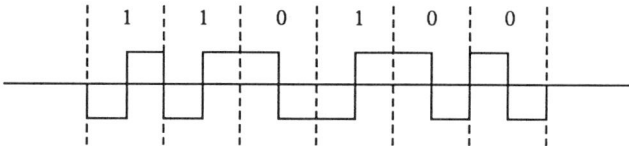

Figure 8.4 Manchester coding

a mix of the two results in a constant stream of *square waves*. This type of signaling imitates a carrier, using a radio analogy, so that when a station transmits, each station on the bus can sense if the LAN is in a *silent* or *busy* state. For this reason, an 802.3 LAN is called a *carrier-sense* LAN.

8.2.2 Media Access

When a computer has data to send, the MAU waits for a quiet condition on the medium and then broadcasts a frame. Because the MAU is a transceiver, it can listen and transmit simultaneously. This enables the MAU to hear a collision with any frame that might be simultaneously transmitted from another station. Such a collision might happen because an electrical signal takes approximately 12 μs to pass from one end of a 2500 m LAN to the other. In the worst case, a time equal to the round-trip time of the signal on the cable may elapse before a collision is detected. This condition occurs when a station at one end of the cable transmits and then another at the opposite end transmits just before the first signal arrives. The first station does not recognize the collision until the signal from the second arrives. This time is referred to as the **slot time** and is the maximum system time to recognize a collision and proceed to resolve it.

If the frame collides with that of another station, both frames become unrecognizable. Each transmitting station intentionally sends a 32-bit *jam* signal to propagate the collision throughout the system. The stations remain silent (**back-off**) for a random amount of time and then attempt to retransmit.

The back-off time is computed from a back-off algorithm. If a collision is detected, a station will delay an integral number of slot times before retransmission. An integral number of slot times is chosen randomly between 0 and 2 (0, 1, or 2) the first time a collision is detected. The next time the integer is between 0 and 4, inclusive. The next is between 0 and 8, and so on. The back-off limit is ten tries, after which the event is reported as an error to the station.

8.2.3 CSMA/CD Frame Format

The 802.3 frame format is illustrated in Fig. 8.5.

The *preamble* is a sequence of seven identical octets that allows the physical signaling circuitry to establish bit synchronization. Each octet is transmitted lsb first:

```
                        lsb                 msb
                         ↓                   ↓
           Bit  —>      1 2 3 4 5 6 7 8

            0    1      1 0 1 0 1 0 1 0
            c    2      1 0 1 0 1 0 1 0
            t    3      1 0 1 0 1 0 1 0
            e    4      1 0 1 0 1 0 1 0
            t    5      1 0 1 0 1 0 1 0
            |    6      1 0 1 0 1 0 1 0
            V    7      1 0 1 0 1 0 1 0
```

The *start frame delimiter* is an octet used for frame synchronization. It is transmitted lsb first and indicates the start of a frame.

Number of
Octets

Octets	
7	Preamble
1	Start frame delimiter
2 or 6	Destination address
2 or 6	Source address
2	Length
User option	Data including pad
4	FCS

Notes:
1. Frame length is measured from the destination address through the FCS, inclusive.
2. The minimum frame length is 64 octets; maximum length is 1518 octets.

Figure 8.5   IEEE 802.3 frame format (Reprinted with permission of the Institute of Electrical and Electronics Engineers, Inc.)

IEEE 802.3 permits 2- or 6-octet addresses for *destination* address and *source* address. All ones in the destination field indicate a *broadcast* frame addressed to all stations. In Ethernet, the addresses are six octets.

The 2-octet *length* indicates the number of octets in the data and pad fields. The data field contains user data and pad is a field of extra octets that may be required to increase the frame length to meet minimum length requirements.

The *frame check sequence (FCS)* is a 4-octet (32-bit) CRC-like check.

8.2.4 CSMA/CD Performance

The information transfer period t_3 includes the time to transmit the 56-bit preamble and the rest of the frame. The medium is released after a system-mandated 9.6-μs *interframe gap* time. The interframe gap provides recovery time for processing and time for the entire medium to become quiet.

From Eq. 8.1,

$$\text{TRIB}_{\text{LAN}} = \frac{n_{\text{info}}}{t_3}$$

where, from Eq. 8.2, for an 802.3 LAN,

$$t_3 = t_{\text{access}} + t_{\text{oneframe}} + t_{\text{interframegap}} \tag{8.3}$$

For one station with no contention, note that $t_{\text{access}} = 0$ s because the media is always available for transmission.

When multiple MAUs are actively contending for access, some frames may collide. Probability analysis is needed to estimate delays due to collisions and retransmissions. The analysis must take into consideration that time is lost because of the collision itself, and time is lost waiting out the back-off time before retransmitting.

The *average* time lost because of the collision itself is the average time to sense that a collision has occurred plus the jam time. The competing MAU can broadcast from almost 0 μs to the round-trip propagation time (the *slot time*) before a collision is detected. Thus, the average time is approximately $.5t_{slot}$ (ignoring the jam time).

If the probability that any one station wants to transmit during the next available slot interval is p, then the probability v that exactly one station successfully transmits is

$$v = Np(1 - p)^{N-1} \tag{8.4}$$

where N is the number of stations.

Using an analysis similar to that of Example 2.10, it can be shown that the average number of retransmissions is $1/v$, and the average delay before successfully transmitting is $(1/v)t_{slot}$. A thorough theoretical analysis is presented by other authors (e.g., [68] and [75]) and the reader may wish to refer to them.

There are several features of Eq. 8.4 that you should note. First, if all the stations wish to transmit with a probability of nearly 1, $v \rightarrow 0$ and the average number of retransmissions gets enormously large. Thus the average access time for each station gets inordinately large, and the network gridlocks.

The probability that exactly one station transmits successfully is maximized when $p = 1/N$. Using this load estimate and letting N be large ($N \gg 1$), v approaches $1/e$ in the limit. Therefore, the average number of retransmissions is e (~ 2.72).

Therefore, the average access delay

$$t_{access} \sim .5t_{slot} + et_{slot} = 3.2t_{slot} \tag{8.5}$$

where

$$t_{slot} = \text{slot time}$$

The 802.3 definition of slot time is 512 bit times, or 51.2 μs, so in the special case where each of a large number of stations has a probability of $1/N$ of transmitting,

$$t_{access} = 165 \ \mu s \tag{8.6}$$

EXAMPLE 8.1   Ethernet TRIB$_{LAN}$

A computer on a 100-computer Ethernet transmits 100 octets of data to another computer on the LAN. Compute TRIB when (a) one computer is transmitting and (b) when each has a probability of transmitting of 0.01.

The frame length is 118 octets (excluding preamble and start frame delimiter).

$$n_{\text{info}} = (8 \text{ bits/octet})(100 \text{ octets}) = 800 \text{ bits}$$

$$t_{\text{oneframe}} = \frac{(64 \text{ bits} + (8 \text{ bits})(118 \text{ octets}))}{(10^7 \text{ bps})}$$

$$= 98 \ \mu s$$

$$t_{\text{interframegap}} = 9.6 \ \mu s$$

a.   For one computer, from Eq. 8.3,

$$\text{TRIB}_{\text{LAN}} = \frac{n_{\text{info}}}{t_{\text{oneframe}} + t_{\text{interframegap}}}$$

$$= \frac{(800 \text{ bits})}{((98 + 9.6) \times 10^{-6} \text{ s})}$$

$$= 7,410,000 \text{ bps}$$

or 74% of the 10-Mbps signaling rate.

b.   For 100 stations transmitting, use Eq. 8.6.

$$t_{\text{access}} = 3.22 t_{\text{slot}}$$

$$= 165 \ \mu s$$

$$t_3 = t_{\text{access}} + t_{\text{oneframe}} + t_{\text{interframegap}}$$

$$= 273 \ \mu s$$

$$\text{TRIB}_{\text{LAN}} = \frac{800}{((165 + 98 + 9.6) \times 10^{-6} \text{ s})}$$

$$= 2,930,000 \text{ bps}$$

or 29% of the signaling rate.

The TRIB of a heavily loaded Ethernet decreases (as we expect) because if the medium is busy, there are collisions and stations are participating in the back-off algorithm.

The 802.3 CSMA/CD LAN is very simple and rugged because it does not depend on active elements to relay frames. If a computer malfunctions, it does not necessarily bring down the whole LAN. However, it has a potential for significantly delaying access if the traffic gets heavy with a large number of users. This is a serious concern if the network deals with urgent data.

8.3 TOKEN-PASSING BUS LAN

The token-passing bus LAN has many of the successful features of the CSMA/CD LAN but provides, through a token-passing scheme, guaranteed access to the medium. The Manufacturing Automation Protocol initiated by General Motors in 1980 implements IEEE 802.4. Several physical layer standards are associated with 802.4, and they provide data rates at 1, 5, or 10 Mbps. Each physical implementation is on coaxial cable bus (Fig. 8.6).

Control is passed via a *token*, a control frame with a special bit field. A station interface must receive the full token frame before it can act on the token (either pass the token on to the next station or transmit its data). In the worst case, the time to receive the token equals the time for the signal to propagate from one

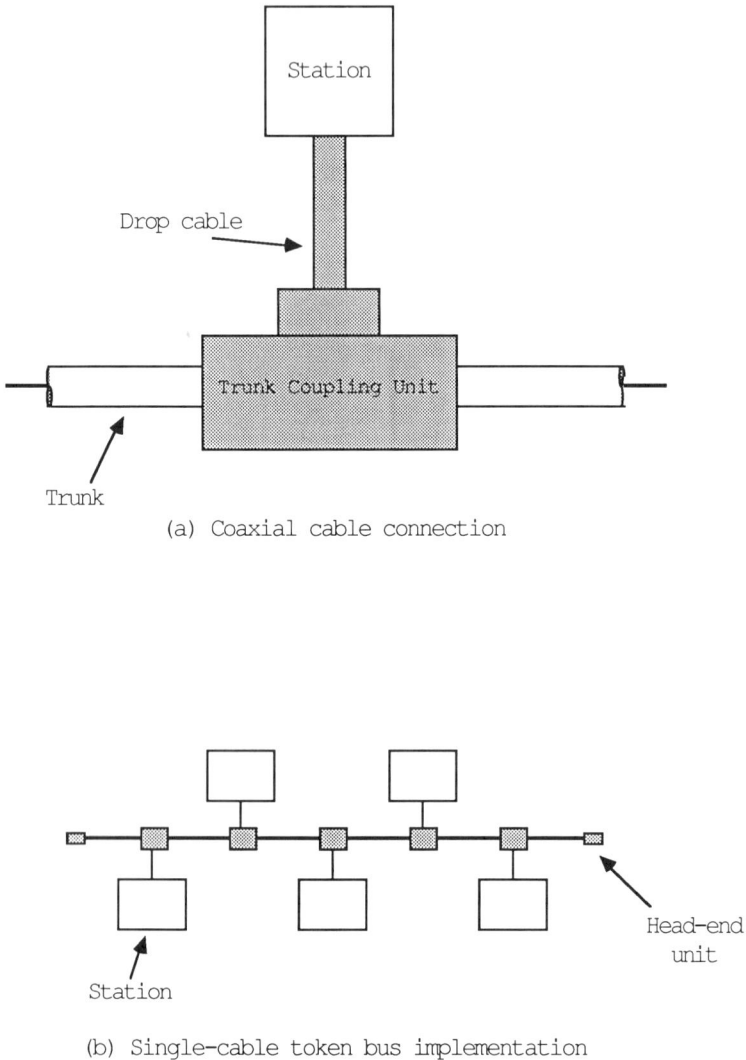

(a) Coaxial cable connection

(b) Single-cable token bus implementation

Figure 8.6 Token-passing bus network

end of the bus to the other, the time for each station interface to do the required signal processing, time to pass the token around to all the other stations, and time for all the other stations to transmit their data.

8.3.1 Media Access

In normal operation, the path of the passing token forms a *logical ring,* where the token circulates from station to station in descending order of station address (not necessarily along physically adjacent stations). Not all stations need to be involved in token-passing—only those that desire to initiate transmissions. Some of the stations on the bus may simply listen. In normal operation, as a station is finished transmitting it sends the token to a specific successor station.

When a station has the token, it may temporarily delegate its right to transmit by setting *request-with-response* bits in the frame it is sending. The destination station may immediately respond, without waiting for the token. This procedure also permits either acknowledged or unacknowledged connectionless service.

8.3.2 Token-passing Bus Frame Format

The frame format for the 802.4 token-passing bus is shown in Fig. 8.7. The *preamble* is a minimum 1-octet pattern to establish bit synchronization, and the *start delimiter* indicates the start of the frame.

Number of
octets

1 (minimum)	Preamble
1	Start delimiter
1	Frame control
2 or 6	Destination address
2 or 6	Source address
User option	Data
4	FCS
1	End delimiter

Note: The maximum number of octets between SD and ED (exclusive) is 8191 octets.

Figure 8.7   IEEE 802.4 token-passing bus frame format (Reprinted with permission of the Institute of Electrical and Electronics Engineers, Inc.)

The *Frame Control* (FC) octet indicates the type of frame, e.g., control or data.

Destination and *source* addresses are two or six octets, similar to 802.3. All addresses on a given LAN are the same length.

The *data* field is limited between the start delimiter and end delimiter, exclusive, to 8191 octets. Therefore, the 2- or 6-octet length of the address fields has a small impact on the maximum length of the data field.

As in 802.3, the FCS is a 32-bit CRC-like error-detection sequence.

8.3.3 Token-passing Bus Performance

In the worst case, media access delay for a token-passing bus includes time for the token to circulate completely around the logical ring. Other delays, such as propagation delays and circuit delays at each interface, are important, but for the sake of simplicity, will be assumed to be zero in the following analysis. Also, in an operating LAN, immediate responses may be requested using frame-control options, but for simplicity, we will ignore this operational complexity when computing $TRIB_{LAN}$.

In a token-passing bus, the time to release the LAN is the time to transmit the token to the next station; therefore,

$$t_{release} = t_{token} \tag{8.7}$$

where t_{token} is the time to transmit the token to the next station.

With only one active station the station must wait, in the worst case, while the token goes all the way around the logical ring.

$$t_{access} = N\,(t_{token}) \tag{8.8}$$

where

$$N = \text{number of transmitting stations}$$

$$t_{token} = \text{time to pass token to the next station}$$

When all the stations are transmitting, in the worst case, the token will go to successive stations in the logical ring and each will respond with data. Access time will simply be the sum of the token-passing time and the average time for each of the other stations to transmit.

$$t_{access} = N(t_{token}) + (N-1)(t_{avgframe}) \tag{8.9}$$

EXAMPLE 8.2   Token-passing bus TRIB

Compute worst-case TRIB for a 10-Mbps token-passing bus with 100 stations when (a) one station is transmitting and (b) all have data to transmit. Assume that all are transmitting 100 octets of data. Compare the two.
Assume:

1. Address field length $=$ 6 octets

2. One $=$ octet preamble

The frame length is 120 octets.

$$n_{\text{info}} = (8 \text{ bits/octet})(100 \text{ octets}) = 800 \text{ bits}$$

At 10 Mbps,

$$t_{\text{oneframe}} = \frac{(8 \text{ bits/octet})(120 \text{ octets})}{(10^7 \text{ bps})}$$

$$= 96 \ \mu s$$

The token is 20 octets. Therefore,

$$t_{\text{token}} = \frac{(8 \text{ bits/octet})(20 \text{ octets})}{(10^7 \text{ bps})}$$

$$= 16 \ \mu s$$

and, from Eq. 8.7,

$$t_{\text{release}} = 16 \ \mu s$$

a. Compute TRIB for the case of one station transmitting.

$$t_{\text{access}} = N \ t_{\text{token}}$$

$$= (100 \text{ stns})(16 \times 10^{-6} \text{ s})$$

$$= 1600 \ \mu s$$

From Eq. 8.2,

$$t_3 = t_{\text{access}} + t_{\text{oneframe}} + t_{\text{release}}$$
$$= (1600 + 96 + 16) \times 10^{-6} \text{ s}$$
$$= 1712 \ \mu s$$

From Eq. 8.1,

$$\text{TRIB}_{\text{LAN}} = \frac{n_{\text{info}}}{t_3}$$

$$= \frac{(800 \text{ bits})}{(1712 \times 10^{-6} \text{ s})}$$

$$= 467,000 \text{ bps}$$

or 5% of the signaling rate.

b. Compute TRIB when all stations have 100 octets to transmit. From Eq. 8.9,

$$t_{access} = N(t_{token}) + (N - 1)(t_{avgframe})$$

$$= (100 \text{ stns})(16 \times 10^{-6} \text{ s}) + (99 \text{ stns})(96 \times 10^{-6}\text{s})$$

$$= 11,104 \text{ } \mu s$$

From Eq. 8.2,

$$t_3 = t_{access} + t_{oneframe} + t_{release}$$

$$= (11,104 + 96 + 16) \times 10^{-6} \text{ s}$$

$$= 11,216 \text{ } \mu s$$

From Eq. 8.1,

$$TRIB_{LAN} = \frac{n_{info}}{t_3}$$

$$= \frac{(800 \text{ bits})}{(11,216 \times 10^{-6} \text{ s})}$$

$$= 71,300 \text{ bps}$$

or .7% of the signaling rate.

In the worst case, with multiple users, $TRIB_{LAN}$ for a given station decreases roughly by a factor of 10 because of the exceptionally long wait while the other 99 stations transmit their data. Note that it is still transmitting data, where in the case of IEEE 802.3, the network is gridlocked. This is one of the main reasons why General Motors promoted this standard for MAP: it has a predictable worst-case TRIB.

8.4 TOKEN RING LAN

In a token ring network, each computer has an active processor that passes digital signals continuously to adjacent computers. The topology for the IEEE 802.5 token ring is a unidirectional ring (Fig. 8.8). IBM announced an 802.5-compatible token ring for its personal computers in 1986.

Each station is physically connected to two adjacent stations and receives signals from one and transmits to the other. Each station regenerates and repeats each bit to keep the network active.

Permission for accessing the network medium is passed via a token. Each station interface requires time to detect the token and decide whether to (1) pass the token to the next station or (2) transmit data. The interface delay time for this decision is typically a 1-bit time interval. The 1-bit interface delay at each station is called the station *latency*. The total delay around the ring is called the ring latency, or the *walk time*. Walk time is an important token ring LAN parameter because it creates a delay in delivering data that increases as more computers are added to

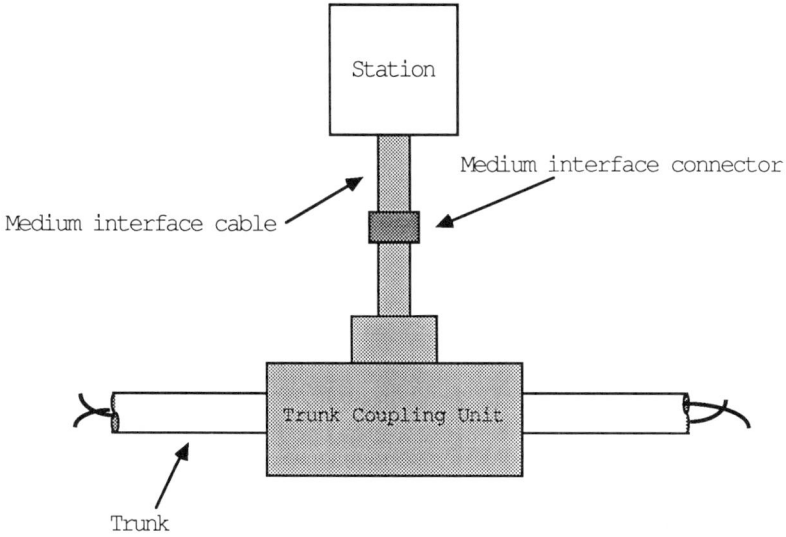

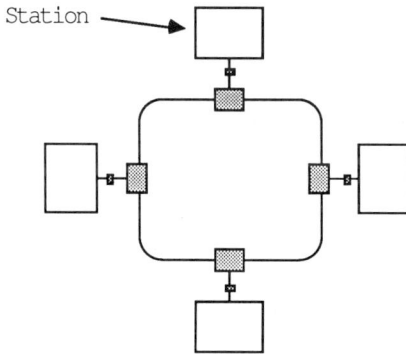

Figure 8.8   Token ring network

the LAN. The total delay for a signal to travel around the ring is the walk time plus the propagation delays.

8.4.1 Token Ring Physical Layer

Data is signaled on the medium using **differential Manchester coding** (Fig. 8.9). If the symbol to be transmitted is a logical 0, the polarity of the leading signal is opposite to that of the trailing element of the previous symbol. If the symbol

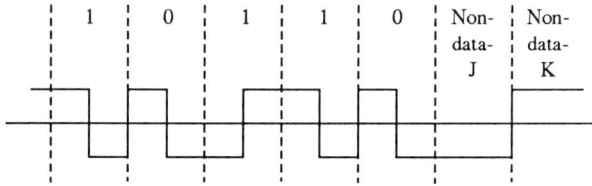

Figure 8.9 Differential Manchester coding

is a logical 1, the polarity of the leading signal is the same as that of the trailing element of the previous symbol. The midbit transition provides bit synchronization.

An interesting convention is the use of "non-data" signaling in the starting and ending delimiter for frame synchronization. *Non-data-J* and *non-data-K* do not have the normal midbit transition. A non-data-J has the same polarity as the trailing part of the preceding symbol and non-data-K has the opposite.

8.4.2 Media Access

The 802.5 token is a 3-octet sequence whose starting-delimiter octet and access-control octet are identical to the two octets that start a data frame, except that a 1-bit token field in the access-control octet provides an indication that the frame is a token. Conversion of that one bit converts the access-control octet from a token indicator to a start-of-frame octet.

When a frame (data or control) is ready to be sent by the station, software prefixes the information field with the appropriate frame-control and address fields and inserts it into a queue to wait for the arrival of the token. When a token with the right priority arrives, the protocol converts the access-control octet to indicate that the access-control octet is the start of a frame rather than a token.

At this time the station begins to transmit the rest of the frame. During transmission, the 32-bit FCS is computed and appended to the end of the information field.

Each station in the ring repeats the incoming signal stream and checks it for frames that it should copy. If the frame is addressed to the station, it copies the appropriate fields to a buffer while repeating the signal to the next station.

The original sender discards all incoming signals as it transmits its frame. When it has received the end of its original transmission, it inserts a new token onto the line and adds *fill* bits until it senses the token or the frame of a new sender.

When there is a time-out, such as when the token is lost due to noise on the line, a station with data to send regenerates the token. It transmits the starting delimiter and access control fields as if it had received a token, sends its frame, and then terminates by generating a new token.

8.4.3 Token Ring Frame Format   *Token Format.*   The token has a 3-octet frame format (Fig. 8.10).

Number of
octets

1	Starting delimiter
1	Access control
1	Ending delimiter

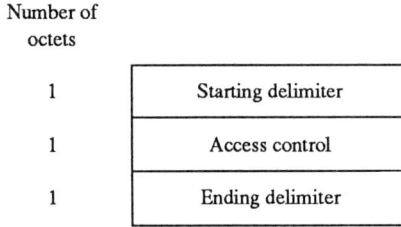

Figure 8.10   IEEE 802.5 Token ring token format

The *starting delimiter* indicates the start of a frame:

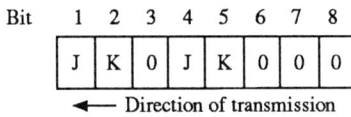

Bit   1   2   3   4   5   6   7   8

J	K	0	J	K	0	0	0

◄— Direction of transmission

Access control indicates if the frame is a token and provides other control functions.

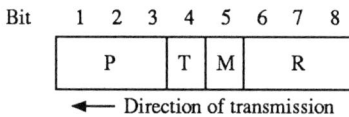

Bit   1   2   3   4   5   6   7   8

P	T	M	R

◄— Direction of transmission

- *P* is a 3-bit field of priority bits to indicate the priority of the token.
- *T* is a 1-bit token field, logical 0 in a token, logical 1 in other frames.
- *M* is a monitor bit to keep a high-priority token from continuously circulating on the ring.
- *R* is a field for reservation bits used by stations with high priority data to request that the token be reissued at high priority.

The *ending delimiter* indicates the end of a frame and provides an error-detected bit to the sender of data.

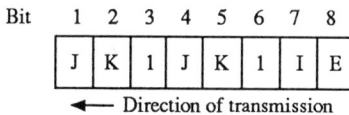

Bit   1   2   3   4   5   6   7   8

J	K	1	J	K	1	I	E

◄— Direction of transmission

- *I*-bit indicates that this is a multiple-frame transmission.
- E is the error-detected bit.

Information and Control Frame Format.   The information and control frame format is shown in Fig. 8.11. The *frame control* octet defines the type of frame, i.e., control or data. The *destination* address and *source* address may be either 2-octet or 6-octet addresses.

Number of octets	
1	Starting delimiter
1	Access control
1	Frame control
2 or 6	Destination address
2 or 6	Source address
User option (max 133)	Data
4	FCS
1	Ending delimiter
1	Frame status

Figure 8.11 Token ring information and control frame format (Reprinted with permission of the Institute of Electrical and Electronics Engineers, Inc.)

The data field is a maximum of 133 octets. The FCS is a variation of a 32-bit CRC. The FCS covers the frame control octet through the data. The last octet is the *frame status*. This octet is used by the receiver to indicate to the sender that it copied the frame.

8.4.4 Token Ring Performance

As with a token-passing bus, media access time includes time for the token to circulate around the ring. Other delays, such as propagation delays and circuit delays (walk time), should be included. We will ignore propagation time in the following discussion.

In a token ring, the time to release the LAN is the time to transmit the token to the next station; therefore,

$$t_{release} = t_{token} \qquad (8.10)$$

where

$t_{token} = $ time to transmit the token to the next station

When only one station is active, in the worst case it must wait while the token goes around the ring, and

$$t_{access} = N\, t_{token} + N\, t_{interface} \qquad (8.11)$$

where

$$N = \text{number of transmitting stations}$$

$$t_{\text{token}} = \text{time to pass token to the next station}$$

$$t_{\text{interface}} = \text{1-bit circuit delay at each interface}$$

When all the stations are active, in the worst case the token will go to successive stations in the ring and each will respond with data. Access time will simply be the token-passing time, average time for each of the other stations to transmit, plus the circuit delays at each interface.

$$t_{\text{access}} = N(t_{\text{token}}) + (N - 1)(t_{\text{avgframe}}) + N(t_{\text{interface}}) \qquad (8.12)$$

EXAMPLE 8.3   Token ring TRIB

A computer on a 100-computer 802.5 token ring transmits 100 octets of data to an adjacent computer on the net. Compute TRIB when (a) one computer desires to transmit and (b) all are trying to transmit. Compare the two cases. Assume the address field is 6 octets. The signaling rate is 4 Mbps.

$$n_{\text{info}} = (8 \text{ bits/octet})(100 \text{ octets}) = 800 \text{ bits}$$

The frame length is 121 octets.

$$t_{\text{oneframe}} = \frac{(8 \text{ bits/octet})(121 \text{ octets})}{(4 \times 10^6 \text{ bps})}$$

$$= 242 \ \mu s$$

The token is 3 octets:

$$t_{\text{token}} = \frac{(8 \text{ bits/octet})(3 \text{ octets})}{(4 \times 10^6 \text{ bps})}$$

$$= 4.5 \ \mu s$$

The station latency is 1 bit time:

$$t_{\text{interface}} = \frac{(1 \text{ bit})}{(4 \times 10^6 \text{ bps})}$$

$$= .25 \ \mu s$$

a.   For one computer, from Eq. 8.10,

$$t_{\text{access}} = N(t_{\text{token}}) + N(t_{\text{interface}})$$

$$= (100 \text{ stns})(4.5 \times 10^{-6} \text{ s})$$

$$+ (100 \text{ stns})(.25 \times 10^{-6} \text{ s})$$

$$= 474 \ \mu s$$

$$t_3 = t_{\text{access}} + t_{\text{oneframe}} + t_{\text{release}}$$

$$= (474 + 242 + 4.5) \times 10^{-6} \text{ s}$$

$$= 720 \; \mu\text{s}$$

$$\text{TRIB}_{\text{LAN}} = \frac{n_{\text{info}}}{t_3}$$

$$= \frac{(800 \text{ bits})}{(720 \times 10^{-6} \text{ s})}$$

$$= 1,110,000 \text{ bps}$$

or 27% of the signaling rate.

b.   When all the stations have data to transmit, from Eq. 8.11,

$$t_{\text{access}} = N(t_{\text{token}}) + (N - 1)(t_{\text{avgframe}}) + N(t_{\text{interface}})$$

$$= (100 \text{ stns})(4.5 \times 10^{-6} \text{ s}) + (99 \text{ stns})(242 \times 10^{-6} \text{ s})$$

$$+ (100 \text{ stns})(.25 \times 10^{-6} \text{ s})$$

$$= 24,433 \; \mu\text{s}$$

$$t_3 = t_{\text{access}} + t_{\text{oneframe}} + t_{\text{release}}$$

$$= (24,433 + 242 + 4.5) \times 10^{-6} \text{ s}$$

$$= 24,700 \; \mu\text{s}$$

$$\text{TRIB}_{\text{LAN}} = \frac{n_{\text{info}}}{t_3}$$

$$= \frac{(800 \text{ bits})}{(24,700 \times 10^{-6} \text{ s})}$$

$$= 32,400 \text{ bps}$$

or .8% of the signaling rate.

In the worst case, i.e., with multiple users, TRIB_{LAN} for a given station decreases dramatically because of the exceptionally long wait while the other 99 stations transmit their data. Note the better TRIB-to-signaling ratio for the ring compared to the token bus, especially with one user. This is primarily due to the shorter token (3 versus 20 octets).

8.5 LOGICAL LINK CONTROL

The logical link control (LLC) sublayer builds on the services of the various MAC sublayers and provides a common interface to the network layer. The protocol is specified in IEEE 802.2.

As mentioned earlier, LLC provides unacknowledged connectionless and connection-oriented service to the network layer. LLC services are made available directly to the network layer at logical service access points (SAPs), or LLC addresses. LAN devices may have one or a number of LLC SAPs. For example, if one system on the LAN is a printer, it may have only one SAP, and after a connection is made to it, any other process that tries to establish a connection receives an indication equivalent to a busy signal.

MAC sublayer protocol headers wrap the LLC frame in a typical OSI fashion, as shown in Fig. 8.12.

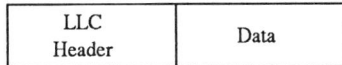

LLC Header	Data

(a) LLC protocol data unit

MAC Header	LLC Header	Data	MAC Trailer

(b) MAC protocol data unit

Figure 8.12   Wrapping of OSI LLC sublayer PDU

In unacknowledged connectionless service, the link software may exchange frames without establishing a data link–level connection. It is basically the datagram approach. The frames may be delivered from a sender to one receiver (*point to point*), specific network computers (*multicast*), or all network computers (*broadcast*).

When a station requests that a frame be delivered by the data link layer in an unacknowledged connectionless mode, it passes the frame to the LLC SAP with the request and simply receives an indication that the LLC has accepted it.

Connection-oriented service, similar to LAPB, requires establishment of a link between the sender and receiver SAPs. Once the connection is made, information is exchanged.

The network layer makes the connect request at the LLC sublayer SAP (LSAP) and indicates the destination LSAP as a parameter (Table 8.2). It receives confirmation that the connection is established or refused. For incoming calls, the LLC will indicate to the network layer that a connection has been made. Other commands between the network layer and LLC include disconnect requests, data transfer requests, and reset requests.

The LLC protocol data unit has the format shown in Fig. 8.13.

The *control* field consists of one or two octets that are used to designate command and response functions and may contain sequence numbers when required for connection-oriented service.

Number of
octets ——▶

Destination LSAP address	Source LSAP address	Control	Data

| 1 | 1 | 1 or 2 | User option |

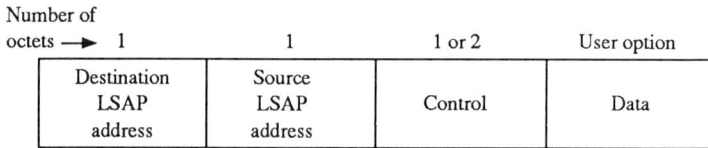

Figure 8.13 IEEE 802.2 LLC frame format (Reprinted with permission of the Institute of Electrical and Electronics Engineers, Inc.)

8.6 SUMMARY

The number of LANs is growing because of the sharp increase in the number of personal computers and the need for sharing of resources. Medium access procedures vary, but three standard IEEE 802 MAC protocols have been specified.

CSMA/CD LANs are the simplest LANs because their medium is passive and it is easy to add or remove nodes. If a station becomes inoperative, the network continues to operate because the physical layer does not depend on individual stations for overall control. Users must contend for the medium, which can lead to overloading and denial of service to high-priority users. Analysis of TRIB and channel efficiency depends on the probability that users who are connected want access at a given moment, and this leads to unpredictability.

Token-passing buses and rings have more predictable access; however, they are less efficient with a large number of computers because all users, even those with no data, must process the token. These networks have an obvious single point of failure. Token rings require active circuitry to keep the LAN operational.

The logical link control sublayer provides a common interface to the network layer for any MAC protocol. LLC provides connectionless or connection-oriented service.

KEY WORDS AND CONCEPTS

back-off
IEEE 802.3 carrier-sense
   multiple-access with collision detect
   (CSMA/CD) bus
IEEE 802.4 token-passing bus
IEEE 802.5 token ring

logical link control (LLC)
Manchester coding
media access control (MAC)
service access point (SAP)
slot time
token

PROBLEMS

1. Explain the meaning of each of the words in the acronym CSMA/CD.
2. If you were to transmit only your last name in an Ethernet frame on a LAN with 6-octet addresses, compute how much pad is required and compute the length parameter.

3. Describe the voltage on a line for 0 1 1 0 1 0 0:

(a) With Manchester coding

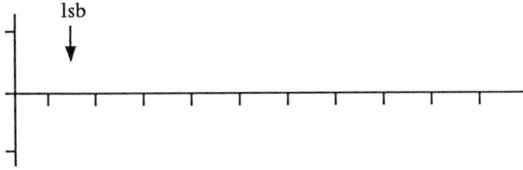

(a) With Manchester coding:

lsb

(b) With differential Manchester coding

(b) With differential Manchester coding:

lsb

4. What is TRIB$_{LAN}$ for the 10-Mbps Ethernet multistation transmission case with the assumptions of Example 8.1b if the data field is (a) 500 octets and (b) 1000 octets? Compare the results with Example 8.1b. What effect does data field length have on Ethernet performance?

5. Compute TRIB$_{LAN}$ for an 802.4 token-passing bus, where all 100 stations are transmitting, the frames have information fields of 100 octets, and addresses are six octets. Assume for this problem that the signaling rate is 4 Mbps (a nonstandard rate). Compare the results with the token ring in Example 8.3. Which LAN carries more information under a heavy load? Why?

6. Compute TRIB$_{LAN}$ for a 10-Mbps token-passing bus when all 100 stations are transmitting and the frames have data fields of (a) 50 octets and (b) 500 octets. Use the assumptions of Example 8.2 and compare results with it. What effect does data field length have on token-passing bus performance under a heavy load?

7. On a 4-Mbps token ring, each station delays the token by one bit. With 100 stations, how long after the token bit leaves the first station will it take for it to return, assuming no one wants to convert it? Assume a total network propagation delay of 10 μs (approximately 2 km).

8. Compute TRIB$_{LAN}$ for a 4-Mbps token ring where one station transmits and the frames have 50-octet data fields. Use the assumptions of Example 8.3 and compare the impact of information field length.

9

TRANSPORT AND SESSION LAYERS

The protocols in the OSI layers that we have discussed so far provide a backbone capability for moving data from a sender to a receiver over a multicomputer network. How will the user be sure that the data is delivered error-free? If the data originates on a LAN and goes through a datagram subnet, it may get lost. What if the link is broken because of a problem in the carrier's equipment? How will the user's system detect it and recover? Answers to difficult questions like these are provided in the transport and session layers of the OSI model. The common characteristic of these upper-layer protocols is that *they reside in the user's host computer*, rather than in a network node communications processor.

The purpose of the OSI transport layer is to give the user a reliable communication channel from a user process in one host to a user process in another, even when the subnets rearrange or lose packets, or reinitialize in the middle of a transmission. The protocols establish a **transport connection** between user processes, analogous to a virtual circuit.

The OSI session layer builds on the transport connection and organizes and synchronizes the flow of data between user processes. The session layer software may monitor the transport connection and enable recovery from specific synchronization points if there is a disruption.

9.1 TRANSPORT LAYER

When the underlying network service is connectionless, packets may be lost or delivered out of sequence. An appropriate transport protocol is required to detect and recover from the errors and then sequence the data. When the underlying network service is already connection-oriented (i.e., X.25), less service is required from the transport protocol. **ISO 8073 connection-oriented mode transport protocol (TP)**, covered next, provides five classes of transport service, so that the user may select as much service as necessary, depending on the quality of service provided by the underlying network.

As we discussed in Chap. 7, DoD IP delivers internet datagrams across all types of subnets. Host computers take responsibility for end-to-end reliability and can use the DoD **Transmission Control Protocol (TCP)**, discussed in this chapter.

As an example of how proprietary architectures deal with the reliability problem, the DNA *end communication* layer builds on the connectionless *routing* layer to allow user processes to exchange data reliably and sequentially. The Network Services Protocol (NSP) is DEC's proprietary protocol that provides the equivalent of OSI transport layer services.

9.1.1   ISO 8073 Transport Protocol

The OSI transport layer uses the services of the network layer to let a user process establish a transport connection with a user process on a distant host. Each user process has a logical access point to a transport connection (a **transport service access point (TSAP)** or, in DoD terminology, a *port*. The data is transmitted in OSI **transport protocol data units** (TPDUs) , or *segments*.

The transport protocol establishes a transport connection, transfers data, and releases the connection through commands from the session layer. ISO 8073 is structured to permit cost optimization. It provides varying degrees of quality of service (such as throughput, transit delay, error rates, and reliability) and is organized into the following five classes.

1. Class 0, simple class. This is the simplest type of transport connection. One transport connection corresponds to one network connection. If the network disconnects, class 0 software informs the user that the transport connection is released. There is no error detection and correction. Class 0 is adequate for X.25 networks.

2. Class 1, basic error recovery class. This protocol automatically recovers from a network disconnect or reset by reassigning the transport connection to another network and resynchronizing. There is no error detection and correction. This class provides expedited data delivery when the transport protocol requests the network to send selected data ahead of the normal queue.

3. Class 2, multiplexing class. This is a protocol that multiplexes several transport connections onto a single network connection. Just as in class 0, if the network disconnects, class 2 software informs the user that the multiplexed transport connections are released. There is no error detection and correction. Class 2 has a flow control option that pipelines data TPDUs and utilizes the windowing concept discussed in Chap. 6 with individual acknowledgments (i.e., no piggybacking).

4. Class 3, error recovery and multiplexing class. This is a protocol that provides both the ability to multiplex (a class 2 capability) and to recover from network disconnects and resets (a class 1 capability). The protocol provides the flow control that was an option in class 2.

5. Class 4, error detection and recovery class. The strongest protocol class, it is used on networks with unacceptable error rates and those with underlying network protocols that are inherently unreliable. Class 4 provides all the class 3 functions and detects and recovers from lost, duplicated, or out-of-sequence segments. Normally, when a valid segment arrives, the receiver will send an acknowledgment. If segments are lost or damaged, the sender times out and retransmits the original segment.

When establishing the transport connection, the transport software will attempt to match the user's request for quality of service with network capabilities. The software may also select the network service that optimizes cost, decide whether to multiplex multiple transport connections onto a single network connection, and establish an optimum TPDU size.

Data transfer is performed in a full-duplex mode, which is created in whatever way necessary with the subnets. The transport protocol performs flow control over the transport connection and may segment and reassemble data given to it by the session-layer protocols to utilize the network better.

9.1.1.1 ISO 8073 transport operation.   The ISO 8073 transport service primitives are shown in Table 9.1. These primitives are used by the session layer to request transport services.

In normal operation, the session entity will issue a T-CONNECT.request to the local transport entity at the TSAP. The distant session entity will receive a T-CONNECT.indication and respond with a T-CONNECT.response. The local session entity will receive a T-CONNECT.confirm as an acknowledgment that the connection is established. The session entity uses the T-DATA.request to send data. The distant session entity receives it at its TSAP as a T-DATA.indication.

At the conclusion of data transfer, either side may issue a T-DISCONNECT.request. The receiver, upon receiving a T-DISCONNECT.indication, terminates the transport connection.

9.1.1.2 ISO 8073 transport protocol data units.   The nine types of ISO 8073 TPDUs are shown in Table 9.2.

The structure of the TPDU, which contains an integral number of octets, is shown in Fig. 9.1.

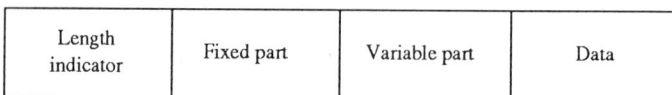

Length indicator	Fixed part	Variable part	Data

Figure 9.1   ISO 8073 transport protocol data unit structure

TABLE 9.1   ISO 8073 Transport Service Primitives

Primitives		Parameters
T-CONNECT	Request Indication	Called address Calling address Expedited data option Quality of service Transport service user data
T-CONNECT	Response Confirm	Responding address Quality of service Expedited data option Transport service user data
T-DATA	Request Indication	Transport service user data
T-EXPEDITED DATA	Request Indication	Transport service user data
T-DISCONNECT	Request	Transport service user data
T-DISCONNECT	Indication	Disconnect reason Transport service user data

(Reprinted with permission)

TABLE 9.2   ISO 8073 TPDU Types

Code	Type	Validity within Classes				
		0	1	2	3	4
CR	Connection request	X	X	X	X	X
CC	Connection confirm	X	X	X	X	X
DR	Disconnect request	X	X	X	X	X
DC	Disconnect confirm		X	X	X	X
DT	Data	X	X	X	X	X
ED	Expedited data		X	NF	X	X
AK	Data acknowledgment		NRC	NF	X	X
EA	Expedited data acknowledgment		X	NF	X	X
RJ	Reject		X		X	
ER	TPDU error	X	X	X	X	X

NF: Not available when the not-explicit flow control option is selected.

NRC: Not available when the receipt confirmation option is selected.

(Reprinted with permission)

The *length indicator* specifies the length of the TPDU header in octets, excluding the 2-octet length indicator field. The maximum length is 254 octets.

The *fixed part* contains frequently occurring parameters such as the TPDU type.

The *variable part* contains less frequently used parameters. For example, it contains a 16-bit checksum for class 4 service.

The *data* field is user-defined.

9.1.1.3 ISO 8073 Data TPDU.

As an example, a Data (DT) TPDU has the structure shown in Fig. 9.2. For a normal format, the fixed part of the DT TPDU uses the following octets:

1. Classes 0 and 1: octets 2–3
2. Classes 2, 3, and 4: octets 2–5

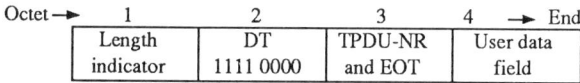

Octet → 1   2   3   4 → End

Length indicator	DT 1111 0000	TPDU-NR and EOT	User data field

(a) Normal format for classes 0 and 1

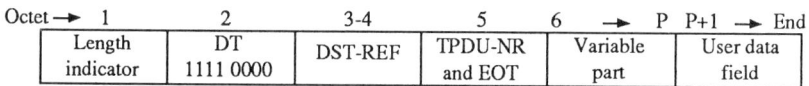

Octet → 1   2   3-4   5   6 → P   P+1 → End

Length indicator	DT 1111 0000	DST-REF	TPDU-NR and EOT	Variable part	User data field

(b) Normal format for classes 2, 3, and 4

Figure 9.2 Data (DT) TPDU structure (Reprinted with permission)

In Fig. 9.2a, the fixed part contains the DT code and the TPDU sequence number. Octet 3 is also used to indicate that this is the last segment of a segmented TPDU sequence.

In Fig. 9.2b, DST-REF identifies the transport connection at the remote transport entity. The variable part contains the 2-octet checksum if class 4 service is used.

9.1.2 DoD Transmission Control Protocol

TCP was created for use on the ARPANET specifically for unreliable subnets. Combined with DoD's IP, it enables the user to reliably transmit large files of data. TCP provides service similar to the ISO 8073 class 4 transport protocol and ensures that the data arrives at the distant user process reliably and in sequence. It includes sequence numbers for each octet of data, LRC checksums for error detection, and acknowledgment and retransmission procedures.

9.1.2.1 TCP operational philosophy.   As with ISO 8073, TCP is used to transfer data between two logically distinct user processes, such as file transfer or electronic mail servers.

Each transport connection is full duplex. When two processes wish to communicate, their TCP entities first establish a connection (which serves to initialize status information on each side). When their communication is complete, the connection is terminated to free the resources for other uses.

TCP formats data into segments of a limited length that contain the user data plus control information. To achieve reliable data transfer, the octets of data in outgoing segments are numbered sequentially and are subsequently acknowledged by number. TCP passes these segments to the IP module for transmission through the subnets to the distant TCP user process.

The interface between a user process and TCP consists of a set of calls, much like primitives or calls that an operating system makes to a user process for manipulating files. There are calls to open and close connections and to send and receive data. For example, an OPEN command includes arguments for the local port number, destination, precedence, and security.

Reliability.   TCP assigns a sequence number to each transmitted octet, and requires a positive acknowledgment message (ACK) from the distant TCP. The ACK is cumulative; an ACK for a given octet implies preceding octets were successfully received.

If an ACK is not received within a time-out interval, the data is retransmitted. At the receiver, sequence numbers are used by the software to eliminate duplicates and order segments correctly that may be received out of order. Errors are detected by adding a checksum to each transmitted segment, checking it at the receiver, and discarding damaged segments. Not acknowledging the segments causes the sender to time-out eventually and retransmit.

Flow Control.   A sender informs the distant end in its outgoing segment of the number of octets it can currently receive. Presumably this parameter indicates how much buffer space is currently available. If the number is low, the distant end throttles down its volume of data. Even without this capability, the distant end may transmit as many octets as it wishes, but if the receiver cannot process them all, they will not be acknowledged.

Addressing.   Multiple processes within a single host may use TCP simultaneously. When TCP is used with IP—which it usually is—a destination is uniquely identified by a *socket*, the combination of the 16-bit *port* and 32-bit *internet address*. Each connection is uniquely identified as a socket pair. A given socket on one host may be simultaneously used in multiple connections. Frequently used processes, such as a bulletin board service, may have fixed sockets that are made public to a number of users.

9.1.2.2 TCP procedures.   A process opens a connection in one of two modes, *passive* or *active*. With a PASSIVE OPEN command, a user process instructs its TCP to be receptive to open requests from other TCP entities. With an ACTIVE OPEN, a process instructs its TCP to proceed to establish a connection to a distant TCP socket. Usually an ACTIVE OPEN is targeted to a PASSIVE OPEN. When data exchange is complete, the connection may be closed by either process to free TCP resources for other connections.

9.1.2.3 TCP header format.

The TCP header from MIL-STD-1778 is shown in Fig. 9.3.

Bits	16								16
Source								Destination	
Sequence number									
Acknowledge number									
DO	XXX	URG	ACK	PSH	RST	SYN	FIN	Window	
Checksum								Urgent pointer	
Options (0 or more 32-bit words)									
Data									

Figure 9.3   TCP header format

Source and *destination* are 16-bit values identifying the port address. The 32-bit *sequence number* specifies the sequence number of the first octet of data in a segment. The *acknowledgment number* is a 32-bit piggybacking field containing the value of the next octet sequence number that the sender of the segment is expected to be received.

The following short fields are grouped into the next 16-bit field:

DO (Data Offset): Three-bit designator of the TCP header length that tells how many 32-bit words are contained in the TCP header. From this value, the beginning of the data can be computed.

XXX: Six bits reserved for future use.

URG: Bit to designate if the URGENT POINTER field is in use.

ACK: Bit for acknowledgment.

PSH: Bit for "push" function. A TCP module is allowed to buffer, segment, and transmit user data at its convenience. The push function allows the sending user process to request that the local TCP promptly transmit all the data it has, and this PSH bit notifies the destination TCP to deliver the data promptly to its user process.

RST: Bit to reset the transport connection.

SYN: Bit to establish transport connections:

SYN = 1 ACK = 0   Connection request to indicate that the piggyback
                       acknowledgment field is not in use.

$$SYN = 1 \; ACK = 1 \qquad \text{Connection reply}$$

FIN: Bit to indicate that no more data will be sent by the sender.

The 16-bit *window* field indicates the number of data octets, beginning with the one identified in the acknowledgment number field, that the sender is willing to accept from the distant end.

The 16-bit *checksum* field carries the 1s complement–based checksum of both the header and data.

An *urgent pointer* 16-bit field indicates an octet offset from the current sequence number at which the receiver can find urgent data. This is in place of interrupt messages.

The *options* field is a variable-length field reserved for miscellaneous parameters. Individual option parameters are in multiples of octets. If the options total less than 32 bits, padding is added. Currently defined option codes in MIL-STD-1778 include the following:

0: End-of-option list
1: No operation
2: Maximum segment size option

EXAMPLE 9.1   Impact of TCP/IP on TRIB

A computer on a 100-computer Ethernet transmits frames with 100-octet data fields to another computer on the net. It is the only computer with data to transmit (similar to Example 8.1a). Compute the impact on TRIB when the 100-octet user field also includes (a) an IP header and (b) TCP/IP headers. Assume:

1. Destination is a local station on the same Ethernet
2. No options field in TCP or IP

a. Add IP.

The data field is 100 octets, but 20 octets of the field is an IP header. Thus the information in the frame is only 80 octets. From Example 8.1, the frame length is 114 octets.

$$n_{info} = (8 \text{ bits/octet})(80 \text{ octets}) = 640 \text{ bits}$$

$$t_{oneframe} = \frac{(64 \text{ bits} + (8 \text{ bits/octet})(114 \text{ octets}))}{10^7 \text{ bps}}$$

$$= 98 \; \mu s$$

$$TRIB_{LAN} = \frac{n_{info}}{(t_{oneframe} + t_{interframegap})}$$

$$= \frac{(640 \text{ bits})}{((98 + 9.6) \times 10^{-6} \text{ s})}$$

$$= 5,959,000 \text{ bps}$$

or 60% of the signaling rate.

b. Add TCP/IP

Now 40 octets of the 100-octet data field are the TCP/IP headers. The user information in the frame is only 60 octets.

$$n_{\text{info}} = (8 \text{ bits/octet})(60 \text{ octets}) = 480 \text{ bits}$$

$$\text{TRIB}_{\text{LAN}} = \frac{n_{\text{info}}}{(t_{\text{oneframe}} + t_{\text{interframegap}})}$$

$$= \frac{(480 \text{ bits})}{(108 \times 10^{-6} \text{ s})}$$

$$= 4,461,000 \text{ bps}$$

or 45% of the signaling rate.

The overall impact of TCP/IP on TRIB is summarized in Table 9.3, including the results from Example 8.1a.

TABLE 9.3   Impact of TCP/IP on Ethernet TRIB

Signaling Rate	TRIB Ethernet Only	TRIB with IP	TRIB with TCP/IP
10 Mbps	8.3 Mbps	6.0 Mbps	4.5 Mbps

9.2 SESSION LAYER

The session layer services operate between the transport connection and the user process in a host. Two of the responsibilities of the session layer are to organize and synchronize data transfer. It may include such procedures as the following:

1. Determine *access rights* when responding to a connect request. The session layer may initially validate access control data and authenticate the distant user process.
2. Monitor the transport connection, re-establish it if it fails, and provide a synchronization point so that the user can resume data transmission.

3. Define periods within the time that there is a session connection for sending logical groups of data.

The session layer acts as an intermediary to the host process. For example, it processes transport connections on behalf of user processes. The *ISO 8327 session protocol* communicates over a reliable connection-oriented transport service.

SNA does many of these functions in its *data flow control* layer. DNA has a session control layer that also performs many of the essential functions just identified. There is no equivalent to the session layer in the DoD Internet architecture.

9.2.1 ISO 8327 Session Operation

The OSI session layer provides the means for organized and synchronized exchange of data between session entities. During a session, the user processes conduct **activities** that are assumed to be a series of **dialogues.** To organize these exchanges, the OSI session protocol provides the user the means to do the following:

1. Establish a session with another session entity, exchange data with that entity in a synchronized way, and release the session connection in an orderly manner.

2. Negotiate for the use of tokens to exchange data, synchronize and release the connection, and arrange for the data exchange to be half- or full-duplex.

3. Establish **synchronization points** within the dialogue, and in the case of errors, resume the dialogue from an agreed synchronization point.

4. Interrupt a dialogue and resume it later at a prearranged time.

The session protocol permits an explicit resynchronization at the end of each dialogue and enables the user to establish minor synchronization points within a dialogue. It provides the means for tokens to synchronize data exchange.

Each of the session services is achieved by invoking session primitives that are identified in Table 9.4.

The session is initiated in typical OSI fashion when a user process sends an S-CONNECT.request with parameters, i.e., destination **session service access point (SSAP)**, desired quality of service, and so on. The distant process receives an S-CONNECT.indication and, if it accepts the connect request, returns an S-CONNECT.response to its session layer. The original sender receives an S-CONNECT.confirm.

During normal data transfer, S-DATA.request commands result in data being passed down to the transport layer. If segmentation of user data is required, the session layer will segment it at the sender's end and reassemble it at the receiver's end. Also, tokens may be exchanged to provide the equivalent of half-duplex operation at the direction of the application layer user process.

TABLE 9.4   ISO 8326 Session Protocol Primitives

Service	Primitives
(a) Session connection establishment phase primitives	
Session connection	S-CONNECT.request S-CONNECT.indication S-CONNECT.response S-CONNECT.confirm
(b) Data transfer phase primitives	
Normal data transfer	S-DATA Request Indication
Expedited data transfer	S-EXPEDITED-DATA Request Indication
Typed data transfer	S-TYPED-DATA Request Indication
Capability data exchange	S-CAPABILITY-DATA Request Indication Response Confirm
Give tokens	S-TOKEN-GIVE Request Indication
Please tokens-	S-TOKEN-PLEASE Request Indication
Give control	S-CONTROL-GIVE Request Indication
Minor sync point	S-SYNC-MINOR Request Indication Response Confirm
Major sync point	S-SYNC-MAJOR Request Indication Response Confirm

(Reprinted with permission)

TABLE 9.4 (continued)   ISO 8326 Session Protocol Primitives

Service	Primitives

(b) Data transfer phase primitives

Service	Primitives
Resync	S-RESYNCHRONIZE Request Indication Response Confirm
P- exception report	S-P-EXCEPTION-REPORT Indication
U- exception reporting	S-U-EXCEPTION-REPORT Request Indication
Activity start	S-ACTIVITY-START Request Indication
Activity resume	S-ACTIVITY-RESUME Request Indication
Activity interrupt	S-ACTIVITY-INTERRUPT Request Indication Response Confirm
Activity discard	S-ACTIVITY-DISCARD Request Indication Response Confirm
Activity end	S-ACTIVITY-END Request Indication Response Confirm

(c) Session connection release phase primitives

Service	Primitives
Orderly release	S-RELEASE Request Indication Response Confirm
U-abort release	S-U-ABORT Request Indication
P-abort	S-P-ABORT Indication

Certain primitives carry a synchronization point serial number that may be used to identify a major or minor synchronization point. For example, the sender may issue an S-SYNC-MINOR.request that requests the receiver to acknowledge that a minor synchronization point has been reached. An S-SYNC-MAJOR.request is stronger; the sender will not send any more data until an S-SYNC-MAJOR.confirm is received.

Either end may terminate the session connection with an S-RELEASE.request command. The local user is given a corresponding S-ABORT.indication.

9.2.2 ISO 8327 Session Protocol

The ISO 8327 session protocol has a large variety of session protocol data units (SPDUs) to provide the services previously described. Figure 9.4 lists the SPDUs that may be sent on normal and expedited transport connections.

The SPDU structure is shown in Fig. 9.5a. By multiplexing, a transport protocol data unit may contain one or more SPDUs, as shown in Fig. 9.5b.

In Fig. 9.5a, the 1-octet *identifier (SI)* field identifies the type of SPDU and the 1-octet *length indicator (LI)* field indicates the length of the following *parameter* field. The *user information* field is not always required in an SPDU.

A DATA TRANSFER SPDU has SI = 1, LI = 1, and a data transfer parameter indicates that this SDPU is the beginning or end of the user record, if the record has been segmented. The user information field contains an integral number of octets.

In conclusion, the ISO 8327 session protocol has a wide variety of options to organize and synchronize information flow. There are 34 SPDUs (a large number), and their headers vary in length. The DATA TRANSFER SPDU has only a 3-octet header, although if certain options are selected, such as half-duplex operation or major synchronization, the impact on TRIB may be significant. The user has the option of selecting the types of service that are required.

9.3 SUMMARY

As we discussed in Chap. 2, the ultimate measure of performance is the transfer rate of information bits (TRIB). Each time that we have added a new layer of protocol—i.e., data link, network (including the internet sublayer), transport, and session—we have added more overhead and more time to the information-transfer period. Finally, however, with the transport and session layer, we have ensured that the users have a continuous, reliable, and synchronized communication service from one user process to another.

In conclusion, ISO 8073 provides five classes of service depending on the characteristics of the underlying network. It has nine types of TPDUs. The data transfer TPDU for class 4 service had a 7-octet header. DoD TCP has a header length of at least 20 octets. TCP and ISO 8073 Class 4 protocols provide almost

Normal Transport Connection	Expedited Data Connection
CONNECT	ABORT
ACCEPT	ABORT ACCEPT
REFUSE	EXPEDITED DATA
FINISH	PREPARE
DISCONNECT	
NOT FINISHED	
DATA TRANSFER	
TYPED DATA	
CAPABILITY	
CAPABILITY DATA JACK	
GIVE TOKENS	
PLEASE TOKENS	
GIVE TOKENS CONFIRM	
GIVE TOKENS ACK	
RESYNCHRONIZE	
RESYNCHRONIZE ACK	
EXCEPTION REPORT	
EXCEPTION DATA	
ACTIVITY START	
ACTIVITY RESUME	
ACTIVITY INTERRUPT	
ACTIVITY INTERRUPT ACK	
ACTIVITY DISCARD	
ACTIVITY DISCARD ACK	
ACTIVITY END	
ACTIVITY END ACK	
*ABORT	
*ABORT ACCEPT	

* If the transport expedited flow is not available, these
additional SPDUs are sent on the transport normal flow.

Figure 9.4 ISO 8327 SPDUs sent on the transport normal flow (Reprinted with permission)

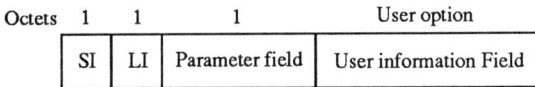

Octets	1	1	1	User option
	SI	LI	Parameter field	User information Field

(a) SPDU

Transport header	SPDU 1	SPDU 2	SPDU 3	SPDU 4

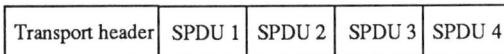

(b) Transport protocol data unit

Figure 9.5 ISO 8327 SPDU structure (Reprintes with permission)

the same service: reliable in-sequence delivery for data transmitted on unreliable networks.

The ISO 8327 session protocol has a wide variety of options to organize and synchronize information flow from the user process over the transport connection. The user has the option of selecting the level of service that is required. ISO 8327 has thirty-four SPDUs, tailored for each service, and their headers vary in length; the session data transfer header is only three octets.

KEY WORDS AND CONCEPTS

activity   session protocol data unit (SPDU)
dialogue   synchronization point
ISO 8073 connection-oriented mode   Transmission Control Protocol (TCP)
  transport protocol (TP)   transport connection
ISO 8327 session protocol   transport protocol data unit (TPDU)

PROBLEMS

1. Draw a diagram similar to Fig. 7.1 that shows the relative position of protocol headers for (a) DoD TCP/IP and (b) OSI session, transport, network, and data link protocols.

2. Compute TRIB for an Ethernet with TCP/IP and 500-Octet data field. Use Ethernet assumptions of Example 9.1, where there is one station transmitting. Assume no options field in TCP or IP and the destination is a local station on the same Ethernet.

3. DUNKNET subscribers (Probs. 6.12 and 7.6) use a transport layer protocol "DUNK-TRANS" with class 4 services, which has a 10-octet transport header.
   (a) For which of the following reasons is DUNKTRANS required? (You may choose more than one answer.)
      (i) To guarantee error-free transmission from end to end
      (ii) To pass messages on to LANs
      (iii) To ensure network does not fail
      (iv) To route messages from one node to another through the network
   (b) Assuming an application message with 150 octets of information, how long will the following be (in octets)?
      (i) DUNKTRANS transport segment
      (ii) DUNKNET network datagram
      (iii) DUNKLINK data link frame
   (c) When DUNKTRANS is used in the following network with a 150-octet message, what is TRIB once the transport connection is established? Assume full-duplex links and BER = 0. Ignore the host-to-node link.

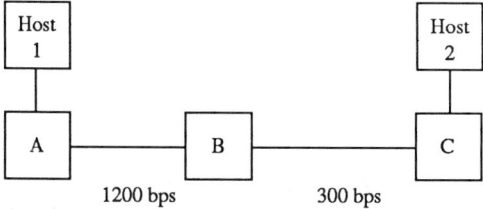

10

PRESENTATION LAYER
AND SECURITY

The presentation layer supports the local application layer by taking application-oriented data and putting it into a format suitable for transit to the distant peer application entity. It is responsible for the *syntax* of the data in transit.

For a user process that includes file transfer, it may compact and decompact the data. In some applications, where sensitive data is being transmitted on the same transport connection, encryption and decryption of data may take place in this layer.

In this chapter we introduce compaction algorithms and examine data encryption concepts. Data encryption is not isolated to the presentation layer. It may take place at the physical or data link layer through **data encryption equipment (DEE)** or at the transport or presentation layer through host software. We discuss the impact of data link encryption on performance. At the end of the chapter we discuss the OSI presentation protocol.

10.1 COMPACTION ALGORITHMS

When transmission capacity is an expensive resource, some applications may implement reversible data compaction that permits the sender to compact the data into a code that can be decompacted at the receiver. A measure of the degree of compaction is the **compression ratio:** the ratio of the bits before compaction to the number of bits after compaction.

$$R_{\text{compact}} = \frac{B_{\text{before}}}{B_{\text{after}}} \tag{10.1}$$

We will examine two different types of compaction algorithms. In one case, the goal is to compress the length of a string of fixed-length symbols. In the second case, the goal is to compress a file of binary data.

An example of the first type is **Huffman code,** where data symbols may be represented with *variable-length code*; common symbols are represented by short codes and infrequent symbols are given long codes. Huffman coding is advantageous when the data is represented by a finite set of fixed-length symbols, such as text messages or files transmitted in ASCII code.

Run-length coding may be used to encode long binary bit strings containing mostly zeros or mostly ones, where a great deal of the data is repetitive. It is useful with data that is not changing value rapidly, such as digitized analog data from slow scientific experiments or signals from facsimile machines or video.

10.1.1 Huffman Coding

In all text, some symbols occur more often than others. In the English language, the ten most frequent letters, digrams, and words, with their percents of occurrence, are shown in Table 10.1. It is one of the applications of Huffman code to reduce the length of a text file, for example, by representing the most frequently used characters with a short code, and the least-used characters with a long code. Note that the telegrapher's Morse code is also an example of a variable-length code; for example, $E = \{\,\cdot\,\}$, $T = \{-\}$, and $Z = \{--\cdot\cdot\}$.

In 1952, Huffman [36] published a procedure for encoding a set of statistically independent symbols in such a way as to yield the minimum average bit length per symbol.

To compute the Huffman code, the sending computer must first determine the frequency of occurrence of each different symbol. The coding procedure is demonstrated as follows:

TABLE 10.1 Percent Occurrence of Letters, Digrams, and Words in English

Letters		Digrams		Words	
E	13.0	TH	3.2	THE	4.7
T	9.0	IN	1.5	OF	4.0
O	8.2	ER	1.3	AND	3.2
A	7.8	RE	1.3	TO	2.4
N	7.3	AN	1.1	A	2.1
I	6.8	HE	1.1	IN	1.8
R	6.6	AR	1.0	THAT	1.2
S	6.5	EN	1.0	IS	1.0
H	5.8	TI	1.0	I	0.9
D	4.1	TE	1.0	IT	0.9
L	3.6	AT	0.9	FOR	0.8

Step 1.   Associate the probability of occurrence with each of *N* symbols to be represented. It simplifies things a little bit, when doing this manually, to write them in a row in descending order of probability.

Step 2.   Add together the two lowest probabilities, form a new row of probability nodes over the original row, and insert the sum on the new line. Draw branches to the lower probabilities. Repeat this step until there is only one node. Note that the probability associated with the last remaining node will be 1.0.

Step 3.   Assign a 1 to the left branch and a 0 to the right branch of each pair of lines. (It works just as well if the convention is reversed.)

Step 4.   Trace the path from the top node to each of the bottom nodes, recording the ones and zeros along the path, depending on whether the branches are to the right or left.

After computing the Huffman code for each symbol, the computer converts the data, one symbol at a time, to fill the information field of the frame. The resulting compressed symbols may not fall on octet boundaries. A table, or *map*, to translate the code back to the original symbols may be included in the initial transmission so that the code can be decompacted by the receiver. The software in the distant host will receive the mapping table and decompact the code, symbol by symbol.

EXAMPLE 10.1   Huffman coding

A message is to be prepared with only the letters A, B, C, and D. Find the Huffman code that should be used to represent each character when

$$A = 60\% \text{ occurrence}$$

$$B = 20\% \text{ occurrence}$$

$$C = 10\% \text{ occurrence}$$

$$D = 10\% \text{ occurrence}$$

Step 1

Step 2

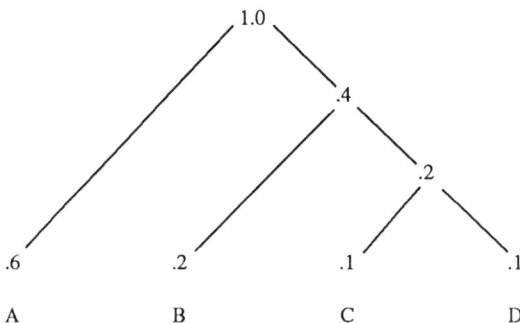

Step 3

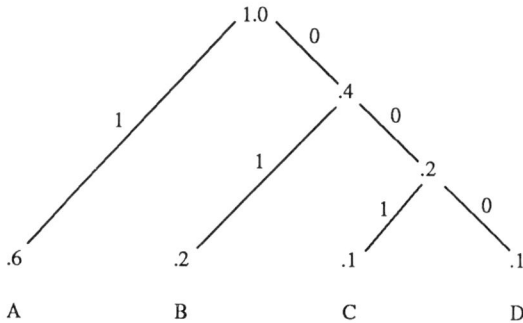

Step 4

$$A = 1$$
$$B = 01$$
$$C = 001$$
$$D = 000$$

To check this, out of 100 symbols, on the average,

$$\text{Total bits} = 60(1 \text{ bit}) + 20(2 \text{ bits})$$
$$+ 10(3 \text{ bits}) + 10(3 \text{ bits})$$
$$= 160 \text{ bits}$$

$$\text{Average bits per symbol} = \frac{(\text{total bits})}{(\text{number of symbols})}$$

$$= \frac{160}{100} = 1.6$$

When this code is compared with 7-bit ASCII code:

$$B_{\text{before}} = (7 \text{ bits/symbol})(100 \text{ symbols}) = 700 \text{ bits}$$

From Eq. 10.1,

$$R_{\text{compact}} = \frac{(700 \text{ bits})}{(160 \text{ bits})} = 4.38$$

If the user information is ABCDAAABAA, the encoded message is

$$1\;01\;001\;000\;1\;1\;1\;01\;1\;1$$

10.1.2 Run-Length Code

Run-length code is often used to encode long binary bit strings such as video or facsimile data. Basically, the number of identical successive bits are counted.

The count is coded into n-bit symbols and only the number is transmitted. If the string of identical bits is equal to or larger than $2^n - 1$ (the largest number per symbol), the symbol for $2^n - 1$ is followed by the symbol for the remainder.

EXAMPLE 10.2   Run-length code

Run-length code the following bit stream. Compress the zeroes and let the count symbol be 3 bits.

    User data:

```
0000001100000000100001000000000100001010100000000000000
        10000001
```

    Run-length coding:

```
110  000  111  000  100  111  001  101  001  001  111  111  000  110
```

    From Eq. 10.1,

$$R_{\text{compact}} = \frac{62 \text{ bits}}{42 \text{ bits}} = 1.48$$

10.2 SECURITY

The goal of security is to protect the confidentiality and integrity of data. Security is becoming increasingly important in military, government, banking, and corporate activities. An adversary frequently has access to the physical medium, especially in microwave and radio transmission. When the transmission medium is exposed, the adversary may seek to read or modify the data.

    In general, security requires the following:

1. Protection of the message against unauthorized disclosure
2. Protection of the message against unauthorized modification
3. Protection of the message against undetected loss or repetition
4. Assurance of the correct identity of the sender
5. Assurance of the correct receiver of the data

    Security can be applied at the physical, data link, transport layer, or presentation layer. The only national standards relate to encryption at the physical and data link layers and are specified in ANSI X3.105, discussed later.

10.2.1 Encryption of Data

Encryption is the process of converting text or symbols into unintelligible symbols based on a set of predetermined rules. The original message, called **plaintext,** is converted into a form called **ciphertext** (Fig. 10.1). Decrypting converts ciphertext back to the original plaintext. These operations are based on specific parameters that are stored in an encryption key. In digital communications, the key is a binary string.

In some cases (for additional security), both the encryption algorithm and key are closely guarded secrets. In others, only the key is secret.

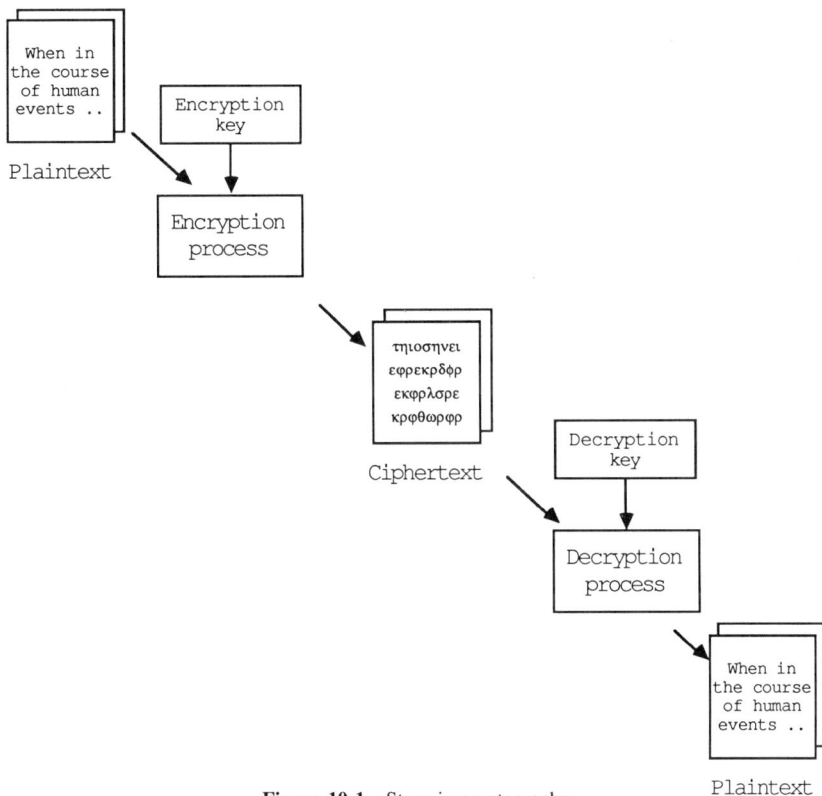

Figure 10.1   Steps in cryptography

10.2.1.1 Substitution codes.   Encryption algorithms based on **substitution codes** are the oldest known methods of coding. The technique replaces data in a message with some other symbols in a systematic way. *Monoalphabetic substitution* replaces each symbol with another from the same ordered set.

Caesar's Cipher.   For example, *Caesar's cipher* shifts the alphabet by three letters and uses the new alphabet to convert the message.

Original alphabet: ABCDEFGHI J KLMNOPQRS TUVWXYZ
                     | | | | | | | | | | | | | | | | | | | | | | | | | |
Substitute: DEFGHI JKLMNO PQRSTUVWXY Z ABC

Plaintext: ATTACK AT DAWN
Ciphertext: DWWDFN DW GDZQ

The number 3 is a key to encrypting and decrypting the text. An improvement is to shift the position of the letters in the alphabet by some variable number, such as 5, for the duration of the message, with the number known only to the sender and receiver.

Another monoalphabetic cipher is to have 26 letters map into 26 letters in a less systematic way, such as:

Original alphabet: ABCDE F GHI J KLMNOPQRS TUVWXYZ
                     | | | | | | | | | | | | | | | | | | | | | | | | | |
Substitute: CGKOSW AE IMQU Y B F J NRVZDH L PTX

Plaintext: ATTACKATDAWN
Ciphertext: CZZCKQCZOCLB

Unfortunately, if the language of the text is known, the encryption method is fairly easily broken by applying the frequency of occurrence of letters and words in that language (Table 10.1).

In *polyalphabetic substitution*, each symbol conversion comes from a revised ordering of the substitute alphabet. The *Vigenere code* is an example of a polyalphabetic substitution cipher. It was published by its inventor in A.D. 1586. It has 26 ordered alphabets as shown in Table 10.2. A secret alphabetic key is chosen to select the appropriate alphabet for each character of a message. The plaintext is encrypted according to the alphabet on the row corresponding to letters of the key. It is extremely important to synchronize the message and the code key.

EXAMPLE 10.3   Vigenere code

Encrypt ATTACKATDAWN with the key *PACIFIC* using Vigenere code.
The first letter of plaintext is *A*. The substitution alphabet is Row *P*, the first letter of PACIFIC, and *A* translates to a *P* with that alphabet. The process is repeated with subsequent letters of the message.

Plaintext: ATTACKATDAWN
               | | | | | | | | | | | |
Key: PAC I F ICPAC I F
               | | | | | | | | | | | |
Ciphertext: P TV I HUC IDC E S

TABLE 10.2 Vigenere Code

Row	A	A B C D E F G H I J K L M N O P Q R S T U V W X Y Z
Row	B	B C D E F G H I J K L M N O P Q R S T U V W X Y Z A
Row	C	C D E F G H I J K L M N O P Q R S T U V W X Y Z A B
Row	D	D E F G H I J K L M N O P Q R S T U V W X Y Z A B C
Row	E	E F G H I J K L M N O P Q R S T U V W X Y Z A B C D
Row	F	F G H I J K L M N O P Q R S T U V W X Y Z A B C D E
Row	G	G H I J K L M N O P Q R S T U V W X Y Z A B C D E F
Row	H	H I J K L M N O P Q R S T U V W X Y Z A B C D E F G
Row	I	I J K L M N O P Q R S T U V W X Y Z A B C D E F G H
Row	J	J K L M N O P Q R S T U V W X Y Z A B C D E F G H I
Row	K	K L M N O P Q R S T U V W X Y Z A B C D E F G H I J
Row	L	L M N O P Q R S T U V W X Y Z A B C D E F G H I J K
Row	M	M N O P Q R S T U V W X Y Z A B C D E F G H I J K L
Row	N	N O P Q R S T U V W X Y Z A B C D E F G H I J K L M
Row	O	O P Q R S T U V W X Y Z A B C D E F G H I J K L M N
Row	P	P Q R S T U V W X Y Z A B C D E F G H I J K L M N O
Row	Q	Q R S T U V W X Y Z A B C D E F G H I J K L M N O P
Row	R	R S T U V W X Y Z A B C D E F G H I J K L M N O P Q
Row	S	S T U V W X Y Z A B C D E F G H I J K L M N O P Q R
Row	T	T U V W X Y Z A B C D E F G H I J K L M N O P Q R S
Row	U	U V W X Y Z A B C D E F G H I J K L M N O P Q R S T
Row	V	V W X Y Z A B C D E F G H I J K L M N O P Q R S T U
Row	W	W X Y Z A B C D E F G H I J K L M N O P Q R S T U V
Row	X	X Y Z A B C D E F G H I J K L M N O P Q R S T U V W
Row	Y	Y Z A B C D E F G H I J K L M N O P Q R S T U V W X
Row	Z	Z A B C D E F G H I J K L M N O P Q R S T U V W X Y

EXAMPLE 10.4   ENIGMA machine

During World War II, the Germans used an encryption machine called the ENIGMA for military encryption that was based on polyalphabetic substitution. The original machine was invented and patented in Holland in 1919 and appeared as a complicated typewriter. Messages were converted character by character as three rotors with 26 positions turned much like an odometer (although in a more complex way) to advance the adjacent rotors and select the substitute characters. The initial rotor positions were coded in the message header, which was a weak point exploited by the Polish, French, and British cryptoanalysts.

10.2.1.2 Transposition codes.

Transposition codes permute, or reorder, the message symbols but do not disguise them. In transposition, the common letters of the alphabet will still occur most often. The message is broken by finding a probable key, rearranging the message, and then looking for a probable word.

One transposition coding method is to write a plaintext message aligned under a key word and wrap text around if the message exceeds the length of the key.

Filler is added at the end to complete the message. Columns of characters may then be transmitted. The columns are transmitted in the order of the alphabetic sequence of the key.

EXAMPLE 10.5   Transposition code

Encrypt the message THE ENEMY IS EAST TEN KM.
The plaintext is written out in rows under the key *JOURNEY* and extra characters are added at the end of the message to complete the row.

$$
\begin{array}{ccccccc}
\text{Key:} & J & O & U & R & N & E & Y \\
& T & H & E & E & N & E & M \\
& Y & I & S & E & A & S & T \\
& T & E & N & K & M & K & K \\
\end{array}
$$

The coded text is formed by transmitting the columns under the key, with the lowest letter in the alphabet E , followed by J, N, O, etc.

Plaintext: THEENEMYISEASTTENKM
Ciphertext: ESKTYTNAMHIEEEKESNMTK

10.2.1.3 Data Encryption Standard.   Substitution and transposition codes have their weaknesses, especially with the availability of computer analysis. This has led to the development of **product ciphers** that combine a series of substitutions and transpositions into the encryption algorithm.

In 1977 NIST, the former National Bureau of Standards, published the **Data Encryption Standard (DES)** a Federal encryption algorithm for unclassified, but sensitive, information. ANSI adopted it as a national standard, known as the Data Encryption Algorithm (DEA). One of the objectives in its development was to make it available to users and suppliers. The encryption algorithm is public knowledge; therefore, the security of the data depends completely on the security of the key. As such, it facilitates interoperability, because users with equipment from different vendors can interoperate with the same key.

DES is designed to encrypt and decrypt 64-bit blocks of data using a 64-bit key. The key is structured into octets, and each octet consists of seven key bits and one parity (odd) bit for error detection. The same key is used for encryption and decryption; therefore, each member of a group of authorized users must have the key that was used to encrypt the data in order to decrypt it. It has been calculated [23] that it would take 228 million years to test all possible keys (at a rate of one test every .100 ms). This demonstrates the importance of the security of the key.

DES is called a product cipher because it computes ciphertext in a sequence of transpositions and substitutions. The fundamental components are *P-boxes* and *S-boxes*. A P-box permutes bits and an *S-box* substitutes.

An S-box takes a binary number and substitutes another. In DES, the S-boxes have 6-bit inputs and 4-bit outputs. In base 2, two bits (the first and last) are taken together to point to a row of the substitution matrix. The other four bits

TABLE 10.3 Sample DES S-box Table

		Column $\rightarrow$															
R		0	1	2	3	4	5	6	7	8	9	10	11	12	13	14	15
o																	
w	0	14	4	13	1	2	15	11	8	3	10	6	12	5	9	0	7
$\downarrow$	1	0	15	7	4	14	2	13	1	10	6	2	11	9	5	3	8
	2	4	1	14	8	13	6	2	11	15	12	9	7	3	10	5	0
	3	15	12	8	2	4	9	1	7	5	11	3	14	10	0	6	13

point to the column. For example, using the sample table from DES (Table 10.3), 101100 (row 2, column 6) becomes 0010 (decimal 2).

The P-box (Fig. 10.2) permutes the position of bits in an ordered manner. Note that if three bits are logical 1s before the operation, three are logical 1s afterward.

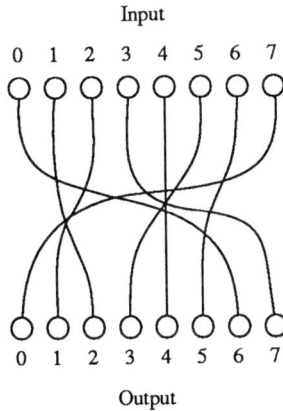

Figure 10.2 An 8-bit P-box

In DES, the 64 bits of the input block are first permuted. The resultant block is then subjected to 16 iterations of a set of permutations and substitutions whose output depends on the key. Each iteration involves a different subset of bits from the key. The output goes through a final permutation which is the inverse of the initial permutation.

10.2.2 Data Link Encryption

The characteristics of a DEE configured between the DTE and a DCE (Fig. 10.3) are defined in ANSI X.3.105. There are two types: one operates at the physical layer on raw bits and the other at the data link layer, interfacing to the link protocol. DEE may be implemented as stand-alone equipment or may be integrated with the DTE or DCE.

The DEE must appear functionally transparent to the DTE and DCE. Its electrical and physical parameters, including the signaling rate, must be the same

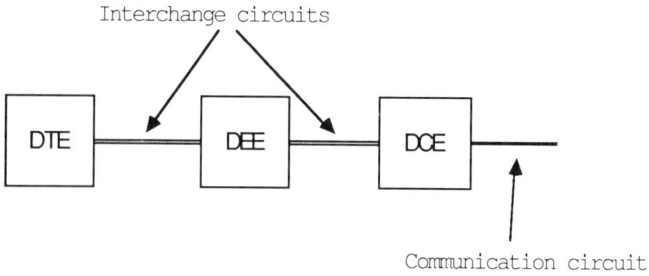

(a) DTE/DEE/DCE schematic

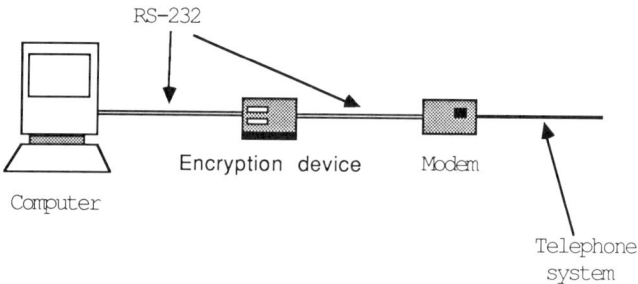

(b) Computer-to-telephone system example

Figure 10.3 Configuration of a link-encrypted circuit

as the associated DTE/DCE. The pin voltages for establishing readiness must also be the same at the interface connector.

If the DEE operates at the physical layer, it encrypts all bits (except the start and stop bits in asynchronous traffic). A data link layer DEE may encrypt the full frame (*full-frame encryption*) or just the information field (*I-field encryption*). In *full-frame encryption,* the DEE encrypts all bits after the flag in a bit-oriented protocol and follows the SOH symbol, or its equivalent, in a character-oriented protocol. It may encrypt many frames in succession. In I-field encryption, encryption is turned on and off for each frame.

10.2.2.1 Data format.   The DES-based DEE that we discuss next operates in a *cipher feedback (CFB)* mode. CFB logically combines a certain number of bits of DEE-generated ciphertext with the plaintext input each time 64 bits are entered into the input stage of the DEE. An unencrypted variable, or **initialization**

vector (IV), is first transmitted from the sender to receiver's DEE to compensate for the initial lack of feedback. Therefore, the IV must precede ciphertext in a transmission to a distant DEE. Note that the CFB process will cause any bit errors in transmission to extend into other data because the deciphering process is combining plaintext output and ciphertext input into its input stage. The extent of bit errors depends on the number of feedback bits involved in the CFB.

With a physical layer DEE, the IV is transmitted after the DTE sends a request-to-send signal through the DEE and the DCE returns with a clear-to-send signal. Note that this will occur once after the circuit is established with a simplex or full-duplex link. With a half-duplex link, whose direction is controlled by the request-to-send pin, the IV will be constantly retransmitted. When transmitting encrypted 8-bit characters, such as with asynchronous traffic, the DEE initially sends a 6-octet IV. The DEE then encrypts the 8 bits between the start and stop bit of each character (Fig. 10.4). In synchronous traffic, a 64-bit IV follows the request-to-send/clear-to-send procedure.

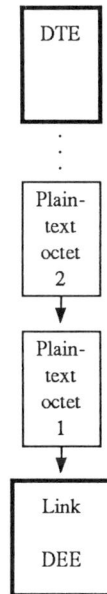

(a) DTE-DEE communication

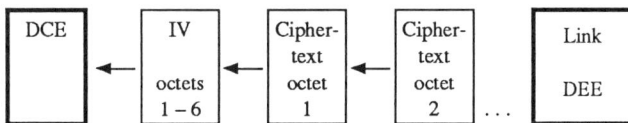

(a) DEE-DCE communication

Figure 10.4 Asynchronous physical layer encryption

In I-field encryption, (Fig. 10.5) the DEE is tailored to the particular link protocol and is capable of determining the start and stop of the information field. The DEE must maintain transparency so that bit patterns in the encrypted data are not confused with control symbols. For example, with bit-oriented protocols, the DEE uses bit stuffing in the I-field output.

10.2.2.2 Performance.   At the sending DTE, plaintext is transferred to the DEE at the signaling rate (Fig. 10.4a). Because of delays in initializing, buffering and flow control are required to keep the DTE from overwhelming the DEE at the beginning of encryption. At the opposite end of the link, after receiving the IV and ciphertext, the DEE delays output to the DTE for asynchronous traffic while decrypting. Once the DEEs are in synchronization they are encrypting and decrypting at the DTE output rate, and TRIB is not impacted.

The information transfer time will increase because of the added time to transmit the initialization vector. With physical layer encryption, an IV is sent once at the beginning of transmission on a link. For asynchronous traffic, this is a 6-octet string. If the link is simplex or full-duplex, the impact on TRIB is minimal. On half-duplex links it will be more significant because IV must be transmitted each time the link changes direction.

For synchronous traffic, a 64-bit IV is sent at the beginning of the encryption period. Full-frame encryption can cover many frames so the impact may be minimal. However, an IV must be sent for every frame in I-field encryption.

For I-field encryption, the information transfer time will include the time to transmit the bit-stuffed frame, including the IV, plus the delays at each end to initialize encryption and decryption. In particular,

$$t_{\text{eachframe}} = t_{\text{oneframe}} + 2t_{\text{proc}} \tag{10.2}$$

where

$t_{\text{oneframe}} = $ time to transmit one bit-stuffed frame with the IV

$t_{\text{proc}} = $ DEE processing time

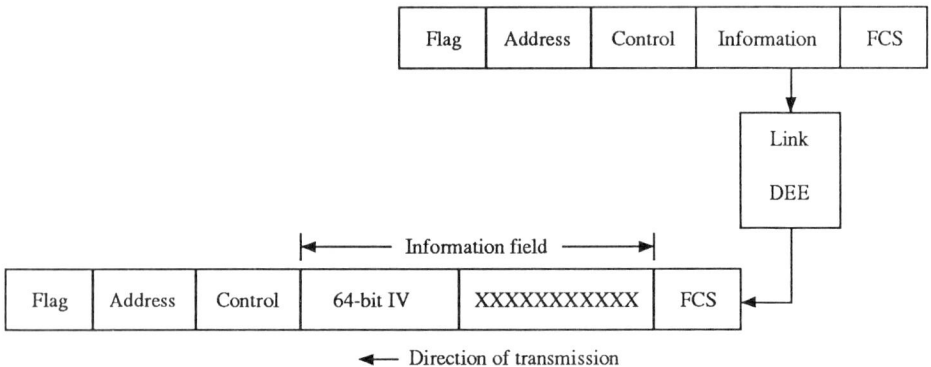

Figure 10.5 Data link layer I-field encryption

EXAMPLE 10.6 Compute TRIB for I-frame encryption

Compute TRIB when sending a file of 65,500 octets using LAPB I-field encryption on an error-free 2400-bps link, similar to Example 6.5a. Assume that an X.25 128-octet packet is buried in the I-field and include the impact of the network headers on TRIB (Fig. 10.6). For simplicity, ignore acknowledgments.

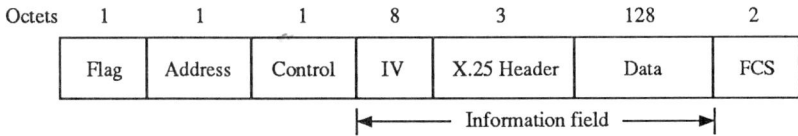

Octets	1	1	1	8	3	128	2
	Flag	Address	Control	IV	X.25 Header	Data	FCS

$\longleftarrow$ Information field $\longrightarrow$

Figure 10.6   I-field encryption with LAPB

Assume:

1. DEE processing time = .040 sec
2. $F_{\text{bit stuff}}$ = 1.02
3. n_{IV} = 64 bits
4. t_{ACK} = 0 s

$$\text{Number of frames} = \frac{(65,500 \text{ octets})}{(128 \text{ octets/frame})}$$

$$= 512 \text{ frames}$$

$$n_{\text{info}} = (8 \text{ bits/octet})(65,500 \text{ octets})$$

$$= 524,000 \text{ bits}$$

$$n_{\text{oneframe}} = (8 \text{ bits/octet})(144 \text{ octets/frame})*1.02$$

$$= 1175 \text{bits}$$

$$t_{\text{oneframe}} = \frac{(1175 \text{ bits})}{(2400 \text{ bps})}$$

$$= .490 \text{ s}$$

From Eq. 10.2,

$$t_{\text{eachframe}} = t_{\text{oneframe}} + 2t_{\text{proc}}$$

$$= .490 \text{ s} + 2(.040 \text{ s}) = .570 \text{ s}$$

$$t_3 = (512 \text{ frames})*(.570 \text{ s/frame}) = 292 \text{ sec}$$

$$\text{TRIB} = \frac{n_{\text{info}}}{t_3}$$

$$= \frac{(524,000 \text{ bits})}{(292 \text{ s})} = 1795 \text{ bps}$$

Note the 18% decrease in TRIB from Example 6.5a. Three factors are involved: There are only 128 true information octets in the frame; the LAPB I-field is 8 octets longer because of the IV; and there is a minor delay as the DEE processes the IV.

10.3 OSI PRESENTATION LAYER

The **ISO 8823 presentation protocol** provides the application layer with a service to transform the application data units into a format, or *syntax*, more suitable for transmission.

The OSI presentation protocol relates the application-unique syntax (the **abstract syntax**) to the syntax that will be used in transmission (the **transfer syntax**). We have discussed several transfer syntaxes already, including ASCII code, Hamming code, compression code, and encrypted code. OSI gives the mapping of the abstract syntax to transfer syntax the name **presentation context**. For example, the application data may have certain fields that are character strings. The specification of the structure of the application record and field type, in this case, "octet string," defines the abstract syntax. Abstract Syntax Notation One (ASN.1) [58] provides a standard notation for abstract syntax definition and ISO 8825 provides standard encoding rules.

ISO 8823 allows the user to alter the presentation context (both the abstract syntax and transfer syntax) at synchronization points in the session activity. For example, if the user wishes to use a Huffman encoder to compress the octet strings, ISO 8823 permits negotiation at synchronization points to alter the context—in this case, to associate a different transfer context (binary Huffman code instead of straight ASCII) with the abstract syntax.

10.3.1 Presentation Operation

ISO 8823 builds on the services of the OSI session protocol by organizing the syntax transformation process around session activities. For example, changes in presentation contexts may be altered at major and minor synchronization points or through the possession of tokens. Note that ISO 8823 does not define any particular transfer syntaxes or algorithms – these are defined by the user as separate entities.

Table 10.4 lists the presentation primitives.

TABLE 10.4   ISO 8823 Presentation Service Primitives

P-CONNECT	Request
	Indication
	Response
	Confirm
P-RELEASE	Request
	Indication
	Response
	Confirm
P-U-ABORT	Request
	Indication
P-P-ABORT	Indication
P-ALTER-CONTEXT	Request
	Indication
	Response
	Confirm
P-TYPED-DATA	Request
	Indication
P-DATA	Request
	Indication
P-EXPEDITED-DATA	Request
	Indication
P-CAPABILITY-DATA	Request
	Indication
	Response
	Confirm
P-TOKEN-GIVE	Request
	Indication
P-TOKEN-PLEASE	Request
	Indication
P-CONTROL-GIVE	Request
	Indication
P-SYNC-MINOR	Request
	Indication
	Response
	Confirm

(Reprinted with permission)

TABLE 10.4 (continued)   ISO 8823 Presentation Service Primitives

P-SYNC- MAJOR	Request Indication Response Confirm
P- RESYNCHRONIZE	Request Indication Response Confirm
P-U- EXCEPTION- REPORT	Request Indication
P-P- EXCEPTION- REPORT	Indication
P-ACTIVITY- START	Request Indication
P-ACTIVITY- RESUME	Request Indication
P-ACTIVITY- END	Request Indication
P-ACTIVITY- INTERRUPT	Request Indication Response Confirm
P-ACTIVITY- DISCARD	Request Indication Response Confirm

10.3.2 ISO 8823 Presentation Protocol

Application software uses the primitives that were listed in Table 10.4 to obtain the services of the presentation layer. In turn, the presentation entity carries out the commands through **presentation protocol data units (PPDUs)** identified in Table 10.5.

The protocol assumes the use of the ISO 8327 session protocol, and it is structured in much the same way in terms of connection establishment, data transfer, and connection termination.

The *alter context (AC) PPDU* is unique to the presentation protocol. It is used to modify the currently defined presentation context. AC PPDU lets the sender negotiate with the receiver and determine the availability of new context definitions in the defined context set.

TABLE 10.5   ISO 8823 PPDUs

Code	PPDU Name
CP	Connect presentation
CPA	Connect presentation accept
CPR	Connect presentation reject
ARU	Abnormal release user
ARP	Abnormal release provider
AC	Alter context
ACA	Alter context acknowledge
TTD	Presentation typed data
TD	Presentation data
TE	Expedited data
TC	Capability data
TCC	Capability data acknowledge
RS	Resynchronize
RSA	Resynchronize acknowledge

When a local presentation entity receives a P-ALTER-CONTEXT.request from the application layer, it sends an AC PPDU to the distant presentation entity with the information and proposed parameters necessary for defining the contexts. For example, before the local presentation entity compresses data by some algorithm, it notifies the distant end to ensure that the destination entity is able to decompress it. If the distant entity can support the new context definitions, it will respond with an *alter context acknowledge (ACA)* PPDU. The originating entity will pass a P-ALTER CONTEXT.confirm to the application layer.

10.4 SUMMARY

Data compression is effective in reducing communication costs because more information is transmitted per unit time. Huffman code compacts a string of fixed-length symbols, and run-length codes are useful for long binary strings.

Security is an important issue. The simplest network security measures are those that restrict access to the computers. In the OSI architecture, this may be supplemented at the session layer by using passwords during log-on. However, encryption is possible at the physical, data link, transport, and presentation layers.

At the transport and presentation layers, software encryption coders and decoders may be user-provided. Commercial devices that use the DES are available for encrypting data on the physical circuits. One type is a physical layer DEE that encrypts all bits (except asynchronous start and stop bits). Other types operate at the data link layer and may encrypt the full frame or only the information field.

The presentation layer takes application-oriented data and puts it in a format more suitable for transit to a distant application process. These coding formats may include compaction and encryption. The ISO 8823 presentation protocol provides the capability for incorporating these services, although it does not provide them itself.

KEY WORDS AND CONCEPTS

abstract syntax
ciphertext
compression ratio
Data Encryption Equipment (DEE)
Data Encryption Standard (DES)
encryption
Huffman code
initialization vector
ISO 8823 presentation protocol
key

plaintext
presentation context
presentation protocol data unit
   (PPDU)
product cipher
run-length code
substitution code
transfer syntax
transposition code

PROBLEMS

1. The following grades were found in the gradebook of a class of 300 students with the stated probability of occurrence:

$$A\ (.1)$$

$$B\ (.2)$$

$$C\ (.5)$$

$$D\ (.1)$$

$$F\ (.1)$$

   (a) Determine the Huffman code for each grade.
   (b) Determine the average bits per character.
   (c) Compute the compaction ratio, and compare this with ASCII code.
2. Determine Huffman code for characters in this sentence. Start with "D" and end with ".".
3. Run-length encode the zeros in the following data with 4-bit symbols and compute the compaction ratio:

        1001000010000000000101100000000010110
         1000000000000000000011000001

4. Determine the optimum symbol length for run-length coding the data in Prob. 3; that is, which symbol length gives the highest compaction ratio?

5. THISISASAMPLE became KVCFLTADLDDFRD using either a substitution code (Vigenere code) or a transposition code. Which code was it and what is the 9-character key?

6. A transposition code output is ENFKWESEMEDRYKIE and the key is SURF. What was the plaintext?

7. The following is an electronic S-box. The 3-bit input, treated as a binary number, is converted to a 3-bit output. Show the substitution table for this S-box.

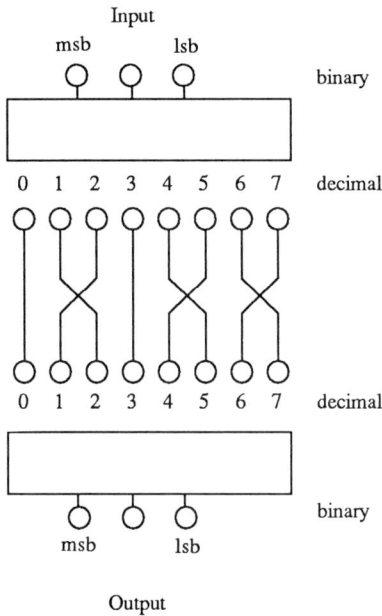

Output

8. Compute TRIB for an error-free 4800-bps link with I-frame DES encryption. Assume each frame is acknowledged individually with an RR packet, as in Example 6.5a. Assume that an X.25 128-octet packet is buried in the I-field (Fig. 10.6). Also assume:

$$\text{Number of frames} = 500$$

$$\text{DEE processing time} = .040 \text{ s}$$

$$F_{\text{bitstuff}} = 1.05$$

$$n_{\text{IV}} = 8 \text{ octets}$$

11

APPLICATION LAYER

Application layer protocols are available for user processes to access all of the services that we have described in this text. Standard protocols that are normally used in a networking environment, such as electronic mail and file transfer, have been standardized for proprietary, OSI, and DoD architectures. In the following section, we discuss the OSI and DoD application layer protocols.

We also summarize, and conclude, the open systems concept in this chapter.

11.1 OSI APPLICATION LAYER STANDARDS

The OSI application layer is comprised of a number of entities known as **service elements.** Some elements, such as electronic mail and file transfer protocols, provide unique services to network users. These entities are known as **specific application service elements (SASEs).** Another type of service element is the **common application service element (CASE);** an entity such as this provides general supporting services to SASEs. An example of a CASE is the abstract syntax notation standard ASN.1 that was briefly referred to in Chap. 10. CASE service elements are also available to establish logical connections between two SASE entities prior to their carrying out their specific application function, and are called the *association control service elements (ACSEs).* Note that with ACSEs, the OSI application layer has the connection-oriented features that characterize the lower layers. Two OSI SASEs are the **Message Handling Service (MHS)** and **File Transfer, Access and Management (FTAM)** protocols. These are directly comparable to DoD protocols.

11.1.1 Message Handling Service

MHS is specified in the CCITT X.400-series Recommendations. MHS enables OSI users to exchange messages on a store-and-forward basis, utilizing intermediate hosts in the network called *message transfer agents (MTAs)*. The MTAs accept, relay, and deliver the messages to the destination users.

A *user* in the system may be either a person or a computer process. The computer program that interfaces between the user and the message transfer system is an application layer entity called the *user agent (UA)*. An originator generates the message using the UA, and the UA interacts with the MTAs to deliver the message to the intended recipient(s). The collection of UAs and MTAs is called the *message handling system*.

The UA submits the contents of the message (Fig. 11.1) and the equivalent

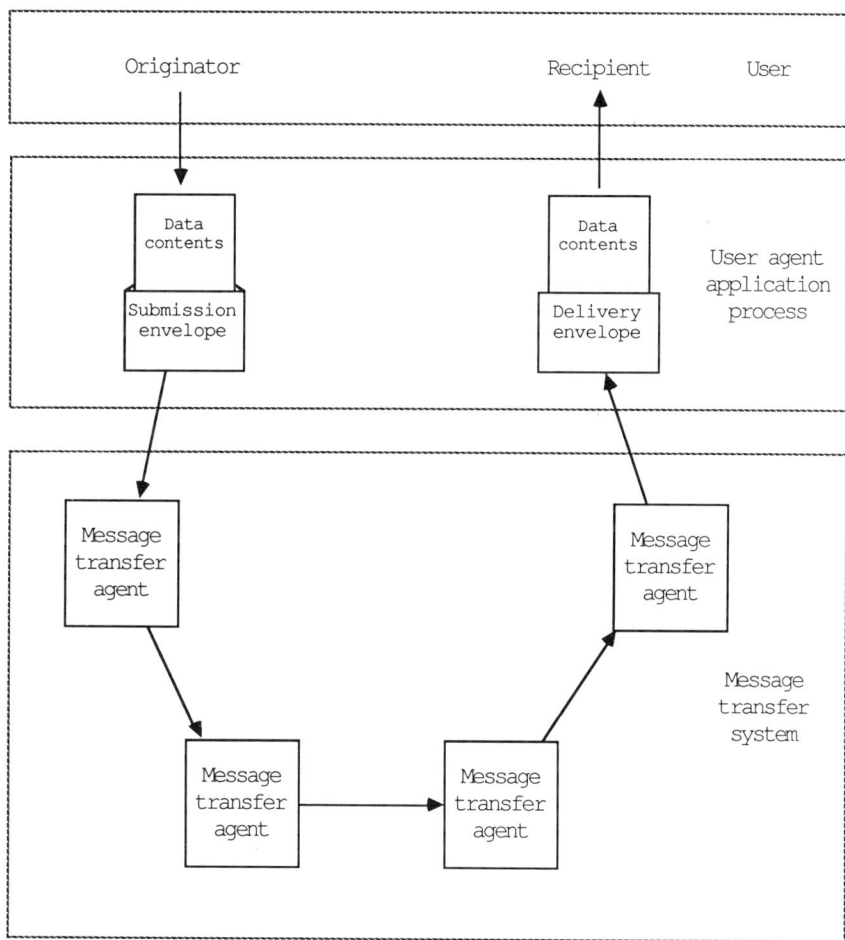

Figure 11.1   X.400 message handling system message flow

of a *submission envelope* with instructions to the local MTA (this may be the same computer, only different user programs). The envelope is the means for exchanging instructions. The envelope becomes a *relay envelope* in the transition between MTAs and a *delivery envelope* between the destination MTA and its UA.

The message-handling protocols are located in the application layer. ACSE and underlying layers establish connections between individual systems to transfer the messages reliably. The underlying network is assumed to be X.25 with a class 0 transport service.

11.1.2 File Transfer, Access and Management

FTAM, specified in ISO 8571, supports transfer and modification of file data through a network where the individual hosts may have different methods of describing and accessing data. FTAM assumes that each FTAM participant has the same type of imaginary file server, a *virtual filestore*. The characteristics of the individual host servers are mapped into the virtual filestores (Fig. 11.2). Commands that are sent between hosts all have the same structure and act on the virtual filestores.

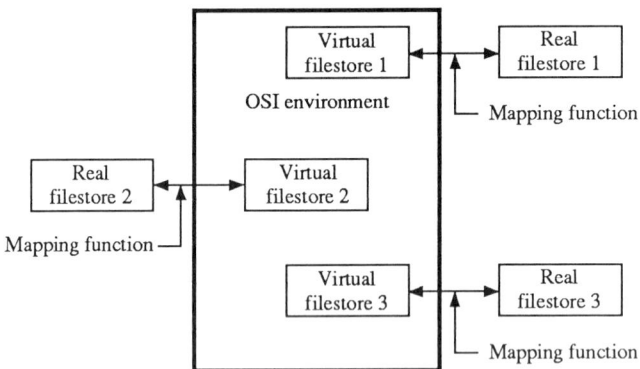

Figure 11.2 FTAM mapping between real and virtual filestores

As a simple illustration, in Fig. 11.2, real filestores exist in systems 1, 2, and 3. Their filenames, attributes, and so on, are mapped into virtual filestores that are readily manipulated by FTAM file service primitives. When system 1 initiates a file activity (as the *initiator*), it interacts with FTAM software in system 2 (the *responder*).

Within each filestore may be a number of files; each file has

1. A single filename.
2. Other descriptive file attributes, which express properties of the file such as accounting information and history.

3. File attributes expressing the actions capable of being performed on the file.

4. File attributes describing the logical structure and dimensions of the data stored in the file.

5. File access data units forming the contents of the file.

The list of FTAM primitives that may manipulate the data units in a file are contained in Table 11.1. The use of each primitive is subject to access control by the responder. The primitive's action may also be limited because of parallel activities occurring at the same time. For example, a certain file may not be read until a current update is complete.

TABLE 11.1   ISO 8571 FTAM Primitives

Primitive	Confirmed	Requested by
File Service Primitives		
F-INITIALIZE	Yes	Initiator
F-TERMINATE	Yes	Initiator
F-U-ABORT	Yes	Either
F-P-ABORT	No	Provider
F-SELECT	No	Initiator
F-DESELECT	Yes	Initiator
F-CREATE	Yes	Initiator
F-DELETE	Yes	Initiator
F-READ-ATTRIB	Yes	Initiator
F-CHANGE-ATTRIB	Yes	Initiator
F-OPEN	Yes	Initiator
F-CLOSE	Yes	Initiator
F-BEGIN-GROUP	Yes	Initiator
F-END-GROUP	Yes	Initiator
F-RECOVER	Yes	Initiator
F-LOCATE	Yes	Initiator
F-ERASE	Yes	Initiator
Bulk Data Transfer Service Primitives		
F-READ	No	Initiator
F-WRITE	No	Initiator
F-DATA	No	Sender
F-DATA-END	No	Sender
F-TRANSFER-END	Yes	Initiator
F-CANCEL	Yes	Either
F-CHECK	Yes	Sender
F-RESTART	Yes	Either

(Reprinted with permission)

In summary, both X.400 and FTAM provide specific services to application layer processes utilizing the connection-oriented service of ACSE and lower layers of the OSI model. They have an interface that maps their functions into local system-specific electronic mail and filestore systems and are both applicable to heterogeneous networks.

11.2 DoD INTERNET APPLICATION LAYER STANDARDS

Several of the major DoD application layer standards are summarized next, including **TELNET, File Transfer Protocol (FTP),** and **Simple Mail Transfer Protocol (SMTP).** Each of these protocols depends on underlying TCP transport connections.

11.2.1 TELNET

TELNET is a virtual terminal protocol that interfaces terminal devices and terminal-oriented processes to each other. A TELNET connection is basically a TCP connection used to transmit user information and TELNET control information. TELNET is built on the concept of a *network virtual terminal (NVT)*, an imaginary device that provides a common network terminal to all user processes. NVTs eliminate the need for users and servers to keep a record of the characteristics of the terminals at the destination host. When a TELNET connection is first established, each end is assumed to originate and terminate at an NVT.

The virtual terminal is a half-duplex ASCII character-oriented device and has a printer and a keyboard. All real terminals are mapped by the TELNET implementation into or out of this imaginary terminal.

11.2.2 File Transfer Protocol

DoD created FTP in the early 1970s to support the transfer of file data among the subscribers of the DoD Internet. FTP assumes that the participating network files have few attributes, and it uses a set of well-defined commands and replies. The command and reply mechanism is used to establish the parameters for a file transfer and then to actually initiate the transfer. FTP uses TCP/IP services. FTP, although usable directly by a user at a terminal, is designed mainly for use by user programs.

FTP utilizes two TCP connections, a *control* connection and a *data* connection. Files are transferred over the data connection (Fig. 11.3).

In FTP, the user initiates the control connection through TELNET. Commands are entered by the user and transmitted to the file server by this control connection, and standard replies are returned by the file server to the user.

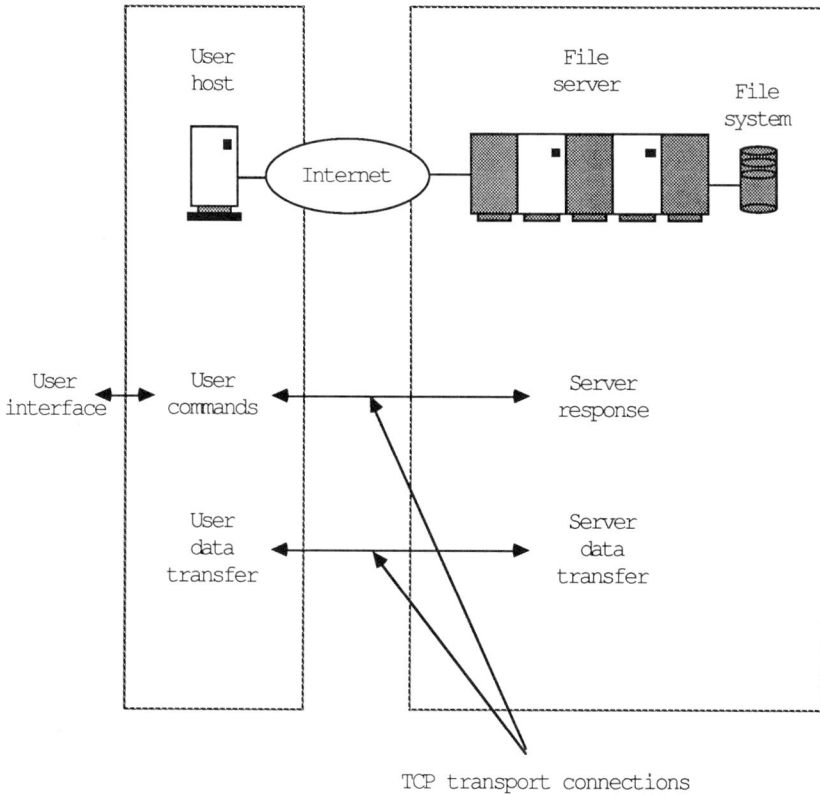

Figure 11.3 FTP functional diagram

FTP commands (Table 11.2) are entered by the user and include a string of parameters. For example, the USER command will include user identification required by the server for access into its file system. Additional identification provided in the form of a password or an account command may also be required by some servers. The file server opens the data port to the designated user process in accordance with the specified parameters. The user data port need not be in the same host that the user uses to initiate commands to the FTP.

11.2.3 Simple Mail Transfer Protocol

One of the important functions of the DoD Internet is support of electronic mail. SMTP can be used to send mail directly from one host to another or via intermediate hosts. It is based on TCP connections (Fig. 11.4).

The sender SMTP module initially establishes a transport connection to a receiver SMTP module with a hello (HELO) command, and the sender identifies

TABLE 11.2   FTP Command List

Code	Commands
Access Control Commands	
USER	User name
PASS	Password
ACCT	Account
REIN	Reinitialize
QUIT	Logout
Transfer Parameter Commands	
PORT	Data port
PASV	Passive
TYPE	Representation type
STRU	File structure
MODE	Transfer mode
FTP File Service Commands	
RETR	Retrieve
STOR	Store
APPE	Append (with create)
ALLO	Allocate
REST	Restart
RNFR	Rename from
RNTO	Rename to
ABOR	Abort
DELE	Delete
CWO	Change working directory
LIST	List
NLST	Name list
SITE	Site parameters
STAT	Status
HELP	Help
NOOP	No operation

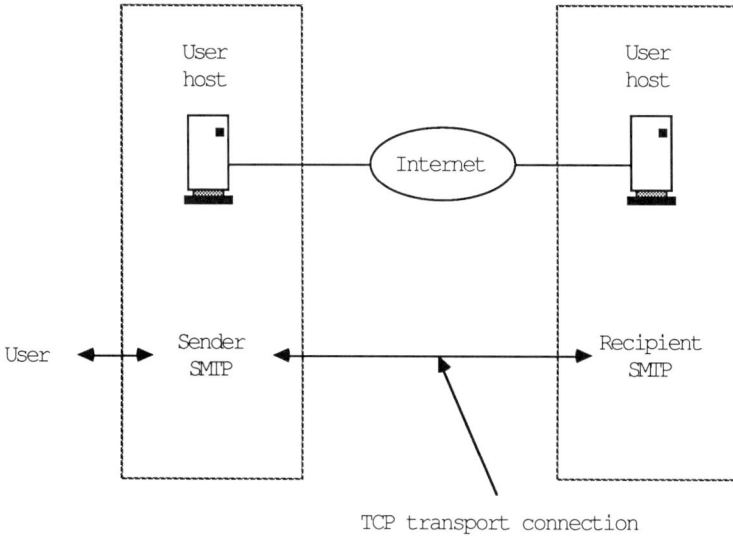

Figure 11.4   SMTP functional diagram

itself. Once the transport connection is established, the sender sends a MAIL command, identifying the sender of the mail. If the receiver's host can accept mail it responds with an OK reply. The sender then sends a recipient (RCPT) command identifying a specific recipient of the mail. When the recipients have been identified, a DATA command is sent, which indicates to the receiver that the succeeding lines are the message text. The message is concluded with an end-of-text indication. A QUIT command terminates the transport connection.

Messages destined to a distant host over intermediate hosts relay in a store-and-forward mode.

11.3 SUMMARY OF SYSTEM ARCHITECTURES

As we have observed, there are several architectural approaches for a total network service (Fig. 11.5). If the proposed network is homogeneous, the vendor may provide all the network protocol capability, including all the upper-layer services. Also, the upper-layer services may be obtained from vendors who will provide host-compatible software.

If the network hosts are heterogeneous, there are two networking alternatives. One is to buy networking software from vendors who provide software to bridge from the network layer of one proprietary system to the host-to-host layers of the other, such as from IBM's SNA to DEC's VAX-based software. These packages, if available, are usually limited to the major vendors. Another option is to buy software that provides a bridge into a standards-based environment.

Typical upper-layer protocols	Vendor-specific products	FTP SMTP TELNET	X.400 FTAM
Typical network	Proprietary	TCP/IP	X.25
Communications architecture	Proprietary	DoD Internet	ISO OSI

Commitment to standards-based architecture

| Types of network computer systems | Homogeneous hosts and nodes | Heterogeneous hosts and nodes |

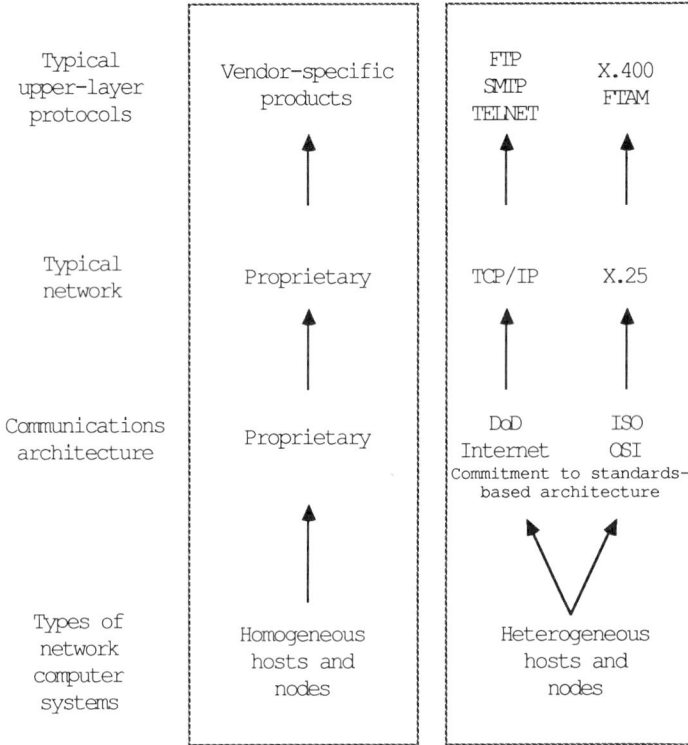

Figure 11.5   Network architectures

An **open architecture** lets the hosts interoperate, basing that interoperation on standard protocols. We have examined the DoD Internet and OSI carefully in this text. DoD's Internet was successfully developed with this commitment, and OSI promises even wider application, since it is based on international standards.

11.4 SUMMARY

User processes access network communication services through the application layer. Services such as electronic mail and file transfer protocols are available in standard and proprietary architectures. OSI and DoD application layer protocols interface to host-unique software through mapping software. OSI protocols also establish connection-oriented application service between hosts, similar to lower level OSI protocols. DoD application modules depend on TCP/IP to communicate between user processes. Most vendors provide proprietary protocols for applications over networks. The benefit of the OSI and DoD standards is that they may be implemented on computers from different manufacturers.

KEY WORDS AND CONCEPTS

common application service element
  (CASE)
File Transfer Protocol (FTP)
ISO 8571 File Transfer, Access and
  Management (FTAM)
open architecture

Simple Mail Transfer Protocol (SMTP)
specific application service element
  (SASE)
TELNET
X.400 Message Handling Service
  (MHS)

PROBLEMS

1. Describe several network *servers*, other than a file server or bulletin board, that can provide services to other network users through the ability to open and close sessions. Select one of these and list commands that may be required to obtain the service you require. Identify some of the parameters that you may need to transmit to the server.

2. Develop the user requirements, system requirements, preliminary design, and design evaluation for an application of your choice, using guidance from the appendix.

Appendix

GUIDELINES FOR
NETWORK PLANNING

Planning a new or improved network requires many technical and management decisions. The starting point for developing the preliminary design is to define the *user requirements* (Fig. A.1). Based on the user requirements, the *system requirements* are developed. An *industry survey*, or trade study, of current technology is usually conducted. *Cost trade-offs* and *design evaluation* may be performed on a preliminary design. The objective is to develop a *final design* that conforms to the system requirements.

A.1 USER REQUIREMENTS

The user requirements cover all the network functions from the user's perspective. This study should accomplish the following:

1. Describe the fundamental reasons, including the current limitations, that lead to a new or improved data communications network. A statement of the problem may include the need to connect available resources into one network to facilitate system utilization, improve communication between people, or give competitive advantage.

2. Provide a concise description of the purpose and objectives of the network. The objectives may be listed in two categories: *mandatory* and *desirable*. For example, an improvement in customer service time may be a mandatory objective, but a reduction in numbers of personnel may only be a desirable objective.

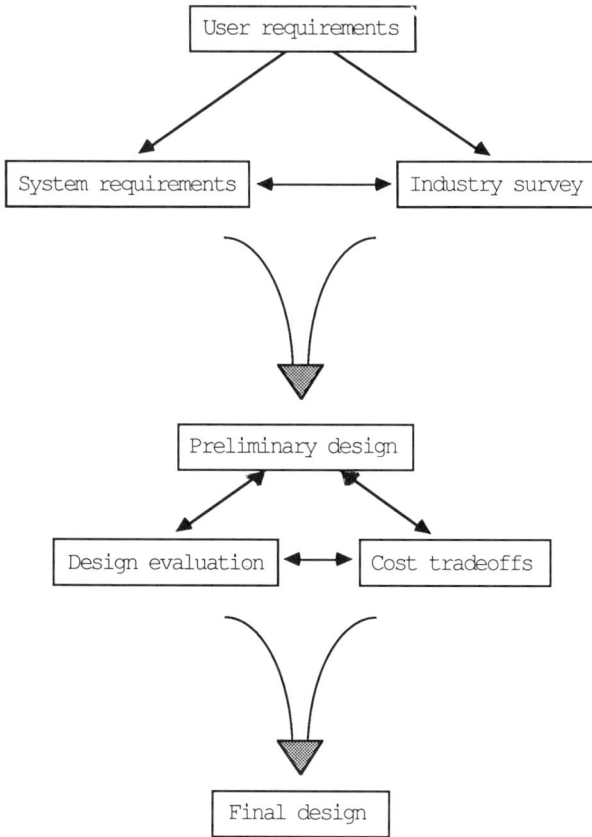

Figure A.1   Systems approach to network design

3. State the geographic scope of the system and generally locate the terminals or computers.
4. Describe each of the network functions to help management visualize the overall network and its operation.
5. Identify the application layer services and characterize the size of data messages to be transmitted. If available, use the current messages as a baseline. Histograms with message-size distribution (Fig. A.2a) may be used to characterize the traffic in each direction.
6. Characterize the frequency with which messages and data are planned to be transmitted over the network. If possible, again, use the current message traffic as a baseline. Histograms with message frequency distribution over time (Fig. A.2b) may be used to characterize the traffic. Identify any response times or delivery time requirements on the messages.

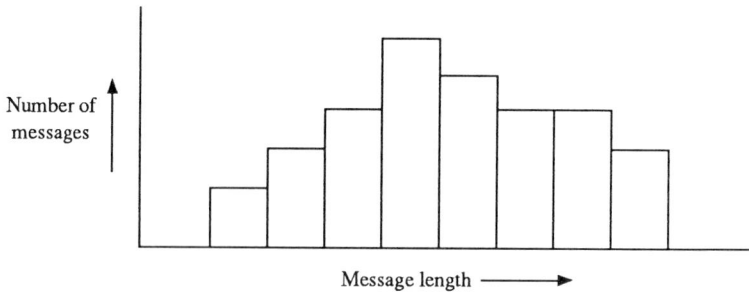

(a) Number of messages versus message length

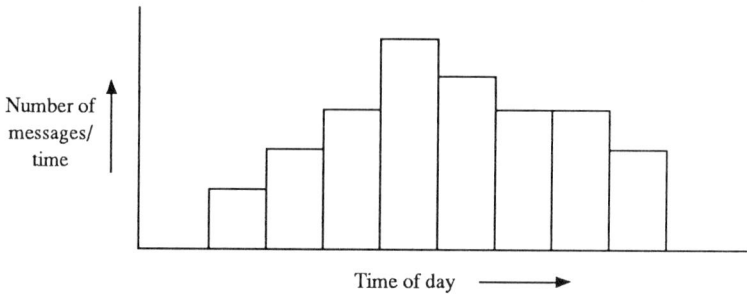

(b) Frequency of messages versus time of day

Figure A.2   Histograms for characterizing messages

7. Identify other user requirements that may impact the communication system, such as:

   Security. Identify where security is required, such as between which computers or user processes.
   Quality of service. Identify delay times to be tolerated, error rates that will be tolerated, need for prioritization of messages, and probability of failure that will be tolerated.
   Reliability. Identify percent downtime permitted. What are the most critical and the least critical times, such as for preventive maintenance?
   Availability. Identify what percent of time the network must be available.
   Maintainability. Identify mean-time-to-repair requirements (including the time to get to the location of the component that failed).
   Logistics. Identify locations of network components, spares, and consumables.

A.2 SYSTEM REQUIREMENTS

The system requirements are a translation of the user requirements into technical language for the designer. This study can be done iteratively with the preliminary design.

One approach is to outline the study into the OSI layers:

1. *Application.* Define services required at the applications layer and abstract syntax.
2. *Presentation.* Define transfer syntax and identify any need for data compaction or security.
3. *Session.* Define characteristics of the sessions between application processes. Define recovery requirements with loss of transport connections.
4. *Transport.* Specify the requirements for host-to-host message delivery reliability. Will end-to-end message or file acknowledgments be required?
5. *Network.* Specify any system-level requirements on the network, such as whether the network will be common-carrier or user-provided.
6. *Data link.* Specify system-level requirements on the links, such as tolerable bit error rates.
7. *Physical.* Based on the services and time constraints of the other layers, specify such physical requirements as data rates and type of communication links (e.g., wireline, VHF radio, microwave, or fiber optics).

A.3 INDUSTRY SURVEY

Contact vendors and other people with experience installing networks, and review trade magazines, journals, and weekly publications to become familiar with the applicable network technology. Articles may describe industries with similar requirements. Collect rough estimates of costs.

A.4 COST TRADE-OFFS

For communications services, there are a number of options that may be considered. In the following examples, a link between Los Angeles, California and Denver, Colorado is examined. Representative cost data were reduced to empirical equations and examined.

> **EXAMPLE A.1   Should a communication link between Los Angeles and Denver be based on land lines or satellite links?**
>
> A trade-off of dedicated land lines versus satellite communications for WAN communications was made from the following equations:

1. The approximate monthly cost for a dedicated land line is

$$\$75 + (\$1.25/\text{mi})(\text{number of miles})$$

From Los Angeles to Denver (820 mi), the cost is about

$$\$75 + (\$1.25/\text{mi})(820 \text{ mi}) = \$1100/\text{month}$$

2. For satellite communications, the monthly cost is

$$\$900 + (0.1/\text{mi})(\text{number of miles}) + \begin{array}{l}(\text{cost of dedicated lines} \\ \text{to exact locations})\end{array}$$

Note that with satellite communications, the major cost is fixed for the special equipment. Distance is a small factor. Between Los Angeles and Denver, including 5 mi of dedicated land lines at each end, the cost is

$$\text{Cost/month} = (\text{L.A. office to antenna}) + (\text{satellite hop})$$
$$+ (\text{antenna to Denver office})$$
$$= (\$75 + \$6.25) + (\$900 + (\$.1/\text{mi})(820 \text{ mi}))$$
$$+ (\$75 + \$6.25)$$
$$= \$1144/\text{month}$$

In conclusion, the land lines are 4% less expensive per month. There is a point at which it is more advantageous to use satellite communications than a dedicated land line. Assuming distances to the local satellite antennas that we used here in the Los Angeles to Denver example, that distance is about 860 mi.

EXAMPLE A.2   Should the Los Angeles-to-Denver link be based on leased or dial-up lines?

1. The cost for each dial-up is:

$$\text{Cost}_{\text{dial}} = \frac{\$.3 + (\$.3 \times \text{number of miles})}{1000} \times (\text{number of minutes})$$

From Los Angeles to Denver for 1 hour,

$$\text{Cost}_{\text{dial}} = [\$.3 + \$.3(820 \text{ mi}/1000)] \times 60 \text{ min}$$
$$= \$32.76/\text{hr}$$

2. From Example A.1, the monthly cost for a dedicated land line is

$$\text{Cost}_{\text{ded}} = \$75 + (\$1.25/\text{mi})(\text{number of miles})$$
$$= \$75 + (\$1.25/\text{mi})(820 \text{ mi}) = \$1100$$

Assuming 20 working days per month, the average daily cost is

$$\text{Cost}_{ded} = (\$1100/\text{month})/(20 \text{ days})$$

$$= \$55.00$$

It is more advantageous to go with a dedicated line than a dial-up line when the average daily dial-up costs exceed the average daily cost of the dedicated circuit. In this example, the number of hours of usage per day on the average has to be at least

$$\frac{(\$55.00/\text{day})}{(\$32.76/\text{hr})} = 1.7 \text{ hr/day}$$

If average telephone usage is expected to be more than 1.7 hours, or 100 minutes, per day, the leased line is less expensive.

A.5 PRELIMINARY DESIGN

Design the preliminary network configuration based on the preceding analysis. Specify the topology and architecture and identify applicable protocols.

1. Describe the major hardware components, including the hosts, network nodes, modems, encryption devices, and communication facilities.
2. Describe the major software modules. If the architecture is "open," specify standard protocols.

A.6 DESIGN EVALUATION

Conduct a thorough review of requirements, by analysis or computer simulation, to ensure that the design meets system requirements.

1. Provide an analysis to be sure that the system accommodates the message traffic requirements with the planned channel capacities.
2. Provide an estimate of total costs for the system. These costs include nonrecurring costs for the initial purchase and installation and recurring costs such as logistics and monthly leases.
3. Provide an estimate of time to install the network. Identify any items whose delivery times strongly impact the schedule. Identify items that should be ordered first.

GLOSSARY

Abstract syntax   The syntax of data used in application layer entities.

Activity   A synchronized exchange of data between users.

American Standard Code for Information Interchange (ASCII)   An alphanumeric code that associates 7-bit binary symbols with 128 alphanumeric symbols and control characters.

Analog-to-digital converter (ADC)   A device that converts analog signals to digital.

Asynchronous   A type of communication in which the time intervals between successive symbols may be unequal.

Attenuation   The loss of signal intensity as a signal travels through the communication system.

Automatic request-repeat (ARQ)   Error-correction technique where the receiver may detect an error and request the sender to retransmit.

Back-off   A procedure for delaying retransmissions after a collision on a CSMA/CD LAN.

Balanced   Describes a circuit that provides an individual return path for the signal, isolated from other grounds.

Bandwidth   Range of frequencies that a communication system can transmit.

Baseband   Transmission when the amplitude of the transmission signal is always proportional to the sender's output.

Baud   The rate of signaling per second on a circuit.

Bit   Binary digit.

Bits per second (bps)   Rate of sending control or information bits.

Bit stuffing   A technique of inserting redundant bits in the data to avoid confusing data with control symbols.

Broadband   Transmission when the wave characteristic of a high-frequency signal is modulated by the sender's output.

Bus   A topology characterized by network nodes communicating through a common transmission medium, and the data and control signals are signaled simultaneously.

Carrier   A frequency in the transmission band of a medium that can be modulated to carry digital data.

Carrier-sense multiple-access with collision detect (CSMA/CD)   A LAN technology that communicates over a passive bus through a contention algorithm; e.g., IEEE 802.3.

Central control   A network-control method where one network node provides the routing tables to all nodes.

Ciphertext   An unintelligible form of a message.

Code rate   A measure of the degree of redundant bits built into a communication code.

Common application service element (CASE)   An application layer entity that provides general supporting services; e.g., ASN.1.

Common carrier   A company that provides commercial communications services using its own communication backbone network.

Compression ratio   A measure of the degree of compaction defined by the ratio of bits before compaction to the number of bits after.

Connectionless service   A network service that routes data in individual packets over a path that is selected as the data arrives at each node.

Connection-oriented service   A network service that establishes a complete path between end nodes before passing the first data packet.

Cyclic redundancy check (CRC)   A method of checking the accuracy of a long sequence of bits in a logical block of data.

Data circuit-terminating equipment (DCE)   Equipment that provides an interface between a computer or terminal and the transmission circuit, such as a modem.

Data encryption equipment (DEE)   A device that provides encryption to a communication circuit.

Data Encryption Standard (DES)   A Federal encryption algorithm for unclassified, but sensitive, information.

Datagram model   A networking model that provides connectionless service.

Data link protocol data unit (DLPDU)   An OSI term for the logical block of data and control symbols transmitted by the data link layer protocol; a frame.

Data terminal equipment (DTE)   Equipment, such as a computer or terminal device, that provides a user with an interface to a network.

Data transparency   A condition where symbols in an information field are not interpreted as protocol control symbols.

Dialogue   A logical subset of a session activity set apart by a synchronization point.

Differential phase-shift keyed modem (DPSK)   A modem that modulates digital data based on phase changes from symbol to symbol.

Distributed control   A network-control method where individual nodes develop their own routing tables based on information from adjacent nodes.

DoD Internet   Formerly ARPANET, a mesh network of heterogeneous hosts developed and maintained by the Department of Defense.

Dynamic routing table   A routing table that is updated frequently to reduce congestion and network difficulties.

Encryption   The process of converting text or symbols into unintelligible symbols based on a set of predetermined rules.

Entity   Active elements, such as software programs and integrated circuits, that provide the services of an OSI layer within a subsystem.

File Transfer Protocol (FTP)   A DoD standard protocol for file transfer (MIL-STD-1780).

Flag   An 8-bit indicator that defines the start and end of a frame in bit-oriented data link protocols.

Flood search   A routing concept where the sender transmits the same call request or datagram on a large number of outgoing circuits.

Forward error correction (FEC)   A technique used to recover data that is based on coding in the original message.

Frame   Logical blocks of data that are transmitted by data link protocols.

Frame synchronization   A condition on a data link where the receiver recognizes the start and end of frames.

Frequency-division multiplexing (FDM)   A technique that divides the frequency bandwidth into smaller bands so that each user has exclusive use of a sub-band.

Frequency-shift keyed (FSK) modem   A modem that modulates digital data based on frequencies for each symbol.

Full-duplex   Transmission in two directions simultaneously.

Gateway   Computer capable of translating among different data link protocols and different network protocols.

Half-duplex   Transmission over a single medium in one direction at a time.

Hamming code   A forward error-correction technique to detect and correct errors in coded data.

Hertz (Hz)   A unit of measurement for frequency.

Heterogeneous   Describes a network with hosts and communication software from different manufacturers.

Hierarchical   A topology which interconnects hosts that progressively increase in data processing capabilities.

Homogeneous   Describes a network with hosts and communication software from the same manufacturer.

Host   A local computer that supports functions such as storing or processing user data.

Huffman code   A compression code where data may be represented with variable-length codes.

Initialization vector   An unencrypted variable that provides code to initialize a distant DEE.

Integrated services digital network (ISDN)   An emerging digital network that provides services, such as information retrieval, banking, and electronic mail.

Interchange circuits   The circuits between a DTE and DCE that transmit data, control signals, and timing signals.

Internet Protocol (IP)   A DoD host-resident protocol for routing datagrams through heterogeneous networks (MIL-STD-1777).

Interoperability   The capability for two or more computers, from the same or different manufacturers, to transfer data and carry out processes as expected by the users.

ISO 8073 connection-oriented mode transport protocol   An international protocol with five classes of service for reliable and sequential data delivery.

ISO 8327 session protocol   An international protocol to organize and synchronize data transfer.

ISO 8473 connectionless-mode network protocol   An international internet protocol similar to DoD's IP.

ISO 8571 File Transfer, Access and Management (FTAM)   An international protocol for file transfer.

ISO 8823 presentation protocol   An international protocol to coordinate transmission formats of data.

Key   A parameter used to encrypt plaintext data.

Layer   A related group of communication functions within a reference model.

Link Access Procedures Balanced protocol (LAPB)   The data link layer protocol for X.25.

Local area network (LAN)   Networks normally limited to a company's or university's site, usually with privately owned circuits.

Logical link control (LLC)   A sublayer in the OSI data link layer that provides connection-oriented or unacknowledged connectionless service on a LAN; e.g., IEEE 802.2.

Longitudinal redundancy check (LRC)   An error-detection technique that checks parity across all the characters in a frame.

Manchester coding   A signaling method where there is a voltage transition at the midpoint of every bit to help maintain bit synchronization.

Media access control (MAC)   A sublayer in the OSI data link layer that defines the means of access control, procedures, and formats for a LAN; e.g., IEEE 802.3, 802.4, and 802.5.

Mesh   A topology where there appears to be no recognizable organization or geometric pattern to the network.

Modem   A device used to modulate and demodulate a carrier.

Modulate   To control such wave characteristics as amplitude, frequency, or phase based on a baseband input signal.

Network protocol data unit (NPDU)   An OSI term for the logical block of data and control symbols transmitted by the network layer protocol; a packet.

Node   A computer that participates in passing data across a network.

Null modem A wiring scheme for a short-distance DTE-DTE connection.

Nyquist relationship The maximum digital signaling rate on a noiseless circuit without incurring interference.

Nyquist sampling theorem A theorem that states that the sampling rate of an analog-to-digital converter must be at least twice the highest frequency in the sampled signal for an accurate restoration of signal frequency characteristics.

Open architecture A network philosophy that bases interoperability on standard protocols.

Open Systems Interconnection (OSI) A reference model developed by the ISO that defines a seven-layer model specifying services and protocols for each layer.

Packet A relatively small unit of control information and data processed by the network protocol.

Packet assembler/disassembler (PAD) A terminal interface associated with X.25 networks.

Parity Calculation of the sum of logical ones in data.

Peer Entities in the same layer on different systems.

Phase-shift keyed (PSK) modem A modem based on phase-change assignments for each symbol.

Piggybacking A technique of including a frame acknowledgment in the header of a data frame.

Pipelining A technique for increasing link throughput by sending multiple frames without waiting for an individual acknowledgment for each frame.

Plaintext An original message prepared for transmission.

Presentation context The mapping of the abstract syntax to a transfer syntax.

Presentation protocol data unit (PPDU) An OSI term for the logical block of data and control symbols transmitted by the presentation layer protocol.

Primitive A command specification, similar to an operating system command, that defines how a higher OSI layer requests services from an adjacent lower layer.

Product cipher An encryption method that combines a series of substitutions and transpositions into the encryption algorithm.

Protocol The formal set of rules governing formatting and relative timing of an information exchange.

Quality of service (QOS) A network parameter based on such factors as transit delay, cost, and the probability of losing, duplicating, or damaging packets.

Reference model   A classification scheme for communication services among computers.

Ring   A topology characterized by a path between network nodes that forms a complete circle, with each node connected to two adjacent nodes.

RS-232   A national electrical, mechanical, and procedural standard between a DTE and a DCE interfacing to an analog circuit-switched network.

RS-422A   A national electrical standard for balanced interchange circuits between a DTE and DCE.

RS-423A   A national electrical standard for unbalanced interchange circuits between a DTE and DCE.

RS-449   A national mechanical and procedural standard between a DTE and a DCE that interfaces to an analog circuit-switched network.

Run-length code   A compression code that is used to encode long binary bit strings where much of the data is repetitious.

Service access point (SAP)   An address for an OSI entity through which a higher adjacent layer can gain service.

Session protocol data unit (SPDU)   An OSI term for the logical block of data and control symbols transmitted by the session layer protocol.

Shannon's law   The theoretical maximum bit-rate capacity for transmitting data on a noisy analog channel of bandwidth W.

Simple Mail Transfer Protocol (SMTP)   A DoD standard protocol for electronic mail (MIL-STD-1781).

Simplex   Transmission where the transmission signal travels in one direction only.

Slot time   The time for an end-to-end roundtrip signal on a bus LAN.

Specific application service element (SASE)   An entity in the application layer that provides specific user services; e.g., MHS and FTAM.

Star   A topology characterized by nodes that route data through a central switching node.

Start bit   Initial control bit sent in asynchronous transmission.

Static routing table   A routing table defined before the network is operational and then updated periodically.

Stop-and-wait   A technique of controlling flow on a link by receiving an acknowledgment before proceeding to send the next frame.

Stop bit   Final control bit sent in asynchronous transmission.

Substitution code   An encryption technique that replaces data in a message with some other symbols in a systematic way.

Synchronization point   A time in a session activity to coordinate progress.

Synchronous   A type of communication in which a large number of symbols are transmitted contiguously.

TELNET   A DoD standard virtual terminal protocol that interfaces terminal devices and terminal-oriented processes (MIL-STD-1782).

Time-division multiplexing (TDM)   A method of giving each input channel a time interval to transmit over a communication system.

Token   A control frame with a special bit field that is used to give permission to the recipient to transmit.

Token-passing bus   A LAN technology that communicates over a bus and uses a token for access control, e.g., IEEE 802.4.

Token ring   A LAN technology that communicates over active circuits and provides access through a token; e.g., IEEE 802.5.

Topology   A description of the interconnection, functionality, and geographic position of computers in a network.

Transfer rate of information bits (TRIB)   A measure used to compare the efficiency of one protocol over another.

Transfer syntax   The syntax, or format, of data in transmission.

Transmission Control Protocol (TCP)   A DoD host-resident protocol for reliable and sequential data delivery (MIL-STD-1778).

Transport connection   A communication path, equivalent to a virtual circuit, between user processes.

Transport protocol data unit (TPDU)   An OSI term for the logical block of data and control symbols transmitted by the transport layer protocol; a segment.

Transposition   An encryption technique that permutes, or re-orders, the message symbols.

Unbalanced   Describes an interchange circuit where voltages on the transmit and receive circuits are measured relative to a common-grounded return path.

Virtual circuit model   A network model that provides connection-oriented service.

Wide area network (WAN)   Networks that cover long distances, usually with common-carrier circuits.

Window   A range of frame numbers that may be legally transmitted or received.

X.21   A CCITT international electrical, mechanical, and procedural standard specifying physical access to circuit-switched digital networks.

X.25   A CCITT connection-oriented packet-switching network standard.

X.400 Message Handling Service (MHS)   A CCITT electronic mail protocol.

REFERENCES

1. Abrams, Marshall, and Ira W. Cotton. *Computer Networks: A Tutorial,* 4th ed. IEEE Computer Society Press, 1984.

2. ANSI X3.4. "7-Bit American National Standard Code for Information Interchange (7-Bit ASCII), Coded Character Sets." American National Standards Institute (ANSI), 1986.

3. ANSI X3.15. "For Bit Sequencing of the American National Standard Code for Information Interchange in Serial-by-Bit Data Transmission." ANSI, 1976.

4. ANSI X3.16. "Character Structure and Character Parity Sense for Serial-by-Bit Data Communication in the American National Standard Code for Information Interchange." ANSI, 1976.

5. ANSI X3.28. "Procedures for the Use of the Communication Control Characters of American National Standard Code for Information Interchange in Specified Data Communication Links." ANSI, 1976.

6. ANSI X3.44. "Determination of the Performance of Data Communication Systems." ANSI, 1974.

7. ANSI X3.79. "Determination of Performance of Data Communication Systems That Use Bit-Oriented Control Procedures." ANSI, 1981.

8. ANSI X3.92. "Data Encryption Algorithm." ANSI, 1981.

9. ANSI X3.102. "Data Communication Systems and Services—User-Oriented Performance Parameters, for Information Systems." ANSI, 1983.

10. ANSI X3.105. "Data Link Encryption, for Information Systems." ANSI, 1981.

11. ANSI X3.106. "Data Encryption Algorithm—Modes of Operation, for Information Systems." ANSI, 1983.

12. ANSI X3.139. "Fiber Distributed Data Interface (FDDI)—Token Ring Media Access Control (MAC), for Information Systems." ANSI, 1987.

13. Bertsekas, Dimitri, and Robert Gallager. *Data Networks*. Englewood Cliffs: Prentice Hall, 1987.

14. CCITT Recommendation T.50. "International Alphabet No. 5." International Telecommunication Union, International Telegraph and Telephone Consultive Committee (CCITT), 1984.

15. CCITT Recommendation X.3. "Packet Assembly/Disassembly (PAD) in a Public Data Network." CCITT, 1984.

16. CCITT Recommendation X.21. "Interface Between Data Terminal Equipment (DTE) and Data Circuit-Terminating Equipment (DCE) for Synchronous Operation on Public Data Networks." CCITT, 1984.

17. CCITT Recommendation X.21*bis*. "Use on Public Data Networks of Data Terminal Equipment (DTE) Which Is Designed for Interfacing to Synchronous B-Series Modems." CCITT, 1984.

18. CCITT Recommendation X.25. "Interface between Data Terminal Equipment (DTE) and Data Circuit-Terminating Equipment (DCE) for Terminals Operating in the Packet Mode and Connected to Public Data Networks by Dedicated Circuit." CCITT, 1984.

19. CCITT Recommendation X.75. "Terminal and Transit Call Control Procedures and Data Transfer System on International Circuits between Packet-Switched Networks." CCITT, 1984.

20. CCITT Recommendation X.121. "International Numbering Plan for Public Data Networks." CCITT, 1984.

21. CCITT Recommendations X.400 to X.430. "Data Communication Networks: Message Handling Systems." CCITT, 1984.

22. Clark, George C., and J. Bibb Cain. *Error-Correction Coding for Digital Communications*. New York: Plenum, 1981.

23. Davies, D. W., and W. L. Price. *Security for Computer Networks*. New York: John Wiley, 1984.

24. Federal Information Processing Standards Publication 46. "Specifications for the Data Encryption Standard," January 15, 1977.

25. *DDN Protocol Handbook*, Vol. 2: "DARPA Internet Protocols," U.S. Department of Defense, Defense Communications Agency, December 1985.

26. "DECnet Digital Network Architecture (Phase IV), General Description." Digital Equipment Corporation, Maynard, MA 01754, May 1982.

27. Dijkstra, E. W. "A Note on Two Problems in Connection with Graphs." *Numerical Mathematics* 1 (1959): 269–271.

28. "DNA Digital Data Communications Message Protocol (DDCMP) Functional Specification." Version 4.1.0, Digital Equipment Corporation, Maynard, MA 01754, No. AA-K175A-TK.

29. EIA 232-D. "Interface between Data Terminal Equipment and Data Circuit-Terminating Equipment Employing Serial Binary Data Interchange." Electronics Industries Association (EIA), January 1987.

30. EIA RS-422A. "Electrical Characteristics of Balanced Voltage Digital Interface Circuits." EIA, December 1978.

31. EIA RS-423A. "Electrical Characteristics of Unbalanced Voltage Digital Interface Circuits." EIA, September 1978.

32. EIA RS-449. "General Purpose 37-Position and 9-Position Interface for Data Terminal Equipment and Data Circuit-Terminating Equipment Employing Serial Binary Data Interchange." EIA, November 1977.

33. "Ethernet, A Local Area Network, Data Link Layer and Physical Layer Specification." Digital Equipment Corp., Maynard, Mass.; Intel Corp., Santa Clara, Calif.; Xerox Corp., Stamford, Conn.; Version 2.0 November 1982.

34. Friend, George E., et al. *Understanding Data Communications.* Howard W. Sams: Sams Understanding Series, 1984.

35. Hamming, R. W. "Error Detecting and Error Correcting Codes." *Bell System Technical Journal* 29 (April 1950): 147–160.

36. Huffman, D. A. "A Method for the Construction of Minimum Redundancy Codes." *Proceedings of IRE* 40 (September 1952): 1098–1101.

37. IEEE Std 802.2 (ISO/DIS 8802/2). "Local Area Networks—Logical Link Control." Institute of Electrical and Electronics Engineers (IEEE), 1985.

38. IEEE Std 802.3 (ISO/DIS 8802/3). "Local Area Networks—Carrier Sense Multiple Access with Collision Detection (CSMA/CD) Access Method and Physical Layer Specifications." IEEE, 1985.

39. IEEE 802.4 (ISO/DIS 8802/4). "Local Area Networks—Token-Passing Bus Access Method." IEEE, 1985.

40. IEEE 802.5 (ISO/DIS 8802/5). "Local Area Networks—Token Ring Access Method." IEEE, 1985.

41. ISO 646. "7-Bit Character Set for Information Processing Interchange." International Organization for Standardization (ISO), 1983.

42. ISO 4903. "15-Pin DTE/DCE Interface Connector and Pin Assignments." ISO, 1980.

43. ISO 7498. "Open Systems Interconnection—Basic Reference Model, Information Processing Systems." ISO, 1984.

44. ISO 8072. "Open Systems Interconnection—Transport Service Definition, Information Processing Systems." ISO, 1986.

45. ISO/DIS 8072/DAD1. "Open Systems Interconnection—Transport Service Definition—Addendum 1: Connectionless-Mode Transmission, Information Processing Systems." ISO, 1986.

46. ISO 8073. "Open Systems Interconnection—Connection Oriented Transport Protocol Specification, Information Processing Systems." ISO, 1986.

47. ISO/DIS 8326. "Open Systems Interconnection—Basic Connection-Oriented Session Service Definition, Information Processing Systems." ISO, 1984.

48. ISO 8327. "Open Systems Interconnection—Basic Connection-Oriented Session Protocol Specification, Information Processing Systems." ISO, 1984.

49. ISO/DIS 8348. "Data Communications—Network Service Definition Information Processing Systems." ISO, 1985.

50. ISO/DIS 8348/DAD1. "Data Communications—Network Service Definition—Addendum 1: Connectionless-Mode Transmission. Information Processing Systems." ISO, 1986.

51. ISO/DIS 8348/DAD2. "Data Communications—Network Service Definition—Addendum 1: Covering Network Layer Addressing, Information Processing Systems." ISO, 1986.

52. ISO/DIS 8473. "Data Communications—Protocol for Providing the Connectionless-Mode Network Service, Information Processing Systems." ISO, 1986.

53. ISO 8473/DAD1. "Data Communications—Protocol for Providing the Connectionless-Mode Network Service—Addendum 1: Provision of the Underlying Service Assumed by ISO 8473, Information Processing Systems." ISO, 1986.

54. ISO/DIS 8571. "Open Systems Interconnection—File Transfer, Access and Management, Information Processing Systems." ISO, 1988.

55. ISO/DIS 8822. "Open Systems Interconnection—Connection-Oriented Presentation Service Definition, Information Processing Systems." ISO, 1986.

56. ISO/DIS 8823. "Open Systems Interconnection—Connection-Oriented Presentation Protocol Specification, Information Processing Systems." ISO, 1986.

57. ISO/DIS 8824.2. "Open Systems Interconnection—Specification of Abstract Syntax Notation One (ASN.1), Information Processing Systems." ISO, 1986.

58. ISO/DIS 8825.2. "Open Systems Interconnection—Specification of Basic Encoding Rules for Abstract Syntax Notation One (ASN.1), Information Processing Systems." ISO, 1986.

59. ISO/DP 8850. "Open Systems Interconnection—Specification of Protocols for Common Application Service Elements, Information Processing Systems." ISO, 1984.

60. Knightson, Keith G., Terry Knowles, and John Larmouth. *Standards for Open Systems Interconnection*. New York: McGraw-Hill, 1988.

61. Lin, Shu. *An Introduction to Error Correcting Codes*. Englewood Cliffs: Prentice Hall, 1970.

62. Lynch, Thomas J. *Data Compression, Techniques and Applications*. New York: Van Nostrand Reinhold, 1985.

63. MIL-STD-1777. "Internet Protocol, Military Standard." U.S. Department of Defense, August 12, 1983.

64. MIL-STD-1778. "Transmission Control Protocol, Military Standard." U.S. Department of Defense, August 12, 1983.

65. MIL-STD-1780. "File Transfer Protocol, Military Standard." U.S. Department of Defense, May 10, 1984.

66. MIL-STD-1781. "Simple Mail Transfer Protocol, Military Standard." U.S. Department of Defense, May 10, 1984.

67. MIL-STD-1782. "TELNET Protocol, Military Standard." U.S. Department of Defense, May 10, 1984.

68. Schwartz, Mischa. *Telecommunication Networks: Protocols, Modeling and Analysis*. Reading, Mass.: Addison-Wesley, 1987.

69. Shannon, C. "A Mathematical Theory of Communication." *Bell System Journal* 27 (July 1948): 379-423 and (October 1948): 623–656.

70. Sinnema, William, and Tom McGovern. *Digital, Analog, and Data Communication*. 2nd ed. Englewood Cliffs: Prentice Hall, 1986.

71. Slana, M. F., and H. R. Lehman. *Computer*. (May 1981): 73–88.

72. "Stable Implementation Agreements for Open Systems Interconnection Protocols." Version 1, Edition 1. National Bureau of Standards Special Publication 500-150, December 1987.

73. Stallings, William. *Data and Computer Communications*. 2nd ed. New York: Macmillan, 1988.

74. "Systems Network Architecture: Technical Overview." IBM Corporation, Research Triangle Park, NC 27709, No. GC30–3073, 1985.

75. Tanenbaum, Andrew S. *Computer Networks*. 2nd ed. Englewood Cliffs: Prentice Hall, 1988.

ANSWERS TO ODD-NUMBERED PROBLEMS

CHAPTER 2

1. Control characters enable control of devices and procedures; to synchronize octets, frames, and messages.
3. 256 vs. 32 symbols
5. Convert your last name to its ASCII binary representation. Assume no parity.

```
S    0 1 0 1 0 0 1 1
M    0 1 0 0 1 1 0 1
I    0 1 0 0 1 0 0 1
T    0 1 0 1 0 1 0 0
H    0 1 0 0 1 0 0 0
```

7. LRC   0 1 0 0 1 0 1 1
9. 250 ms
11. 5933 s
13. 0 0 1
15. 1 1 1 1 1 1 1
17. (a) 1 1 1 0 0 0 0 (b) 1 0 0 0
19. 57.1%
21. 210 bps
23. (b) .3 ms

CHAPTER 3

3. Thermal, due to thermal motion of the electrons; and manufactured or artificial, due to machinery and switches in the circuits.

5. (a) 4800 bps (b) 6200 bps

7. Full-duplex modem operation permits data communication in two directions simultaneously. Half-duplex permits communication in each direction, one way at a time.

9.

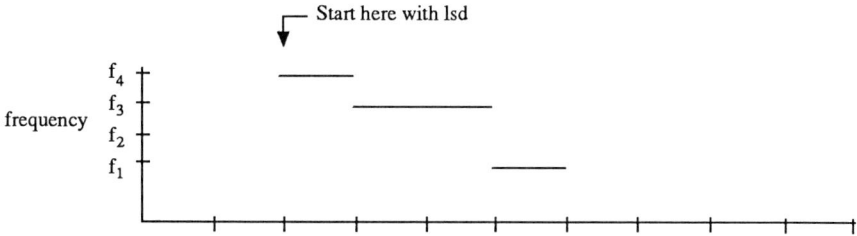

11.

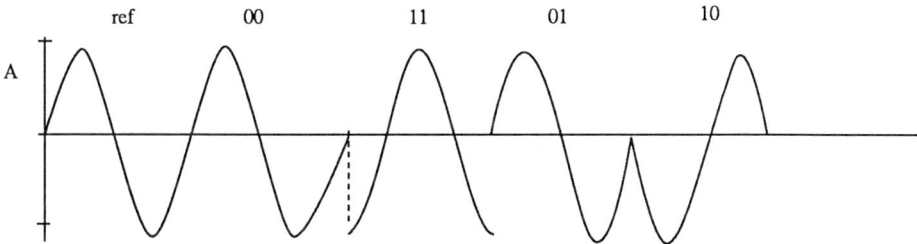

13. Less distortion

15. (a) 6.35×10^9 bits (b) 19.4×10^9 bits

17. (a) 4800 bps (b) 75%

CHAPTER 4

1. The routing that takes place between the source of the package and the final destination. There are regional centers where mail is routed for shipment to other destinations.

3. Presentation

5. Presentation

7. A session layer protocol is when the calling party says, "Hello, this is . . . , may I speak to . . . ?" and the appropriate person comes to the telephone.

CHAPTER 5

1. (b) A&D
3. *DTE ready* and *DCE ready* indicate equipment readiness and *request to send* and *clear to send* indicate channel readiness. The procedures for autoanswer are as follows. Assume: DTE is ready.

TABLE A.5

Description	DTE		DCE			
	DTE Rdy	Req to Send	DCE Rdy	Clr To Send	Rng Ind	Rc'ved Ln Sig Det
Idle	ON	OFF	OFF	OFF	OFF	OFF
Incoming call	ON	OFF	OFF	OFF	ON	OFF
Answer circuit ready	ON	OFF	ON	OFF	OFF	OFF
Channel ready, transmit carrier	ON	ON	ON	ON	OFF	OFF
Detect distant modem carrier	ON	ON	ON	ON	OFF	ON

CHAPTER 6

1. All the control characters are coded in octets and one needs to know where the octets begin.
3. Synchronous idle (SYN) characters are used for octet synchronization in character-oriented synchronous transmission.
5. The frame has to arrive without any errors and an acknowledgment has to be successfully received by the sender.
7. (a) 4
   (b) 6

9. 1 1 0

11.

```
     Flag
0 1 1 1 1 1 1 0 1 1 1 1 1 1 0 1 0 1 1 1 1 1 0 0 1 1
1 1 1 1 1 1 1 1 0 1 1 0 0 0 0 1 1 1 1 1 1 0 1 0 1 1 1
1 1 1 0
                          Flag
```

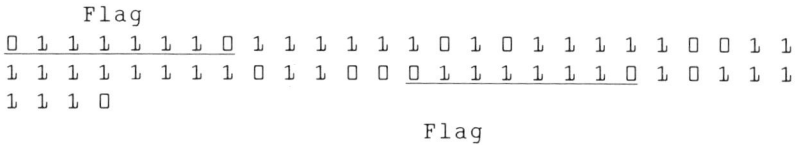

13. 2210 bps, shorter header and fewer services.

15. 819 bits

CHAPTER 7

1. (a) A physical circuit transmits and receives electrical signals. A virtual circuit is established in software in intermediate computers to associate input and output physical circuits with a logical channel (virtual circuit) from a sender to receiver.
(b) Yes

3.

	$N(2)$	Path	$N(3)$	Path	$N(4)$	Path	$N(5)$	Path
$N\{1\}$ 4	4	1-2	1	1-3	∞		2	1-5
$N\{1, 3\}$	2	1-3-2	1	1-3	5	1-3-4	2	1-5
$N\{1, 3, 5\}$	2	1-3-2	1	1-3	5	1-3-4	2	1-5
$N\{1, 3, 5, 2\}$	2	1-3-2	1	1-3	4	1-3-2-4	2	1-5

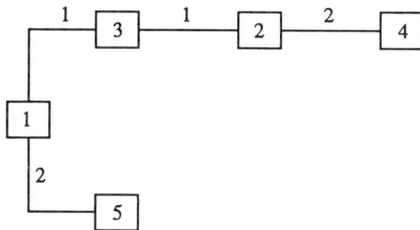

Routing table for computer 1 is:

Destination	Next Computer
2	3
3	3
4	3
5	5

5. TRIB could be affected by computer processing time and quality of service (e.g., bit errors) on the link.

7. (a) The packet is destined for a distant network computer. The PACLINK frame is destined for an adjacent computer.
(b) 528 bits before bit stuffing
(c) (i) 1.000 s; (ii) .1080 s; (iii) 1.080 s;

CHAPTER 8

3. (a) With Manchester coding:

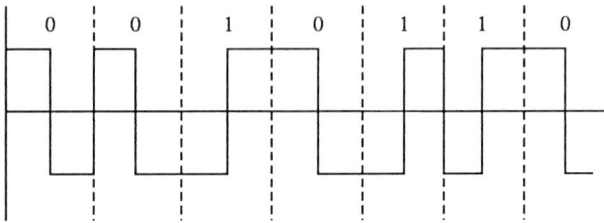

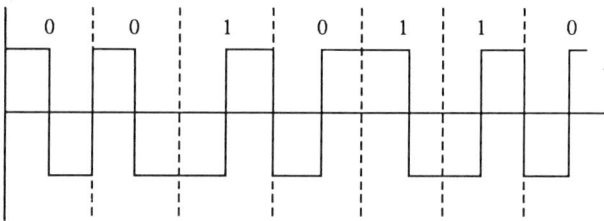

5. (a) 28,500 bps; token ring better (token shorter).

7. 30 μs

CHAPTER 9

1. (a) DoD IP header, TCP header:

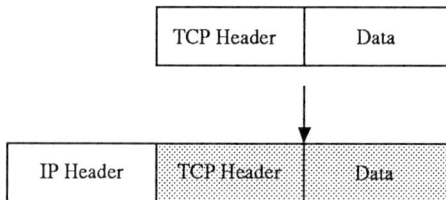

(b) ISO session, transport, network, and data link header:

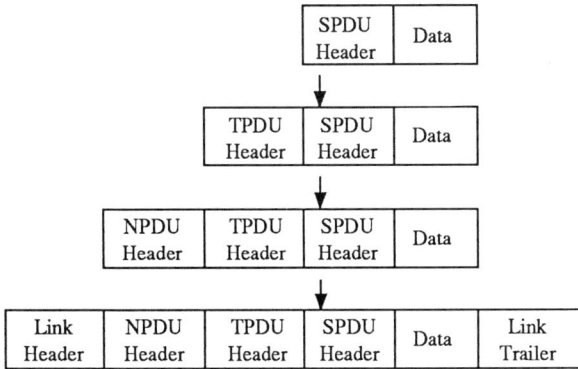

			SPDU Header	Data	

		TPDU Header	SPDU Header	Data	

	NPDU Header	TPDU Header	SPDU Header	Data	

Link Header	NPDU Header	TPDU Header	SPDU Header	Data	Link Trailer

3. (a) *i*

(b) DUNKTRANS transport segment: 160 octets
DUNKNET network datagram: 163 octets
DUNKLINK data link frame: 2171 octets

(c) 702 bps

CHAPTER 10

1. (a)

C 1
B 01
A 001
D 0001
F 0000

(b) 2.0 bits/character (c) 3.50

3. (a)

```
0010 0100 1010 0001 0000 0111 0001 0000 0001 1111
0111 0000 0110
```

(b) 1.17

5. Vigenere code, because a different set of characters is used (substitution) and the key is ROUNDBALL.

7.

In	Out
000	000
001	010
010	001
011	011
100	101
101	100
110	111
111	110

INDEX